ACCLAIM FOR TRACY L. HIGLEY

City on Fire, previously released as *Pompeii*

"Higley's Pompeii ignites with riveting and compelling characters. No one unleashes the secrets of history with a masterful hand the way Higley does! Authentic and powerful, [*City on Fire*] is a fiery tale of a city lost to the power of Vesuvius. I simply could not read fast enough!"

—RONIE KENDIG, AUTHOR OF
THE DISCARDED HEROES SERIES

"[*City on Fire*] is a richly detailed story of powerful redemption and raw courage. Higley takes readers right to the foot of the legendary volcano, Vesuvius, and spins her tale under the shadow of certain disaster."

—GINGER GARRETT, AUTHOR
OF *WOLVES AMONG US*

"Higley brings Pompeii to life again in this exhilarating tale of love and adventure. The story was so enthralling to me—I want to read it again!"

—ELIZABETH GODDARD, AUTHOR
OF *THE CAMERA NEVER LIES*

So Shines the Night

"Higley proves once again that she has a great talent for historical fiction. It is easy to get lost in the ancient world with Daria during her adventures. The story is so well detailed and the struggles between different faiths and cultures is exceptionally illustrated. Daria characterizes all one would hope for in a strong, brave woman of faith."

—*ROMANTIC TIMES* BOOK
REVIEWS, 4-STAR REVIEW

"I love Tracy Higley's novels. Meticulously-researched, spell-bindingly written with luscious prose and compelling and complex characters, each one is a treasure. Higley knows her history, but more importantly, she knows just how to capture the struggles and questions of the human heart—yesterday and today."

—TOSCA LEE, *NEW YORK TIMES* BEST-
SELLING AUTHOR OF *HAVAH: THE STORY OF
EVE* AND THE BOOKS OF MORTALS SERIES

Garden of Madness

"Readers will find much to enjoy here: fine writing, suspense, mystery, faith, love, and a new look at an old story."

—*PUBLISHERS WEEKLY*

"The author's insights into a woman's inner strengths . . . will leave readers rejoicing."

—*ROMANTIC TIMES* BOOK REVIEWS,
4½ STARS, TOP PICK!

"Mystical as the Seven Wonders, exotic as the Hanging Gardens. Higley has outdone herself with this exquisite story of intrigue, elegantly told and rich with all the flavors of ancient Babylon. Simply magnificent."

—TOSCA LEE, *NEW YORK TIMES* BEST-SELLING
AUTHOR OF *HAVAH: THE STORY OF EVE* AND
THE BOOKS OF MORTALS SERIES

"Even more riveting than the historical background is the mystery that Higley creates as the backdrop to her exploration of the ancient world . . . Readers will not be satisfied until they have discovered the truth along with Tiamat."

—DR. SHANNON ROGERS FLYNT,
ASSISTANT PROFESSOR, DEPARTMENT
OF CLASSICS, SAMFORD UNIVERSITY

"Each of Tracy Higley's historical novels is more powerful than its predecessor, and *Garden of Madness* continues the trend. I was drawn into the ancient Babylonian world from the very first page and held spellbound until the last, savoring every moment of Tia's journey from despair to redemption. Whether you've read Higley's previous works, or are just discovering her amazing stories, you must not miss this one!"

—JANELLE CLARE SCHNEIDER,
AUTHOR AND SPIRITUAL DIRECTOR

Isle of Shadows, previously released as *Shadow of Colossus*

"One of the most beautifully written books I've ever encountered. The prose is amazing, the story is riveting, and the characters are complex. I was absolutely and completely satisfied with every aspect of this story, which is rare for me. I am now a HUGE Tracy Higley fan."

—RONIE KENDIG, AUTHOR OF
THE DISCARDED HEROES SERIES

"Fast-paced adventure, fascinating characters and insights into the culture, politics and people of this ancient world make this book a unique and unmissable read."

—REL MOLLET, RELZREVIEWZ.COM

"This is such a unique historical novel that it really sets itself apart from all others. Higley's portrait of day-to-day life in the ancient world drew me in and her strong heroine kept me reading."

—JILL HART,
THESUSPENSEZONE.COM

"Blending suspense, romance, political intrigue, and a healthy dose of drama, Higley brings the struggles, class differences, and pagan culture of ancient Greece to vivid life . . . Strong characterization combined with rich historical detail have won this book a home on my shelves of keepers."

—JENNIFER BOGART,
TITLETRAKK.COM

ALSO BY TRACY L. HIGLEY

Garden of Madness

Isle of Shadows

So Shines the Night

The Queen's Handmaid (Available Spring 2014)

Pyramid of Secrets (Available as e-book only, November 2013)

CITY *on* FIRE

A Novel *of* Pompeii

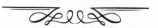

TRACY L. HIGLEY

THOMAS NELSON
Since 1798

NASHVILLE DALLAS MEXICO CITY RIO DE JANEIRO

Published in Nashville, Tennessee, by Thomas Nelson. Thomas Nelson is a registered trademark of Thomas Nelson, Inc.

Thomas Nelson, Inc., titles may be purchased in bulk for educational, business, fund-raising, or sales promotional use. For information, please e-mail SpecialMarkets@ThomasNelson.com.

Library of Congress Cataloging-in-Publication Data

Higley, T. L.
  City on fire / Tracy L. Higley.
    pages cm
  ISBN 978-1-4016-8752-6 (trade paper)
  I. Title.
  PS3608.I375C585 2013
  813'.6--dc23
                              2013013009

Printed in the United States of America

13 14 15 16 17 18 RRD 6 5 4 3 2 1

To Mike and Pam Dittman
and
Pat and Nadine Pileggi

. . . who first taught me that girls could be warriors, too.
You have always encouraged me to find my
adventure and pursue it with passion.
For this I am grateful.

WORD LIST

aedile—city official, mainly responsible for public buildings and festivals

amphorae—a two-handled jar with a narrow neck used to carry wine or oil

apodyterium—changing room for the men in the bathhouses

aureus—gold coin valued at 25 silver denarii

bestiarii—fighters who faced beasts in the arena

calidarium—hot room of the bath complex, with a hot plunge bath

Capitolium—temple of the gods, with great arches on either side

contubernium—a unit of soldiers in the Roman army, composed of eight legionaries

cornu—a curved brass instrument used for communicating in battle

Decanus—Roman military title, leader of the contubernium

denarii—Roman silver coin

duovir—one of two joint city magistrates, mainly responsible for administration of justice

editores—politician sponsoring public games, to curry public favor

Eumachia—building in Pompeii named for priestess of Venus, used by the fullers

frigidarium—cold room of the bath complex, with a cold plunge bath

garum—ancient Greek and Roman condiment, a fermented fish sauce

gradi—unit of distance equal to approximately 2.5 feet

HaShem—literally, "the name," the Jewish word used for God

impluvium—sunken part of an atrium to catch the rainwater coming through the open roof

insulae—tenement-type apartment buildings in ancient Roman cities

Junius—the month of June

Kykeon—ancient Greek alcohol that brought on frenzied hallucinations

lancea—a Roman short javelin

lanista—trainer of gladiators

locarii—ushers who checked on visitors' seating in the Roman games

lupanaria—brothel named for the "lupe"—the she-wolf, whose call the women mimicked

Macellum—main market of the city

Murmillo/Murmillones—gladiator with high-crested and broad-rimmed helmet that resembled a fish

ordo/ordo decurionum—city council

palaestra—the city's main field for athletic training and fitness

palus—poles buried in the ground used for gladiator training

parados—the offstage corridor of the theater

pater familias—literally "father of the family," head of the household

pilum—Roman long javelin

praenomen—first name, given by parents, to a Roman child

pugio—short sword

quadriporticus—four-sided courtyard surrounded by columned walkways

quaestor—city official, mainly responsible for financial matters

Retiarius/Retiarii—gladiator who used a casting net and trident as weapons

rudis—wooden training sword, also used as a token given to a freed gladiator

scaenae frons—two-story façade behind the stage

Secutor—gladiator who fought heavily armed, including a helmet

sestertius/sestertii—brass coin

stola—woman's garment, comparable to the man's toga

suggestum—platform where orators could make their appeals

tabernae—single-room shop in market, with wide doorway and barrel-vaulted ceiling

tablinum—room on one side of the atrium, used as an office

tepidarium—warm room of the bath complex

thermopolium/thermopolia—ancient Rome's "fast food restaurant"—masonry counters with sunken jars holding food

tholos—a circular building with various uses

triclinium—main dining area of a home

Vulcanalia—festival dedicated to Vulcan, god of fire

". . . a peak of Hell, rising out of paradise."
—JOHANN WOLFGANG VON
GOETHE, ON VESUVIUS

From its lofty place above the sparkling crescent Bay of Napoli, Vesuvius loomed over the surrounding towns, pressure building beneath its grassy slopes.

The hot springs that bubbled up from deep within brought pleasure-seekers from the north to bathe in secluded groves, and the mountain boasted lemon trees and long waving grasses where wildlife grazed the foothills. The purple, cloud-kissed peak shone always in the sunlight.

But under it all, where the eyes of no patrician or plebeian saw, it churned with an angry force waiting to be unleashed.

It had been quiet these many years. Too many years for counting, even. Controlled, subdued, silent as generation after generation lived and farmed and reveled in its long shadows.

But not for long. No, not for long.

Though the people who lived beneath it believed they controlled their own destiny, they would soon learn that their fate was not in their own hands.

PROLOGUE

Jerusalem
August 9, AD 70

Ariella shoved through the clogged street, defying the mob of frantic citizens. Men, women, and children crowded the alleys, senseless in their panic to flee the city. They carried all they could, packed into pouches slung across their chests and clutched in sweaty hands. Soldiers ran with them, as though they had all joined a macabre stadium footrace, with participants who clubbed and slashed at each other to get ahead. Beside her, one of the district's tax collectors tripped and fumbled a latched wooden box. It cracked against the cobbled street and spilled its meager hoard of gold. The tax collector was dead before he hit the ground, and the Roman soldier pulled his sword from the man's gut only to scramble for the coins.

Ariella turned her head from the gore but felt little pity for the tax man, cheated of life by the Romans for whom he had betrayed his people. Still, concern flickered in her chest at the sudden violence in the street.

Something had happened.

The city had been under siege for months. Three days ago her mother announced that the sacrifices in the Temple had ceased. But today, today was something new. Perhaps three days of sins not atoned for had brought the wrath of the Holy One down on them all.

Ariella's destination was neither Temple nor countryside, unlike those who ran in the streets with her. She returned to her home—if the dim tenement could be called such—from another useless excursion to secure food.

At sixteen and as the eldest child, it fell on her to search the famished city for a scrap of dried beef to feed her brother, perhaps a thimbleful of milk for the baby, crumbs for her father whose eyes had gone glassy and whose skin was now the color of the clay pots he once turned on the wheel.

But there was no food to be found. Titus, the emperor's son, had arrived in the spring with his army of eighty thousand, and his siege wall served well its double function—the people were trapped and they were starving.

Not even such a wall could prevent news from seeping through its cracks, however. From Caesarea, word escaped of twenty thousand Jews slaughtered in a day. Fifty thousand killed in Alexandria. Ten thousand met the sword in Gamla. Such numbers were incomprehensible.

Here in Jerusalem, the bodies thrown outside the city were too numerous to count, piled high in rotting mounds, as though the city itself were defiled and would forever be unclean.

Yet we are not all dead. Ariella's hands curled into tense fists as she rounded the last corner. She would cling to life as long as she had strength and, like her untiring mother, she would hold tight to that elusive thread for each member of her family.

She pushed against the rough wood of the door and slipped out of the rush of the street. The home's tomb-like interior had the peculiar smell of starvation. In the corner, her baby sister whimpered as if in response to Ariella's entrance. Micah met her at the door, his sunken eyes fixed on her and his lips slightly open, as though anticipating the food she might have brought. Or perhaps he simply lacked the strength to close his jaw. She shook her head and Micah turned away, hiding his disappointment as all boys of eleven do when they are threatened by tears.

Her father did not speak from his mat on the floor. Ariella scooped the listless baby, Hannah, into her arms and gave her a finger to suck. Small consolation.

"Where is Mother?" She scanned the room, then looked to Micah. A low groan from her father set her heart pounding. "Where is she, Micah? Where has Mother gone?"

Micah sniffed and glanced at the door. "To the Temple. She has gone to the Temple."

Ariella growled and pushed Hannah into her brother's arms. "She is going to get herself killed, and then where will we be?"

She bent to her father's side. The man had been strong once. Ariella could barely remember. She touched the cool skin of his arm. "I will bring her back, Father. I promise." Her father's eyes sought her own, searching for reassurance. The hunger seemed to have stolen his voice. How long until it took his mind?

She turned on Micah, grabbed his shoulder. "Do not let anyone inside. The streets—" She looked to the door. "The streets are full of madness."

He nodded, still cradling Hannah.

She kissed the baby. "Take care of them, Micah." And then she left to retrieve her mother, whose political fervor often outpaced her common sense.

The midsummer sun had dropped in the sky, an orange disc hazy and indistinct behind rising smoke. The city burned. She smelled it, sensed it, felt it somehow on her skin as she joined the flow toward the Temple—a heat of destruction that threatened to consume them all.

Her family enjoyed the privilege of living in the shadow of the Temple Mount. A privilege that today only put them closer to folly. She twisted through the crazed mob, darted around wagons and push-carts laden with family treasures, swatted at those who shoved against her. Only halfway there, her heart struck against her chest and her breathing shallowed, the weakness of slow starvation.

She reached the steps to the south of the Temple platform and was swept upward with the masses. Why were so many running to the Temple? Why had her mother?

And then she heard it. A sound that was part shrieking anger, part mournful lament, a screaming funeral dirge for the city and its people. She reached the top of the steps, pushed through the Huldah Gate, dashed under the colonnade into the Court of the Gentiles, and drew up short. The crowd pressed against her back, flowed around her and surged onward, but Ariella could not move.

The Temple was on fire.

The next moments blurred. She was running, running toward the Temple as if she alone could avert this monstrous evil. Joining others who must have shared her delusion. Roman legionaries clubbed women and children, voices raised in a war cry. The yells of zealot rebels and the shrieks of those impaled by swords returned like an echo. The dead began to accumulate. Soldiers climbed heaps of bodies to chase those who fled. She tasted ashes and blood in the air, breathed the stench of burning flesh, and still some pushed forward.

She fought the smoke and blood, climbed the steps, and entered the Court of Women. All around her, peaceful citizens were butchered where they stood. Ahead, a current of blood ran down the curved steps before the brass Nicanor Gate. The bodies of those who had been murdered at the top slipped to the bottom.

Ariella swayed on her feet at the carnage. That her mother was one of these dead she had no doubt. Elana's outspoken defiance of Rome had earned her a reputation among her people, one that matched the meaning of her given name, "torch."

She could go no farther. The entire Temple structure flamed now, from the Court of Israel to the Holy of Holies, its beauty and riches and sanctity defiled, raped by the Romans who even now risked their own flesh to steal its treasures.

A groan at her feet drew her attention, and she saw as if from a great distance that indeed her mother lay there, a bloody slash against her chest and a vicious purpling around her eyes. She lifted a hand, claw-like, to Ariella, who bent to kneel beside her and clasp her fingers.

Ariella had no words. What use to say good-bye, when they would all be in the same place soon?

Strange, she was very cold. With the flames so near and so fierce, still her fingers felt numb as she wrapped them around her mother's hand.

Elana whispered only, "Never forget . . . ," before she was gone, and Ariella nodded because it was the expected thing to do. She studied her mother's face, the eyes open and unseeing, and felt nothing. Was that right? Should she feel something?

After a while she thought perhaps she should go home. She tried to stand, slipped in some blood that had pooled on the marble beneath her, and tried again.

The noise seemed far off now, though she could see the faces of citizens, mouths gaping as though they screamed in agony, and soldiers, feral lips drawn back over their teeth. But the sounds had somehow receded.

She weaved through the upright who still lived, stepped over the prone who had already passed, and drifted back to her house. Behind her, the Temple Mount was enveloped in flames, boiling over from its base, though there seemed to be even more blood than flames.

The stupor that had fallen over her at the Temple seemed to slough away as she traveled the streets. From open doorways she heard an occasional wail, but largely it was quiet. Too quiet. As though a river of violence had washed down the street while she'd been gone and swept away all that lived.

Her own street was not so peaceful. From end to end it burned.

She searched the crowd for her father, Micah, the baby. Grabbed hollow-eyed friends and wailing neighbors. One old woman shook her head and pointed a withered hand to the end of the burning street. "Only Micah," she coughed. "Only he escaped."

Micah. She called his name, but the word choked in her throat. Where would he have fled?

They had whispered together, one unseasonably warm night a few months ago on their roof, of running away from Jerusalem. Child's talk, but now . . . Would he have tried to leave the city, to make it two hours south to family in Bethlehem?

Minutes later she stumbled toward the Lower City. The Dung Gate would lead her south, to the valley of Hinnom and onward to Bethlehem. If she could escape.

Too many joined her. They would never be allowed to pass. She climbed crumbling steps to the rim of the city wall. Would she see a thread of refugees weaving out of Jerusalem, beyond the gates?

There was a procession of Jews, yes. But not on foot, fleeing to safety. On crosses, writhing in death throes. An endless line of them, crucified in absurd positions for the Romans' entertainment, until they had run out of crosses, no doubt. Ariella gripped the wall. She would have retched had there been anything in her stomach.

She considered throwing herself from the wall. Was it high enough to guarantee her death? She would not want to die slowly on the ground, listening to the crucified.

The decision was made for her. From behind, a Roman soldier grabbed both her arms, laughing. She waited for the air in her face, for the spin of a free fall in her belly, that feeling she loved when her father rode the donkey cart too fast over the crest of a hill.

Instead, the soldier spun her to face him, shoved her to the stone floor, and fumbled at her tunic.

No, she was not going to die like that.

She exploded into a flailing of arms and legs, kicks and screams. She used her fingernails, used her teeth, used her knees.

From behind her head another soldier called, "That one's a fighter, eh, Marcus?"

The soldier on top of her grunted.

"Better save her for the general. He wants the strong ones to sell off, you know."

Since the siege began months ago, Ariella had believed one thing with all her heart. She had believed she would meet her death in the City of God. But as Jerusalem died without her, the truth of her future slammed against her chest, stole her breath. Not death. Something far worse.

Life in the slave market of Rome.

1

Rome

Nine years later

Night fell too soon, bringing its dark celebrations to the house of Valerius.

Ariella lingered at the fishpond in the center of the dusky atrium, slipping stale crusts to the hungry scorpion fish one tiny piece at a time. The brown-and-white-striped creature snapped at its prey with precision, the venomous spines along its back bristling.

The fish food ran out. There was no delaying the inevitable.

Let the debauchery begin.

Nine years a slave in this household, nine annual tributes to Dionysius. The Greek god, embraced by the Romans and renamed Bacchus, apparently demanded every sort of drunken vice performed in his honor. And Valerius would not disappoint the god.

Indeed, Valerius flaunted his association with the mystery sect, though its practice was frowned upon by the government and disdained by most citizens.

Ariella inhaled, trying to draw strength from the deadly fish her master kept as a pet. For they were both kept as such, weren't they? The scorpion fish's body swayed like a piece of debris, its disguise needless in its solitary enclosure.

Within an hour Valerius's guests poured into the town house, sloshed up most of the wine she'd placed on low tables in the *triclinium*, and progressed to partaking of the extract of opium poppies, tended in red-tinged fields beyond the city. The sweet, pungent smoke hung like a smothering wool toga above their heads.

A traveling guild of actors somersaulted into the room, their lewd songs and costumes an affront to decency and a delight to the guests. Ariella lowered her eyes, embarrassment still finding her even after all she had endured, and cleared the toppled cups and soiled plates. She passed Valerius, sprawled on a gold-cushioned couch, and he rubbed a hand over her calf. Her muscles twitched like the flank of a horse irritated by a fly.

Her master's high-pitched laugh floated above the general noise of the intoxicated. Ariella winced. Valerius performed tonight for his honored guest, another politician from the south somewhere.

"Perhaps we shall make a man of you yet, Maius." Valerius waved his slender fingers at the larger man. "I shall take you out into the city and declare to all that you are one of us."

The politician, Maius, reddened.

Ariella leaned over him to refill his cup. Clearly, he was here to humor Valerius but not align himself with the vile man.

When the actors had twirled their final dance and claimed applause, the herd of guests took their revelry to the streets. Valerius dragged Ariella through the door, always his special companion this night. Her breath caught in her throat. It was not the streets she feared. It was what would come after.

Why could she not be strong, like her mother?

The insanity built to a crescendo as they wound their torch-lit way toward the Via Appia, where the procession would climax. The Bacchanalians howled and pushed and tripped, their vacant eyes and laughing mouths like the painted frescoes of her nightmares. Hair disheveled, carrying blazing torches, they danced along the stones, uttered crazed predictions, and contorted their bodies impossibly. Back in Jerusalem, her father would have said they had the demons in them. Here in Rome, Ariella rarely thought of such things.

It was enough to survive.

They passed a cluster of slaves, big men, most of them, herded into a circle amidst a few flaming torches. Strange time of day for a slave auction. Ariella met the eyes of a few, but their shared circumstance did not give them connection.

Snatches of speech reached her. A gladiator troupe. A *lanista*, the trainer for the troupe, called out numbers, making new purchases. A memory of home flashed, the day she had been sold to Valerius's household manager. She had thought herself fortunate then, when so many others were sold off to entertain in the arena. Foolish child.

The unruly procession passed the men bound for death and Ariella's gaze flitted through them. Did they feel the violent shortness of their lives pressing down on them? Before her stretched nothing but endless misery. Was their lot not preferable?

A muscled slave with the yellow hair of the west shifted and she glimpsed a face beyond him. Her blood turned to ice, then fire.

Micah?

She yanked away from Valerius's sweaty grip. Stood on her toes to peer into the men.

Valerius pulled away from the raucous group, wrapped a thin arm around her waist, and brought his too-red lips to her ear. "Not growing shy after all these years, are we?" His baby-sweet voice sickened her.

She leaned away. Caught another look at the boy.

Turn your head. Look this way!

Valerius tugged her toward the road, but her feet had grown roots. She must be sure.

But then he turned, the boy about to be a gladiator, and she saw that it could not be Micah. He was too young—older than she remembered her brother, but not old enough to be him, though the resemblance was so strong that perhaps he was a distant cousin. In fact, the boy looked more like *her* than Micah. If she were to cut her hair, she could pass for his twin.

She let Valerius pull her back to the procession, but the moment had shaken her. Memories she had thought dead turned out to be only buried, and their resurrection was a knife-blade of pain.

She sleepwalked through the rest of the procession, until their drunken steps took them to the caves on the Via Appia, dark spots on the grassy mounds along the road where greater abuses could be carried out without reprisals.

Valerius and his guest, Maius, were arguing.

Ariella forced her attention to the men, leaving off thoughts of Micah and home. It did not pay to be ignorant of Valerius's moods.

"And you would sully the position you've been given by your dissolution!" Maius's upper lip beaded with sweat and he poked a finger into Valerius's chest.

Valerius swiped at the meaty finger. "At least I am not a coward! Running home to pretend to be something I am not."

"You think me a coward? Then you are a fool. I know how to hold on to power. Yours will wash away like so much spilled wine."

Valerius cackled. "Power? Ah yes, you are a mighty man down

there in your holiday town by the sea. I daresay you couldn't put a sword to a thief if he threatened your family!"

Ariella took a step backward. Valerius misjudged Maius, she could see. The man's eyes held a coldness that only came from cruelty.

Before Valerius could react, Maius had unsheathed a small dagger from his belt. He grabbed for a nearby slave, one of Valerius's special boys, wrapped a meaty arm around his forehead, and in one quick move sliced the slave's neck. He let the boy fall. Valerius screeched.

"There." Maius tossed the dagger at the smaller senator's feet and glared. "I owe you for one slave. But perhaps now you will keep your pretty mouth shut!"

"What have you done?" Valerius bent to the boy and clutched at his bloody tunic. "Not Julius! Not this one!"

The moon had risen while they marched, and now it shone down on them all, most of the guests taken with their own lustful pursuits and senseless to the drama between the two men. Ariella traced the path of moonlight down to her feet, to the glint of iron in the dirt. Maius's dagger.

She had not held a weapon for many years. Without thought she bent and retrieved it. Held it to her side, against the loose fabric of her robe.

She could not say when the idea first planted itself in her mind. Perhaps it had been back in the city when she had seen the boy who was not Micah. Perhaps it only sprang to life at this moment. Regardless, she knew what she would do.

She would not return to Valerius's house. Not participate once more, behind closed doors, in the mystery rites that had stolen her soul. Her nine years of torture had come to an end.

No one called out, no one pursued. She simply slipped away, into the weedy fields along the Via Appia, back to the city, the dagger hidden under her robe. She unwrapped the fabric sash at her waist and wound it around her hair. A few quiet questions and she found the yard where the newly purchased gladiators awaited their assignment. A little flirtation with the loutish guard at the gate, enough to convince him that she was one of the many Roman women obsessed with the fighters, and he let her in with a wicked grin.

She found the boy within moments. His eyes widened as though she were his first opponent. She pulled him to the shadows, to the catcalls of his fellow fighters.

The dagger was steady in her hand and sharp enough to slice through large hanks of hair. The boy watched, wide-eyed, as she disrobed in front of him, modesty ignored.

He was young enough to easily convince.

Within minutes she had donned his leathers and taken his place on the ground with the other fighters. The boy stumbled across the yard, awkward in his new robes and headscarf.

It was done.

Elana would be proud.

2

Pompeii
June AD 79

I n the protective embrace of Mother Vesuvius, the city of Pompeii
flourished like a well-fed child, glorying in the wealth that was
Rome and offering one of the Empire's ex-politicians an excellent
place to hide.

Cato waited in the cobbled street outside his newly purchased
wine shop, shielding his eyes against the fiery morning sun. The
expected delivery of new *amphorae* should have arrived by dawn.
Already carts rattled over familiar ruts in the center of the street, and
shoppers hummed along the raised sidewalks, making purchases and
trading gossip. But no sign of his delivery. He shook his head at the
inefficiency, then shrugged.

He should relax. It was a vacation town, after all.

The flaking red paint on the wooden sign outside the shop touted
the former owner's skills. Cato scraped at it, adding *repaint the sign* to
his unending mental list of tasks.

Back inside the shop, he blinked to adjust to the dim light. His only employee, Remus, clucked his tongue over the rows of dusty amphorae that leaned against the stone wall and held up a dingy rag. "Not getting clean, master. Not getting clean."

Cato had reminded Remus not to call him "master" a dozen times since hiring him last week, but as a former slave, the man couldn't seem to break the habit.

"So we'll have a pot-breaking holiday after we get the wine into the new amphorae, Remus." He grinned. "Anyone whose head you'd like to invite to the event?"

Remus waved a rag in Cato's direction and shook his head, as though refusing to be baited. "I'm at peace with the world, master. At peace with the world."

Cato should be so fortunate.

In truth, the orderly rows of tan pots, balanced on their pointed ends and leaning against the walls of the shop or resting above in wooden cradles, pleased Cato very much, in spite of the accumulated grime from months of neglect. He had acquired the shop, the vineyard on the outskirts of town, and the home of the former owner all at a good price, and planned to make a success of the whole enterprise in short order. In the weeks of transition from Rome to Pompeii he had concentrated on the success ahead and refused to acknowledge the failure behind.

He ran a finger over the dusty terra-cotta. "Forget the pots, Remus. Let's get the rest of the place clean before the crowds start trampling us down."

Remus snickered. "Grand plans you have for the place, master."

Cato crossed the shop and slapped Remus on the shoulder. "That's the only way to move forward, my friend. Plan for success." He turned to the filthy shop before Remus could see the uncertainty in his eyes. Uncertainty and perhaps not a little desperation.

A voice from the doorway filled the shop, and Cato imagined the pots rattled on their shelves. "Making good progress, I see."

He laughed at the barbed words. "Be careful, Mother, or I'll put a rag in *your* hand."

She huffed. "I agreed to follow you to Pompeii for the weather, remember? You'll not find me scrubbing floors on my knees, no matter how anxious you are to make this mad idea work."

With the light of the morning behind her, Octavia could have passed for a woman half her age. Still stunning, with dark hair falling in waves around delicate features that belied her inner strength, she had left behind a list of potential suitors in Rome—crestfallen noblemen, heartbroken that Rome's most recent widow wasn't interested in aligning herself with a new house. Cato observed her for a moment, grateful she had agreed to come—and to bring his youngest sister with her.

"Why are you staring at me, you silly boy?" She swept into the shop, holding her shining white *stola* around her, as though she could protect it from the grime. The red sash at her waist and the clustered emeralds at her throat seemed as out of place as a long-stemmed rose tossed into a trash heap.

"Just wondering what a woman of your advanced age is doing out of the house at such an early hour."

Octavia's gaze would have cut down a lesser man, but Cato laughed, kissed the top of her head, and answered his own question. "Looking beautiful, as always."

She sighed. "Why are we here, Quintus?"

Behind him, Remus chuckled. Since learning Cato's *praenomen*, he seemed to find it amusing that this eldest son had been given the name of "fifth."

Cato ignored his mother's question as to why they had come. She knew the answer. And rehearsing it would challenge his optimism, already stretched taut.

"The shop will be cleaned up soon enough." He surveyed the red-and-gold frescoed walls hidden beneath their layer of soot. "And then it will be a grand success."

Octavia sniffed, as though the odor of failure lingered around the shop and even around Cato himself, overwhelming her own perfume. "You could have had grand success in Rome."

Cato forced a smile and turned away. "Ah, well. They will have to struggle along without me, I suppose."

She sighed again. "At least tell me you will find a wife here. There are many good families with holiday villas—"

"Ha! Between you and Isabella, I am surrounded by women! Why, by all the gods, would I want to acquire another?" He pulled a small wooden box from under the front counter and dug through the paltry supply of coins, readying the payment for the new amphorae. A twinge of concern bloomed in his chest. The purchases of the shop and fields and home had all but annihilated the family fortune, and there was little left for building the business. Along with his list of tasks, the list of costs was also lengthening. Would there be enough? He slammed the lid on the money box and clenched his fist around the coins. There must be.

As though his heart were the fertile black soil of his vineyard, the determination to thrive here had taken root inside him like a stubborn vine, curling around his heart, drawing nourishment from the pain of the past, longing to bear fruit.

He turned back to Octavia. "Don't worry, Mother. Portia is sure to give you all the grandchildren your arms can hold."

The marble of his mother's stately features seemed to quiver and she dropped her eyes. Cursing his mistake, he set the coins on the counter, crossed to where Octavia stood in the center of the shop, and gripped her arms. "She still believes she cannot conceive?" Cato's eldest sister had been a resident of Pompeii for five years before them, after meeting Lucius while vacationing here and marrying him in what seemed an instant. The two were exceedingly in love—and still childless.

Octavia glanced at Remus, as though reluctant to share family secrets in front of the help. As if on cue, Remus began whistling a tune, a bawdy melody straight out of the taverns. Octavia's eyes returned to Cato and glistened. "She despairs. As do I."

He patted her arm. "The gods will smile, Mother. Portia is a good woman."

She turned away and straightened the folds of her stola.

Cato went to the doorway again, still looking for his overdue delivery. The sea-tinged air was already heavy with the coming heat of the day, and the cloth awning jutting from his shop did little to relieve it. The shoppers who pushed past him seemed damp and harried.

His was only one of the busy streets that crisscrossed Pompeii in a grid that held both shops and homes, some little more than huts and others with doors opening to grand villas. The city moved with surprising intensity, even in these early summer months when the vacationers were fewer, many choosing to remain in Rome while the weather was pleasant.

Unlike Octavia, he had not come to Pompeii for the weather, but he meant to enjoy it nonetheless. In truth, he meant to enjoy everything about his new life.

A familiar figure moved toward him from across the street. Not his delivery, but just as welcome. He waved at Isabella and could see his youngest sister brighten, even from this distance. She skipped across the three large stepping-stones, placed to raise pedestrians out of the daily rush of water that cleaned the streets, and continued toward him on his side. He lost sight of her amidst the other shoppers, but her wide eyes and big smile soon reappeared. At fourteen, she was becoming a woman. This she should not know.

He leaned forward as if to kiss her cheek, but pinched her side instead and waited for her reaction.

"Quintus!" She slapped his arm. "I came to save you from Mother, and that's how you repay me?"

He laughed. "Not even your wisdom could convince Mother that my plans are worthy, I'm afraid."

"Hmm. She was complaining before she even left the villa."

Cato pulled his sister into the shop and didn't miss the way she lifted her own stola off the dirty floor. She was her mother's daughter, after all. Octavia raised her eyebrows at Isabella, and they seemed to share a common opinion.

"I thought you were planning to open soon." Isabella scowled. "This place is disastrous."

Cato shrugged. "We're using that as a selling point." He spread his hands to the room. "'Our wine is so good, even the shop is aged.'"

Isabella rolled her eyes, not amused. "Seriously, Quintus, who is going to come—"

"It was a good price, sister. Bargains come with drawbacks. Nothing we can't fix."

Behind them, Remus cursed suddenly, and the expletive was followed by the sound of smashing pottery. Cato whirled in time to see the line of amphorae balanced on their pointed ends going down like wheat falling beneath a scythe.

"Remus!" He dove for the jars, but Remus was already there, down on one knee with his hands thrust forward to catch the next one. He righted it before it could take down another, then sat back on his heels. Six terra-cotta jars lay cracked on the floor, their blood-red contents leaking or surging from cracks of varying widths.

Cato grabbed two with slow leaks and balanced them against the wall before they could contribute to the mess. The rest were already empty.

"Master, I—" Remus's voice caught. Was the man near to tears?

"An accident, Remus!" He placed a hand on the man's shoulder. "I suppose you were just getting started on our pot-breaking, eh?"

"But the wine, master—"

"Saturninus's wine wasn't very good anyway, and we both know it. No doubt why he went out of business." He stepped across the widening puddle. "Perhaps it will do more good washing away the grime of the floor!"

Octavia and Isabella had backed away to the doorway, and Cato didn't need to look at the two women in his life to know what they were thinking.

He and Remus set to work cleaning up the spilled wine and cracked pottery with the women looking on.

"Saturninus didn't go out of business because of the quality of his wine, master."

"He must have been a poor businessman, then, for he was certainly bankrupt."

Remus knelt to sop up the wine with a rag. "Yes. But driven there. Driven to bankruptcy by the crook who owns half the city and controls the other. Gnaeus Nigidius Maius."

"The *duovir*?" He had heard the politician's name muttered a few times by disgruntled citizens but knew nothing more of the elected official.

"Don't let the position fool you. The city is united in its hatred for him. He would sell his mother for a vote, and when Saturninus refused to give him a take of the shop's profits, Maius destroyed him. That's why you were able to buy everything the man owned for a *sestertius* on every *aureus*."

Cato straightened, two shards of pottery in his hands. "Maius forced him out of business?"

"Indeed. The man's a—"

Remus's sentence hung unfinished as the doorway darkened and Cato looked up, still expecting his delivery. His mother and sister turned and seemed dwarfed by the bulk of the man who filled the frame.

"Please, finish." The large man dipped his head toward Remus. "You have me so curious."

Cato looked from the stylish visitor to the cowering Remus and instinct told him that this was the man himself.

Gnaeus Nigidius Maius. Enemy of the people.

3

The journey from Napoli to the foot of the beautiful mountain had taken half the day, and Ariella was footsore and thirsty by the time Drusus called a halt to the forced march. She waited for instructions, hoping they would be allowed to rest.

The mountain—Vesuvius, they called it—had loomed to the south of the troupe when they left Napoli, looming larger until they traveled the narrow channel of land between the mountain to the east and the sea to the west. Now it was behind them, with the sun beginning to fall toward its pointed peak.

Drusus declared that they were only an hour out from Pompeii. "But we will camp here and enter the city tomorrow." A cheer went up from the troupe, as though tomorrow's arrival would be a triumphant procession of honored soldiers returning from victory rather than a column of ragtag gladiators hauled in to entertain the masses with their blood.

Drusus directed the slaves who accompanied them to begin setting up camp alongside the road. To the troupe, he called out sharp instructions. "Take some water, men." He pointed to an open area beside the road, bordered on one side by a grove of trees. "We begin practice shortly."

The collective groan was more subdued than the cheer had been, for good reason. Drusus was a harsh master, and reluctance to train only resulted in more of it.

One of the other gladiators, Celadus, nudged Ariella. "You'd better get some water, Ari. You're not looking well." Celadus was a bear of a Roman with his front teeth missing, but usually kind.

Another fighter chuckled without mercy. "These young boys are more likely to fall *between* cities than in the amphitheater. I don't know why Drusus keeps buying them."

Ariella lowered her chin to hide the flash of anger in her eyes. It was difficult enough to masquerade as a young man, but to be seen as weak infuriated her. She beat back her exhaustion and shrugged. "I'll outlast you in the arena, Paris. Larger is not always better, you know."

"Hah!" Paris, the Greek favorite, was as chiseled as one of his forefathers' statues, but his grin held ugly animosity. "Perhaps not against animals. Wait until you face a real opponent."

Celadus passed a water skin to Ariella, saving her from a reply.

The afternoon sun hammered down on her head, making her grateful she had chopped her hair off at the neck weeks earlier. With no head covering, her usual mane of thick hair would have been like a heavy blanket in the *Junius* heat.

Was the month still Junius? The thought wandered through her exhausted mind as she swigged from the water skin. She had lost track, which she found both bothersome and somewhat terrifying. As though she were leaving parts of herself along the sides of the road, including her awareness of time.

All too soon, Drusus called an end to the break and instructed the men to begin drills. Each of them went to the equipment wagon and sought out their personal training weapons. Ariella's wooden sword, the traditional *rudis*, was blackened and dented already, even though it had only been three weeks since she had disguised herself, escaped Rome and Valerius and all that made life unbearable, and fallen in with this gladiator troupe.

She secured leather straps around her left hand and turned with her rudis, waiting to be partnered for the drills. The three weeks had passed in a blur of dogged determination to survive, alternating with periods of fatigue so severe she had to call up angry memories of both the distant and immediate past to find the strength to continue.

And today would be no different. She would fight, and she would survive. As she always had.

But for how long?

"Ari, you're with Celadus," the trainer called out.

She gave Celadus a half smile, and he rolled his eyes in mock disgust. "Not again." He spoke so only she could hear it. Drusus had been pairing them often, though Celadus was much bigger. An apparent effort to "broaden the boy's shoulders," as he said, eyeing Ariella with dissatisfaction.

She and Celadus found an open space in the grass among the other twenty-nine pairs and squared off. "You're never going to fight anyone but the animals and the little men," Celadus called to her, in the time-honored insults of gladiator training. She was expected to return with angering words for him, to get the blood boiling, but her thoughts were fuzzy today, and even her vision seemed to blur with weariness.

She raised her arm, though. Raised her wooden rudis above her head and ran at Celadus with a snarl of defiance, as much toward her own fatigue and doubts as toward Celadus and his taunts.

Their battered swords clacked together with the artificial smack of dull wood, and Celadus laughed, revealing the wide gap in his smile, and pulled back to reposition. "Like an angry little dog kicked too many times by a cruel master."

More truth to that than he realized.

They sparred for what seemed hours, but Ariella did not back down. Even when she saw the beige tents go up nearby and imagined falling into one and sleeping until autumn. Her short tunic grew damp with sweat and dingy with kicked-up dust, and the collective odor of the men hung heavy over the field. Her sword felt weighted in her hand, and the grunts and calls of the fighters muddled together.

Would that she had an arm of iron rather than flesh. But still she did not yield.

It was not until the mountain loomed purple to the southwest, with the sun hiding behind it, that Drusus called an end to the drills. For the rest of the troupe, the declaration brought relief. For Ariella, the true challenge had just begun.

To be a woman disguised as a man, in a group of sixty-five men, presented difficulties that far outweighed those of the training—or even her single experience of combat in Napoli, when Drusus had put her in the ring with first a wild boar and then an ibex. Those fights had been only for show. She had not been expected to kill either of the beasts, only to provide a prelude of entertainment before the real fighters flooded into the arena. But the battle she would face in the remaining hours of daylight today, and even beyond, was not for show.

It was life or death.

She trudged to the blazing campfire with the others, passed the equipment wagon, and secured her sword. The five slaves who traveled with the troupe were already passing out plates of spicy meat and bread, and the men fell around the large fire and dug into the food. Ariella took her meat, then pulled away from the crowd and found a lonely spot in the scratchy grass. Her stomach heaved with physical and emotional unrest, but she forced the food down for the sake of her strength.

She watched the gang of men wolf down their meal. Most of these Gentiles were indeed wolves. If they discovered that she was not a slightly built young man but a woman—she shuddered to think of the outcome. They were a long way from Rome and its laws, and even there, women were not so protected that men did not take advantage.

But even life as an effeminate young man among older, well-muscled men who had long been far from women presented challenges. There were a number of them who would not be put off by her gender, even believing she was a man. She was on guard always—slept with muscles tensed, ate with only one eye on her food, and when she slipped into the woods to attend to hygiene, she walked nearly backward to be certain she was not followed.

She shrugged to herself. In her twenty-five years she had survived worse, first in Jerusalem and then in Rome. She would survive this. Perhaps her arm could not be made of iron, but her heart had long been smelted into something harder than flesh and blood.

No doubts allowed.

And what better place to hide from Valerius? Though he must be scouring the Roman countryside for her, he would never think to look in the center of a gladiator troupe.

The meal ended as quickly as it began. The fighters tossed their greasy plates at the waiting servants and began to prepare for much-needed sleep. Ariella returned her own plate to the pile and eyed the nearby verdant grove of trees. She needed to disappear there and attend to personal matters, then find a way to change her clothing without being observed in the tent she shared with five other men, and finally to settle into a night of half sleep before marching into

Pompeii. Such had been the past three weeks. Tonight was no different, she told herself.

And she refused to listen to the small voice that told her perhaps she was not as invincible as she believed.

4

Cato resisted a self-conscious glance around the grimy shop with its spilled wine leaking across the floor. As Maius crowded into the room, past Octavia and Isabella, the interior seemed to shrink upon them all, as though five were a number far too great for the four walls.

The politician Maius had already lost interest in Remus's opinion of him, distracted perhaps by the shop's deficiencies. His attention went to the walls, the floor, the counter, then at last to Octavia—where his gaze stopped.

Cato stepped forward to introduce himself. "Quintus Portius Cato. My mother, Octavia Catonis, and my sister."

Maius nodded toward Octavia, ignoring him. "Nigidius Maius." He reached for Octavia's hand, caught it up in his own, and kissed it lightly.

Cato glanced to his mother to assess her reaction. She was not impressed. He circled Maius to gain his attention. "What can I do for you, Maius?"

The larger man turned on him at last and seemed to take his

measure in an instant, as though sizing him up for a future fight. Maius's dark hair receded from his forehead slightly, but lay slick and oiled as though carved from black marble. His eyes were focused and sharp, and when he smiled on Cato, it was more like the wide snarl of a menacing yet confident beast. "I came for your sake, Portius Cato, not my own."

"Can I offer you a cup of wine?" Cato flicked a glance in Remus's direction and indicated one of the broken pots, standing on its end to retain what wine remained. Remus hurried to get cups and Cato turned back to Maius, whose attention had again drifted to Octavia.

"I look forward to making the acquaintance of your husband, dear lady." He bowed.

Cato rolled his eyes at the obvious ploy.

"My husband is dead." Octavia's words had enough blunt coldness to warn off any pursuer.

Maius smiled, a small, knowing smirk, as if he believed that Octavia played a game with him, holding back her favors to encourage ardor. Cato knew better. His father had been gone for four months, and his mother still cried every night.

"Wine?" Cato took two cups from Remus and passed one to Maius.

The politician accepted with a nod. He buried his nose in the cup and took two short sniffs. His eyes flicked upward to Cato, then he swirled the cup and sipped. And promptly spat upon the floor. "Aahh!" Maius shoved the cup at Remus. "What kind of foolishness is this?"

Cato sipped from his own cup and agreed that the wine was inferior, though not deserving of Maius's reaction. A bit too earthy on the nose, perhaps, with too short a finish. He shrugged. "Saturninus was not so good with the vines, it seems. All the better for me. We will have a finer supply in the years to come."

Maius raised his eyebrows. "Then the rumors are true? This is more than a vacation for the Cato dynasty? You think to remain in Pompeii?" He did not make reference to Cato's flight from his political career in Rome, but the implication was there.

Cato handed his own cup to Remus and smiled coldly. "To stay, to enjoy this fine city, and to thrive."

Maius stepped around the spilled wine on the floor and wandered around the small shop, taking in each cracked fresco, each rotting shelf, and glancing back at Cato, who followed him with his eyes. It was as though they circled each other in that moment, fangs bared and hackles up.

But Maius was all pleasantry when he turned his attention back to Cato. "Good luck to you, then, Cato. Saturninus never found much success here."

"Saturninus didn't have my talents."

Maius bowed his head in Cato's direction. "I am sure you are correct."

"Remus tells me that besides your responsibilities as duovir, you have many other . . . successful ventures in Pompeii. I appreciate such a prominent businessman stopping by to wish me good fortune in my own small efforts."

Maius crossed back to the doorway, where the morning light seemed to glow around him, and stood too close to Octavia, letting his arm brush against hers. She shifted away, silent and haughty. "Do not be modest, Cato. Your new villa and vineyards, these are not small investments. You strike me as a man who wishes to make a name for himself. A *respected* name, that is."

Cato swallowed a heated reply. "I can only hope to achieve a bit of what you have accomplished."

Maius held his silk-edged toga over one bent arm and smoothed the heavy fabric with his free hand. "You honor me." He brushed at imaginary soil. "It is true, I have given myself, body and soul, for the good of this city. It is sometimes thankless, but rewarding all the same." He sniffed and fluttered his eyes in self-deprecation, then gave his attention to Octavia. "You have heard of the games I am sponsoring a few evenings hence, no doubt?"

Octavia's only response was a small puff of breath escaping her tight lips.

Maius seemed not to notice her distaste. "I would be most honored if you would be my guests." A look toward Cato broadened the offer. "I've sponsored thirty pairs of gladiators, including the fighter Paris, a favorite coming in from Rome. There will be a hunt as well. And executions." He bowed toward Octavia. "Not that you would enjoy such things, but we have some troublesome Jews here, refusing to worship the emperor. You will see that even in our small town, the laws must be honored."

Octavia glanced at Cato, the concern in her eyes evident.

But he must ignore Maius's last comment and focus on the games themselves. He had always been drawn to the games and had seen Paris fight in Rome. He wouldn't miss the event at the end of the week, even if it were a politician's ploy to curry the favor of the people. "Generous of you, Maius."

Maius shrugged. "As I said, I do the best I can for my beloved Pompeii." His eyes bored into Cato's. "I'm sure you would do the same, had you my position."

The mutually insincere flattery seemed to have played itself out, though the heat of the encounter still sparked between them. Had he become an enemy to Maius simply by opening a small wine shop? Surely Maius wasn't threatened by Cato's presence in Pompeii?

As if the shop weren't crowded enough, another figure peeked out from behind Maius, still in the street. "Quintus? Mother?"

Cato sighed. He should have expected his married sister, Portia, to make an appearance.

Maius slid to the side to allow her to enter, and Cato did not miss the naked admiration that overtook the older man's face as Portia ducked her head politely and joined Octavia.

"Ah, it is like a double rose has bloomed right before my eyes." Maius rubbed his hands together and looked between Octavia and Portia. "Two blooms ready for picking."

Despite the sordid insinuation, Cato nearly laughed aloud at the look on his youngest sister's face. Isabella had been ignored far too long, and this last insult of attention lavished on both her mother and older, married sister was too much for her. She crossed her arms and shot daggers at the politician from her eyes. Cato did her a favor by neglecting to introduce her older sister.

Portia lifted her chin and ignored Maius's comment. Octavia seemed too insulted to respond. Best to position himself between Maius and the women before his mother recovered and took a swing at the offender.

"You'll forgive us if we excuse ourselves from your kind visit, Maius." He held a hand toward the doorway. "As you have certainly noticed, there is much work to do here." He indicated Maius's fine woolen toga, with its purple silk edging, and fought to keep the scorn from his voice. "We wouldn't want you to get soiled by standing too close to the effort."

Maius bowed to Cato, then to the women, including the young Isabella, then reached again for Octavia's hand.

She deftly wrapped an arm around Portia's waist and lifted a serene smile. "We have heard so much about you, Nigidius Maius." Her expression was like ice. "Meeting you indeed confirmed all we have heard." The words were honey-coated barbs, but her pleasantry did not waver.

Cato lowered his head and coughed into his hand to hide his amusement.

Maius's face darkened for a moment, then cleared. "I look forward to furthering our acquaintance at the games this week." His eyes roamed over Portia now, as though he had traded in Octavia for the younger version.

They stood suspended, all of them, until he removed himself from the shop, then for a few more beats while Cato imagined him strolling down the sidewalk, and then they seemed to exhale all as one, and the women started talking.

"What a vile man!" Octavia brushed at her clothing as though Maius had left behind some vestige on her person.

"Hush, Mother." Portia eyed the doorway. "He may hear you."

Octavia huffed. "Let him hear me. It seems he does not hear the truth often enough in this town."

Portia gripped her mother's arm. "He is not a man to be opposed, Mother. He has been duovir for longer than the five years I have been here and commands much fear in this city."

The young Isabella spoke for the first time, her voice low. "Someone should poison his mushrooms."

"Isabella!" Octavia's rebuke was halfhearted.

Cato winked at his sister. She had become fascinated of late with the history of the Empire and had been all talk about the Emperor Claudius, murdered twenty-five years ago in such a way.

Portia turned her eyes on him, and there was neither amusement nor petulance there. "He is just the sort of man you always opposed in Rome, Quintus. You could do something."

Cato turned back to the spilled wine, but Remus had it all cleaned.

Portia had not finished. "It would give your coming here purpose. More than a rich nobleman's idle pastime with the vines."

Cato scowled. "Not as rich as you seem to think, Portia. And my 'idle pastime' will no doubt yield more fruit than any of my efforts in Rome. Or have you forgotten?"

Portia started again, but her mother stilled her with a gentle hand on her arm. "It grows close in here, girls." She straightened. "Let us leave the men to their work and take some air."

Cato passed her a look of gratitude, but the intensity of her eyes was as pointed as Portia's remarks.

She felt it too, he could see. That he was wasting his life here.

He walked with them to the doorway and watched as the three women who both loved and frustrated him walked arm in arm down the raised sidewalk of the Arnius Pollio block where his shop huddled between others of its kind.

Portia's words chased around themselves in his mind. *"It would give your coming here purpose."*

But he did have a purpose.

He would get his hands dirty, but it would be in the fertile black soil at the foot of Vesuvius, not in the futile political maneuverings of the city government.

No matter how much Gnaeus Nigidius Maius deserved to be brought down.

5

The evening was a fine one for theater entertainment, and Cato escorted his mother and Isabella toward the southern end of town, eager for a diversion.

The bulk of their belongings had arrived from Rome yesterday, and between directing the slaves to place the furniture and prized statuary throughout the new villa and instructing Remus in the final details of opening the shop, Cato had found the past few days to be more work than play. A situation he meant to rectify this evening.

He did not acknowledge that an inner restlessness also plagued him, a stirring of unease, as if none of his frantic activity amounted to anything worthwhile.

A half-moon hung already over the back wall of the city's large theater as they approached. They could see nothing but the high wall with its curved vaults and outer staircases from this side, but beyond the wall and sloping downward lay a fine example of Roman-adopted Greek culture. The Romans had long ago left behind their barbarism and embraced the sophistication and the architecture of the Greeks, whose far-flung city-states the Roman military machine had swallowed.

Cato led the two women to the outer wall. They would not enter the theater at the front. The only access to the highest tiers of seats, reserved for the nobility, was from the outside. He stepped aside at the base of the stairs and allowed them to precede him. The two were radiant tonight, with eyes shining in anticipation of the performance and hair braided into delicate spirals atop their heads. He gave young Isabella a quick peck on the cheek as she passed.

Her face lit at his attention. "You are in fine spirits tonight, Quintus."

A few steps above, Octavia turned to call over her shoulder, "Quintus, tell me there is not going to be some vulgar competition here tonight, in addition to the play."

Cato laughed and tightened his toga to climb the stairs. "Fear not, Mother. I am simply a boy on holiday after too much time indoors with an ill-tempered tutor."

Octavia shook her head and continued upward. She was aware of his proclivity for competitive entertainment. He was, after all, a Roman, raised on lust and blood. And Maius's comment about the Jews who would be executed had her worried, though they would not speak of it between them.

The truth was that he would have rather been at the arena, but the new gladiators had just arrived and would not perform for another two days.

They cleared the stairs and stood above the highest gallery of the theater, gazing down into the middle tier of twenty rows, accessible by vaulted corridors at the side of the building. Below the middle tier a covered gallery curved around the half circle, separating it from the lowest tier for slaves and the poor and providing special box seating for the magistrates whose generosity sponsored the event. Far below, the orchestra seating was reserved for aristocrats.

Taken in all at once, it was a spectacular sight. The five thousand seats had nearly filled, and the citizens had arrived in their best clothes, melting the marble theater into a sea of white, with red and blue and gold sashes weaving and twisting through the bright sea like languid, colorful fish.

Cato put a hand on his mother's back and guided her to a bank of empty seats.

"Oh!" Isabella pointed. "There is Portia! And Lucius!" She waved frantically, and her older sister smiled and nodded. The two joined them a moment later. Cato slapped his quiet brother-in-law's back in greeting, kissed Portia's cheeks, and the group squeezed into a near-empty row.

As they sat, the hum of the waiting audience increased. Cato searched for the cause and saw Gnaeus Nigidius Maius had entered from the side corridor and crossed to a private box at the side, where nearly everyone in the theater would be able to see him. Cato fought to hold on to his mood of frivolity.

Something about that man drove ice down his back and fire into his veins.

The curtain hiding the two-story façade at the back of the stage soon dropped into the trench and the performance began—a typical one, with the itinerant actors performing the familiar roles of Maccus the Jester, Bucco the potbellied simpleton, and Dossenus the trickster. Behind them, on the freestanding *scaenae frons*, the two-story façade, marble statues of the honored prominent family of the gens *Holconii* watched the proceedings, mute spectators from an era now past. The Holconii family had renovated the theater as a gift to the town.

The play failed to capture Cato's attention. Instead, his eyes continued to travel to the seats where Maius held court, whether with petitioners or family members Cato could not tell at this distance.

At a break in the performance, Cato stood. "I am going to walk in the *quadriporticus*." He glanced at his family. "Anyone care to join me?"

Portia stood at once. "I must stretch my legs." His sister hated confined spaces. Cato held out a hand. "Then let's go for a run."

She batted his hand away. "A stroll will do."

They left the others in their seats to gossip and socialize, descended the stairs, and circled around the theater to the colonnaded grassy enclosure. It had once been a *palaestra*, the city's main field for athletic training and fitness, with the covered porticoes surrounding it providing shady areas for more academic instruction. But a larger palaestra had since been built, out near the amphitheater, and this one had been given over to the training of gladiators. Still, the tradition of strolling the area during theater breaks remained, and many followed Cato and his sister into the rectangular area.

Portia clucked her tongue as they entered, then pointed to the fighters at the end of the field. "That's why you wanted to come down here." Her tone was indulgent. "You didn't tell me there would be gladiators."

Cato laughed. "How could you have missed them entering the city yesterday?" He eyed the men, who looked small at this distance, curious to see if he could pick out the champion, Paris. The men trained in pairs, their movements fluid and graceful, like the dancers who sometimes entertained in the baths. Outstanding. He watched one pair with interest, for they seemed a strange mismatch—a muscle-bound, seasoned fighter with a young man struggling to hold his own, inexperienced. They did not wear their costumes to train, so he could not tell their positions—*Retiarius* or *Secutor*, Gaul or *Murmillo*, it was impossible to guess. He followed every parry and thrust, the rhythm of the fight he had loved since childhood. It would take more research to decide where to place his bets. The blood sport was more than entertainment. Fortunes could be won or lost.

A silky voice spoke between them, and a hand came to rest on his shoulder. "I see you are an admirer."

Cato turned to find Maius smirking at his back. The older man jutted a heavy chin toward the gladiators. "All of Pompeii is talking about the fight I have sponsored. It will be worth all my expense, I am certain."

Maius could save his politicking. Cato shrugged the hand off his shoulder.

Maius's attention shifted to Portia. "Ah, here you are again." He sidled closer. "As if Fortuna herself smiles down on me."

A small crowd had grown around them, no doubt curious to see who the great Maius deigned to address. But it was Maius's interaction with Portia that troubled him. The politician was welded to his sister.

Portia pulled her head back, as though to remove herself from him without the insult of stepping backward. She was elegance personified, as always.

Cato saved her the trouble and inserted himself between them, resting a hand on his sister's lower back. He could feel her tension. "Come, Portia, I shall give you a lesson in the way of the games. I know how much you love blood and glory."

Maius extended his arm toward the fighters, like a host inviting a guest into his home.

Cato bristled at the condescension but strolled toward the end of the grassy field, his hand guiding Portia. He would not give Maius the satisfaction of seeing him perturbed.

A group had formed to watch the fighters and Cato joined it, hoping that Maius would drift away. The man was ruining his good mood.

But Maius remained close, even introducing him to several prominent men of Pompeii. "Portius Cato," Maius offered to one of the nearby men. "Come to our little town to grow grapes and sell wine."

The patrician's eyebrows raised. "I knew your father in Rome, Cato." His expression grew haughty. "And many of the Catonii clan. None of them were farmers that I remember."

Cato bowed slightly at the veiled insult. "An indulgence of mine, I will admit. But I am certain you will be glad of my new hobby once you have tasted my wine."

Maius laughed and elbowed the patrician. "Ah, but the wine supply in Pompeii is more than adequate with my vineyards and shops, is it not, Gracchus? Cato here refuses to see that his predecessor failed for just this reason. People simply prefer my wine." His voice was softness undergirded with iron.

Gracchus bowed. "And your fruit stands. And bakeries. Even your brothels."

Cato stifled a snort at Gracchus's fawning tone. "Perhaps they have been kept from a better alternative." His voice hardened and he smiled. "They need to be freed to try something new. Something superior."

From Maius's glare the man understood the deeper meaning of his words. But Maius recovered and again attached himself to Portia. "Well, if the Catonii family can create wine half as delectable as their women, my business will indeed be in jeopardy." He ran a finger up her arm to the elbow, and Cato saw a small shudder. "You are simply delicious, my dear girl."

"Pity for you she is a married woman." Cato pulled his sister from the man's grasp, his fingers twitching with the urge to strike Maius. But he should have kept silent. The husbands of beautiful women were never safe from unscrupulous men, and Maius struck him as a man devoid of integrity. His brother-in-law, Lucius, was in danger.

"Come, Maius." The sound of applause drifted from the theater, and Gracchus and the others backed away. "The performance is about to resume."

Cato held Portia back for a few moments to give Maius and his sycophants time to clear the quadriporticus. He returned to watching the mismatched gladiators in silence. Had Portia's thoughts gone in the dark direction of his own?

He became aware of a small group of men in a huddle nearby, talking together, their eyes on him. He gave them a casual nod, and they glanced at each other and then approached, as if he had invited them to speak. From their dress he could see that they were wealthy men. One of them seemed to lead the group forward.

"Portius Cato? Newly come from Rome?"

Cato bowed. "Indeed. And anxious to make the acquaintance of the town's leading men."

The spokesman smirked. "Spoken like a true politician."

Cato straightened and raised his eyebrows.

"I meant no insult. In truth, just the opposite."

Cato lifted his chin and observed the man through lowered lids. "You have me at a disadvantage."

"My apologies. My name is Tullius Taurus." He nodded to each of his four companions and introduced them all in turn.

Cato knew none of them.

Taurus inhaled deeply, as though bracing himself. "We saw you speaking with Nigidius Maius."

Cato tried to read Taurus's eyes, unsure whether to share his mind about the man who seemed to control the town. "Maius was speaking to me, not I to him." He held up his palms. "As you said, these politicians must try to make connections."

"And did he succeed?"

Taurus's direct question surprised him. Alliances in Rome were a tricky game. Were things simpler here in Pompeii, so far south of the mother city?

He examined Taurus's eyes once more, then decided on forth-rightness. "He did not."

Taurus's chest seemed to deflate, and Cato had the sense it was in relief. "So you do not intend to be a Maius man?"

Cato laughed. "I am my own man. Always."

There were guarded smiles around the little group. Cato glanced at Portia. She'd been here for years and must know these men. Her eyes betrayed that she knew more of the encounter than Cato did. He furrowed his brow with an unspoken question, but she tilted her head, all wide eyes and innocence.

Taurus was speaking again, this time in a lower tone. He took a step closer to Cato. "There are many who would see Maius extricated from the office he's gripped with greedy fingers for many years."

Cato nodded. "I do not believe he is the man of the people he purports to be."

"He is evil, crawled out of a pit from the underworld."

Cato bit back a laugh, for the man's face bore an intensity that matched his words. "So why is he not voted out?"

Taurus spoke through clenched teeth. "Because he buys votes with money, blackmails to gain those who can't be bought, and threatens those with nothing to hide."

Cato eyed the quadriporticus, empty now except for the gladiators and the lanista who trained them. He should be back in the performance with his family, away from the talk of corrupt politicians. Yes, he should leave.

He must have leaned that way unconsciously, for he felt Portia's hand on his back, as though she would keep him here with her delicate fingers.

It was time to escape. The next words were inevitable, even before they emerged from the lips of Taurus.

"We want you to run against him."

His head was shaking before Taurus finished. "I came to Pompeii to enjoy life." He nodded toward the theater. "To bask in the balmy weather and grow luscious grapes and get fat with contentment."

Taurus inclined his head and watched Cato as though he were a specimen to be studied. "You are young to be so disillusioned with higher purpose." His voice quieted. "Only two years as *aedile*, then two as *quaestor*. You had a long career ahead of you in Rome."

And you know too much about me. He searched for a clever response, but had nothing. "I served the Empire as best I could. And now I wish for other things."

But Taurus would not be put off. "There is no one else in Pompeii qualified to run for duovir who has not already sold himself to Maius. There is only you."

A twinge of the old ambition, the old passion to right wrongs and destroy corruption, burrowed through his heart and threatened to surface. He beat it back with the hammer of the past. "I am honored by your request, citizens. Truly, I am. And I support your efforts to remove Maius from office so that he can face the prosecution he deserves for his many crimes. But you will have to find someone else."

Taurus would speak again, but Cato bowed and took Portia's arm. "My sister is no doubt grieved to be missing the third act." He pulled Portia along. "Please excuse us."

"Do not think you can avoid him, Cato," Taurus called after him. "Maius will destroy you as surely as he did Saturninus."

Cato strode from the quadriporticus, dragging Portia with him. But it was not his pace that caused her objections.

"Cato, how can you dismiss their request? You could do so much good here—"

Cato released her arm and escaped through the entrance to the grassy area outside the wall with Portia on his heels. "Almost I could believe this was *your* doing, Portia." He headed for the steps to the theater.

Her silence condemned her.

How could you do it, Portia?

He reached the top of the stairs, emerged onto the highest tier of the theater, and stopped to take in the thousands of people who laughed at the farce before them.

They were only a quarter of the city. So many more, with Maius's greed oppressing them all in some fashion. He stared at the man in his special cubicle, elevated above the people.

In that moment Maius turned his eyes upward toward Cato as well, and though Maius could not identify him from this distance, nor did he know of the request just made, there still seemed to be a coldness emanating from the man, directed toward Cato.

He thought again of the two gladiators, the way the younger fought with everything in him, even though outmatched.

He would not allow Gnaeus Nigidius Maius to oppress him. But he would find some other way to avoid the man's malice.

Not an election. Definitely not an election.

6

Pompeii did not have the expansive sprawl of Rome, nor was it weighted with the abundant amounts of marble, but Ariella would not have traded the one day spent here for a hundred in Rome. The town felt safe, as though she were tucked away beneath the beneficent gaze of the mountain Vesuvius, safe from Valerius and his searching eyes.

The troupe had spent their second day in the town much as their first, training in the barracks that also had become their new home. The rectangular building housed dozens of cells off the roofed passage that ran around the open courtyard, with a kitchen, an armory, even a prison. This evening, when the afternoon's heat fell behind the theater along with the sun, Drusus, their lanista, called them back from their cells to work out in the cooling air.

Ariella glanced at the back of the theater's two-story façade. What kind of play was being performed there? Valerius had dragged her to several in Rome, each one more embarrassingly vulgar than the next, further proving that Roman society had traded morals for thrills.

She faced off against her usual partner, Celadus, again, and not many minutes into their sparring, a crescendo of laughter from the theater beyond peaked with a thunder of applause. Ariella pulled back from Celadus and panted.

"By the end of the week they will be yelling for us." Celadus grinned, gap-toothed.

Ariella shrugged. "Yelling for our blood."

He raised his sword. "For honor. For glory. They live it through us. You will see."

A steady stream of people began to flow into the large enclosure from the far end, nearest the theater. They strolled along the columned porticoes, talking and laughing. Some of them made their way to the end where the fighters practiced and formed a line along the muddy area to watch the training.

Though it wasn't a true performance such as they would offer in a few days, Ariella's nerves fluttered at the gaze of so many people, far closer than they would be in the arena. She tried not to take note of those who watched, but one man caught her attention and she glanced toward him more than once. He had seemed interested at first, but another, larger man had drawn him away. Even from the distance of twenty *gradi*, she could see that animosity between the men lay beneath their civility.

"Over here, Ari," Celadus called. "The fight's over here."

"Sorry." She refocused.

But her eyes strayed to the leaner man again. There was something about him that she liked. His wavy hair was styled in the Roman fashion, and his clothes spoke of wealth but were not ostentatious. He carried himself with confidence, like a man who has tried himself on and found it to be a good fit. Strong jawline. Ready smile.

He had a woman with him, a stunning beauty. She wore a pale blue robe the color of sky, gathered at the shoulders and secured with gold pins. Ariella studied her through a twinge of jealousy. From the way she put her hand to the man's back, she was likely his wife.

"Ahh!" Celadus's wooden sword clapped down on her shoulder.

"Keep your eyes where they belong, boy!" Celadus said. "There'll be bigger crowds than this on the sand, and animals besides. You must learn not to be distracted."

She rubbed her shoulder and grimaced at Celadus. "Fine." She circled so that she could watch the man and the beautiful woman over Celadus's shoulder as they sparred. Drusus would not leave Celadus paired with her for long. The bigger man needed opponents who would challenge him. She had better learn to fight well or she wouldn't fight long enough to survive.

But the interaction behind Celadus still distracted her. The big man had left with his friends, and another, smaller group had approached, but these seemed to frighten the Roman somehow, and before long he turned and left, nearly running from the enclosure.

She felt a sharp poke in her side and shot a look at Celadus.

"You are worthless tonight." He waved his sword. "And lucky I fight with wood."

Drusus called a break, and Celadus huffed away in disgust toward the lanista, complaining about having to look after an idiot who could not fight.

Ariella crossed to the covered walk and collapsed onto a bench. Since arriving in Pompeii yesterday she had recovered much of her energy, but the training was vigorous. She swiped at her damp brow with her forearm and leaned her back against the stone wall.

An older slave approached with a bucket of water and a metal dipper. She glanced at him from under lowered lids, then lifted her head for a better look. He was strong but a bit grizzled, with deep lines about the eyes. And there was something about him . . .

Jewish.

She waited for him to look at her. He bent to his knees and offered her a dipperful of water, lifting it above his head for her to hold as she drank. She took the lukewarm water in her mouth and swallowed. Then said softly, *"Shalom."*

His head jerked upward and he peered into her eyes. "A fellow traveler." He smiled slightly.

She nodded. "Still longing for home."

Word had come from Rome that Emperor Vespasian had died, and his son Titus succeeded him. Titus, who had led the rampage across Judea. It was best to speak carefully, though she would spit upon the man if he stood before her today.

The slave pulled a rag from his belt and dipped it into the water, then stayed on his knees to wash her lower legs, grimy from the mud of the practice field. It was an odd feeling, but she allowed it for the chance to speak to him.

"How long since you have seen Jerusalem?" His question was a whisper.

"Nine years." He would grasp the significance.

He sighed heavily. "Did you see the Temple . . . after?"

"I saw it burn before my eyes." Her voice caught, and the slave paused in his work but did not look up.

"Your family?" he asked.

"All lost but a younger brother. But I know not where he is, nor if he still lives."

The slave resumed, nodding. "I share your grief. We long for the Messiah's return."

Ariella snorted. "I have long ceased waiting for a prophet's dream."

He did not speak at first, but then said quietly, "Perhaps He has already come, and we did not know Him." He rinsed her feet. "Though it is dangerous to speak of such things here."

Ariella shrugged. "I have more faith in those who fight here and now."

He finished and stood, looking down on her face for the first time. His expression shifted. Did he know her secret? "Surely you have not been with the troupe these nine years?"

She shook her head. "Less than four weeks."

His lips twitched into a small smile. "Take care." He inclined his head toward the city. "The arena can be a cruel place for a—for anyone."

And then he was gone, moving on to offer water to the next thirsty trainee, and Ariella was left with a deep sorrow for home and family, one that hollowed out the inside of her heart.

The break ended and Ariella returned to the field, this time left to herself to train against the *palus,* a wooden post driven deep into the ground.

She became aware, gradually, of someone watching her, and was startled to find it was the nobleman from earlier. He had returned alone and stood apart, his face creased with an emotion she could not read. Sadness? Anger?

She paused in her drill when she noticed him, and he acknowledged her attention with a small nod.

She looked away, her thoughts jumbled. If her life had not become what it was, she would have felt herself his equal. Before the siege that took their futures and their lives, her family had been wealthy and prominent. She was accustomed to interacting with men such as this from a young age. The pull of attraction would not have seemed misplaced, except for his Roman patronage.

But here, in Pompeii, she was not the daughter of a wealthy Jew. She was not even a woman. While in her eyes he was an attractive man, she was only a slave boy to him. The thought discomfited her.

"You are young for the arena." He studied her, as if reading her thoughts in part.

She lowered her rudis but said nothing.

"How old are you?" His face had lost the pensive look, and he seemed now to be only seeking distraction.

"Sixteen," she answered, as though her years had ceased to advance when Jerusalem fell.

"So do the crowds come to see you fight, or to see you die?"

"Why did *you* come?"

He laughed. "Quick boy. Not to see you, of course. Two stray dogs in a street fight would be more entertaining."

She attacked the palus again. "Do not let the lanista hear that." Another strike. "He expects me to earn my keep."

"I would think the fighter Paris makes him more money than he needs."

She huffed and turned on him. Always it was Paris. "Is that why you keep coming? To see Paris?"

He narrowed his eyes. "*Keep* coming?"

Ariella turned away, chiding herself. "I saw you here earlier. Watching."

"And you thought I was watching you?"

She struck the wooden pole once more. "I thought you were one of the many who enjoy bloodshed and revere those with more muscle than mind."

He laughed again. "An undersized gladiator with an oversized mouth! It is a pity your lanista cannot make money on the strength of your wit rather than your arm."

"But it is as you said. You have come to see Paris."

"You are jealous?"

Ariella dropped her sword, remembered her stab of jealousy at the woman in sky blue who had been with him, and laughed at the irony. "Paris is a stupid brute."

"Ah, but that is the best kind of brute, don't you think?"

She refused to humor him. "He is over there." She pointed to where Paris trained in the shadow of the covered walkway. "Enjoy your conversation."

He looked at her strangely. "Something tells me it will be dull in comparison."

Ariella shrugged. "You have been warned."

He moved away and she watched him go, then flushed when he turned back and took a few steps toward her. "I am Portius Cato."

She nodded. Why give his name?

"And you are . . . ?"

"Ari."

"Ari." He nodded, inhaled, and looked to Paris. "Ari, if you need anything while in Pompeii, send a message to the house of the Catonii. I will do what I can."

And then he turned again and strode toward Paris, leaving Ariella to stare after him, more confused than before he had spoken.

She pointedly ignored the interaction between Paris and the nobleman for the next few minutes, and did not look at him when he strolled from the barracks. But she soon found a way to draw near to Paris and make a casual comment about his admirer. "Perhaps he means to sponsor the games." She kept her voice light. "He seemed quite interested in you."

He grunted. "He is a rich man who follows the games. That is all. He made no mention of sponsoring me." He scratched his neck and grinned. "But do not worry. I will not be with the troupe much longer."

Ariella looked sideways at the handsome fool.

"I have a good feeling about this town. If I can keep winning here, there'll be extra purses for me. I need to win the crowd. And then I'll buy my freedom."

Ariella had heard talk of this possibility, but none of the other fighters seemed to believe it likely. Of course, Paris would believe he could.

"Maybe I will win the crowd as well."

"Ha!" Paris slapped her shoulder, knocking her forward. "You won't last that long, my boy. The best you can do is learn to die well and bring honor to the lanista and the *editores* who sponsor the games."

She bristled. "All I have to do is evade the sword and entertain well. Perhaps I can do that with the animals."

He grew serious, and were his eyes daggers they would pierce her through. "This is no place for weaklings. Drusus shames the troupe by putting you out there. And I don't intend to let you steal any of my crowd by gaining sympathy for the underdog." He gripped her shoulder, as if in camaraderie, but his fingers shot pain into her muscles. "Ari, my boy, I doubt you'll even see the arena. You'll be finished off in training one of these days."

It was more than a prediction.

It was a threat.

7

Gnaeus Nigidius Maius did not care to get his hands dirty. For that, he had others. Both the slaves who followed him northward through the city's Forum this morning, and those who answered his summons for work best accomplished without attention.

The Forum lay before him today as a mute reminder of all he had not yet accomplished in this city. Its broad central court of white paving stones, bordered on three sides by civil offices, markets, and warehouses, still bore the marks of the earthquake seventeen years ago that had ravaged their town. Thanks to Maius, much rebuilding had been accomplished, but there was still much to be done. At the far end of the Forum, the Temple of Jupiter, with its still-broken right arch, attested to the new ideology—one that favored improving the centers of leisure, like the baths and theaters, over the temples dedicated to the worship of the emperor. And he must give the people what they wanted. Beyond the Forum, mothering the city, lay Mount Vesuvius.

He headed for the northeast corner of the Forum, where the town's main market, the *Macellum*, would already be churning with shoppers, and where the slaves who hurried to keep pace with him would pick out his purchases for the day.

In truth, he trusted his household slaves to choose the fish and cuts of meat for him, and even the luxury purchases he demanded. No, today he had another goal for his visit to the Macellum.

"The people do not care so much about the Temple," Gracchus was saying at his right. Maius had forgotten the man was there. "But they are unhappy that the Macellum is still void of decoration. It is an ugly place to shop, some say—"

Maius held up a hand to stop the putrid flow from the man's mouth. How did he ever tolerate Gracchus's incessant rasping in his ear? If not for the tidbits of factual gossip his advisor had a talent for unearthing, Maius would have found a charge worthy of execution for the man long ago.

They passed the *Eumachia* and the Temple of Vespasian, crossing between marble columns to walk in the shaded portico that ran the length of the Forum on both sides. The Macellum lay just beyond the grand arch, one of a pair of arches that flanked the Temple of Jupiter at this end of the Forum. Maius halted his progress at the Forum Gate of the market and surveyed the inside. Gracchus was right.

"Why have the sculptors not completed the dome of the *tholos*?" He spoke more to himself than to Gracchus. "The gods know I've funneled enough money to the project." The round structure in the center of the market enclosure, with its ring of columns supporting a domed roof, was both practical and decorative. The official weights and measures were kept there, around a central fountain that boasted live fish. But the dome still bore the ragged chisel marks of its creation, not yet smoothed into twining vines and blooming flowers. Maius fumed over the delay. The people must feel contented with their city. It was the only way to keep them contented with its government.

Gracchus started into a sputtering response, but Maius crossed the threshold without hearing it. It was time to begin his rounds.

The Macellum's three sides were lined with a series of *tabernae*, single-room shops with barrel-vaulted ceilings. Maius nodded to the servant whom he kept to staff his wine shop on the right side of the market, pricked with annoyance at the memory of Portius Cato at the theater. When he first heard of Cato's arrival in Pompeii, he had thought to crush the younger man for his ignorance in setting up a competing business. But after last night's unpleasant encounter, and Cato's preening arrogance, the desire had grown to take Cato down.

Maius sighed over the ever-present pressure of public life, then put it aside and turned to the left side of the square, reserved mainly for butchers, with marble counters provided to keep the meat cool and special troughs for drainage. He crossed to the first of them, hung with hunks of blood-red meat, their own marbling of yellow-white fat mimicking the counters.

Men of any status could be controlled, Maius had long ago learned. Each required a different tactic, but he had mastered them all. For the pleasure-seeking vacationers from the city, Maius was the beneficent host, and few of them cared to concern themselves with local politics. His money had purchased much of the town and its surrounding fields, and most of the lower classes were in his employ. For the wealthy townspeople, whose chief pursuits were leisure and distraction, he had informants well placed in many households, and the secrets he kept were as good as chains around the nobility. And for those who could be neither bought nor blackmailed, there was always the effective, if conventional, threat of violence.

Each of these merchants contributed to Maius's coffers, and in return he protected them from any violence that might somehow find them. Over the years his wealth grew, and his influence with it. He had been one of two duoviri for sixteen years, but the other, Balbus, was easily controlled. Maius's elected position assured that he could not be prosecuted for any crime of which he might be accused. Not that anyone would have the audacity to accuse him. And the wealth and power left him free to pursue his other . . . interests. Interests more secretive than lucrative.

This particular merchant, the largest butcher in Pompeii, held an interest beyond monetary for Maius. He was brother to one of the two aediles, the other leading politicians who held the city's purse strings. And Maius had learned that like a bloated water skin, pressure applied here at the butcher's counter could result in movement elsewhere in the city. Namely, in the basilica, where financial decisions were made.

The butcher saw him approach and was all wide-mouthed smile and extended hands. Maius ignored the proffered hunk of crusty bread, disinterested in the salted meat that would follow. The calls of merchants and the buzz of shoppers filled the Macellum, and Maius leaned in close to deliver a few words of what he called *encouragement*. The butcher's face turned sallow and he scraped at the blood trapped under his fingernails.

"Father!" The word sang out over the noise of the market, but Maius would have known it in any pitch. He turned from the butcher, his message conveyed, and spread his arms to his precious Nigidia.

The girl pranced across the Macellum, reminding him of one of the horses that performed in the arena games he sponsored. Her dark hair threatened to escape its gold combs and tumble to the fine silk of her stola, and her unusual blue eyes sparkled. "Nigidia, my pet."

She kissed his cheek, then pouted. "You said there would be a delivery from Rome today." Her voice elevated yet another few pitches and her sulky frown was meant to manipulate.

He traced the line of her aquiline nose, so like his own. Except for the strangely blue eyes, she was his daughter, from looks to tactics. He stroked her arm. "I shall have the heads of those who caused any delay, my dear."

She grunted, and Maius understood her impatience. He had an insatiable hunger for luxuries himself. This was why he must remain in power. It was for his family, all that he did. The wealth he accumulated and the way in which he accomplished it. All for them.

The nagging pinch of guilt that occasionally plagued him had no power today, thankfully. Nigidia's presence calmed and pleased him as it always could.

The girl threaded her arm through his own and led him away from the butcher's shop. "Camilla says that I do not deserve any more silk from Rome."

Maius patted her hand on his arm. "Your tutor forgets that young girls must be beautiful if they are to make good matches." They strolled toward the fabrics, Nigidia leading the way and Gracchus following. Maius pictured his daughter's stern tutor, pointing her disapproving finger at the lovely Nigidia. Another woman, Cato's sister Portia, strayed across his thoughts. He had seen her again last night and she lingered in his memory like an unplucked cluster of grapes, like an untasted jar of wine, like a—

"Do not speak of marriage to me, Father. I cannot bear to think of being separated from you."

Maius breathed away thoughts of Portia and focused on his daughter. "Who speaks of separation, my pet? A good marriage expands our family, it does not sever it."

They had arrived at the central tholos and stared down into the pool, churning with black scales and watery eyes.

"My lord," Gracchus rasped behind him.

"What is it?" Maius had a laughable vision of throttling his advisor until his eyes bulged like the fish in the pool.

"There are some here to see you."

Nigidia released his arm and melted away, attuned as always to the needs of his position.

Maius swiveled to meet a few of his loyal men on the *ordo* council, their eyes downcast as though the news were bad.

"Not here." He stalked to a corner of the Macellum, where an unused tabernae lay dusty and dim. Away from the noise of the market, he turned on them. "You have interrupted my shopping."

"Forgive us, Maius." One of the men held up his palms. "But there is talk."

"Who is talking?"

The lackey shifted and swallowed. "His name is being carried through the back rooms of power as we speak."

Maius knew the name before he spoke it out.

"Portius Cato."

The gods curse that presumptuous young whelp. Cato had not yet settled into his new home and already he had people talking.

The councilman continued, "Did you know that he was quaestor in Rome, before—"

Maius growled. "I make it my business to know such things."

"He has been approached. By Taurus and his league."

Yes, of course. They would waste no time once they saw the possibility. For all his supposed knowledge of the city's goings-on, he should have seen this coming.

First ignorant, then arrogant. The young Cato had spawned Maius's instant dislike. But this was something altogether different. Politics left no room for personal grudges.

Politics was war.

8

Cato opened the wood-post gate that allowed entry into his new vineyard and swung it wide to allow the servant Remus to follow.

Since last night's theater performance his thoughts had not strayed far from Gnaeus Nigidius Maius and his unspoken threats. The vines and soil had better distract him this morning.

"Huh!" Remus grunted, taking in the plot of land before them.

"It's grown a bit wild, I suppose." Cato put a hand to his eyes to block the bright morning sun and surveyed the trellised rows that trailed away from him, toward Vesuvius in the distance, outlined in lovely purple against a pale blue sky. The vineyard was oriented in the same direction as the Forum on the other side of the city, and Cato amused himself that the vineyard was *his* Forum, the place where his fortune would be made. Vesuvius looked down on his vineyard like a mother, and Cato would be the midwife, helping her give birth to the grapes. He laughed at his mind's strange imagery. He lived with too many women.

"You'll need the hands of the gods to reach down and make this mess right." Remus scratched at his ear. "Hands of the gods."

"Ah, but look with a more kindly eye, my friend." Cato crossed the grass to the nearest row of vines. He reached between glossy leaves, cradled a cluster of small, green fruit in his hand, and tilted it to reveal the slight purpling at the base of each, and thankfully, no mildew. "We have everything we need here, Remus. Warm sunlight. Well-drained soil, black with fertility." He leaned his head back and sniffed, his heart as much as his nose filling with the scents of fruit and earth and salt. "Do you feel that breeze off the sea? Perfect."

"The posts are rotting and the vines are untrained."

Cato laughed at Remus's pessimism and held up the cluster. "But the grapes, Remus. It is the grapes that matter most."

Remus walked to the row beside him and pulled at a chunk of the black locust post that held the vine. It fell off in his hand. "Next year's harvest?" He held up the rotted wood.

"Next year's harvest will put Maius and his wine to shame!" Cato pulled a grape from the cluster in his hand, popped it into his mouth, and bit down too hard. The unripe fruit shot tartness into his cheek. The vines grew well, though wild. The jolt of taste took him back for a moment to Rome, to his uncle's fields outside the city, where he had first plunged his hands into the soil to test its moisture level, first learned to prune and train and love the woody stalks into vines that would later reward both his nose and his palate. His uncle Servius was a good man, if a bit strange with his religious beliefs, and he had been an excellent tutor. But Cato was ready to create his own *symphony of fruit*, as Servius used to say. His would be an earthier floral, with a longer finish, buttery in the mouth.

"You'll have to convince the nobility." Remus wrinkled his nose. "They've got a bad taste in their mouths from Saturninus's wine and his reputation."

Outside the fence, a line of leather-and-metal-clad figures caught

Cato's eye. He released the grapes and turned to the narrow strip of grass that lay between the border of his vineyard and the arena, also on the outskirts of the city.

The gladiators. They marched in succession toward the arena, and for a moment Cato worried that he had missed the news of their first performance. But there were no crowds, no noise. They must have come for drills only. He watched the men, maybe a hundred of them, clomp past in full costume, from the Retiarii with their nets, to the Murmillones with fish helmets. There was the hero, Paris, larger and angrier than the rest. And that little one, what was his name? Ari. The boy seemed focused on his own sandals today, but Cato chuckled at the memory of his brash talk.

The line of men snaked into the arena's lower entrance and was lost to Cato. He mused for a moment on the irony of his vineyard of beauty and fertility so close to the arena built for gore and death.

Maius belonged more to the arena than to the vineyard. The thought had sprung unbidden but with the ring of truth. He had known many such men in Rome. Had fought against them all. Unsuccessfully.

He shook his head. Those memories were buried deep. Let them rot there.

"And so we will convince them, Remus." He turned once more to the untamed plot of land. "How about a competition? Bring the people out for a friendly contest between wines."

Remus snorted. "With Saturninus's wine? Or do you propose to wait until next year for your contest?"

"Good point, my friend." He strolled down the first row, Remus trailing behind. "So perhaps we shall give it away."

"You are a strange man, master. With a strange way to make money."

Cato stopped and turned on his laborer. "No, it is a good idea, Remus! I will hold my first dinner party as a citizen of Pompeii. We shall invite the nobility, and we'll make sport of Saturninus's bad wine. I'll send them all home with jugs of the stuff to give to their slaves and servants, demonstrating that my wine will be far superior."

Remus said nothing, only scrunched up his forehead against the sun. The idea *was* a good one, from the man's lack of objection.

"You see, Remus? We will show them that they have a choice. Maius does not own the town."

Remus shrugged. "It could work."

From the arena beyond, the first shouts of training and clash of swords reached them.

Cato slapped his laborer on the shoulder and hurried back through the row of vines. "Tend to the vines. I will start immediately."

It took Cato half of a Junius hour to crisscross through the narrow streets and reach his new Pompeiian villa on the upper end of the town. Like all wealthy homes, the façade and the entrance made a statement about the status of the owner. The front door stood open as usual, with the line of sight designed to allow passersby to glimpse the interior of the house and form an opinion. Cato paused in the doorway and tried to see the home through the eyes of his impending guests.

The mosaic greeting in front of the door, lettered in the Latin for welcome, invited guests. The entry hall's high walls were sculpted like miniature temples, and it opened to a large garden courtyard overflowing with green shrubbery and small trees, and in the atrium between the entry and the garden lay the most impressive piece in view, a bronze statue of a dancing faun poised on the lip of the *impluvium*, the tiled basin in blues and greens designed to catch rainwater. The faun must have been an especial commission by Saturninus, representing as it did the wild followers of Dionysus, Greek god of wine.

The peristyle garden was bordered on three sides by opulent receiving and dining rooms, with elegant furnishings, elaborate frescoes of deep reds and warm golds on the walls, and intricate floor mosaics. Before reaching the dining area at the rear, guests would cross a huge piece depicting a four-hundred-year-old battle between Alexander and Darius of Persia, a tesseraed mosaic that would make a Roman nobleman envious.

All in all, the house made a statement favorable to its owner, if only he could erase the stigma of Saturninus's failure.

A figure crossed the atrium before him and must have sensed his shadow in the doorway.

"Quintus, what are you doing standing there?" It was his mother.

"Admiring the view." He smiled and winked, and thought he saw his mother blush even from this distance. Since his father had passed, he had tried to remember to compliment his mother from time to time. The elder Portius Cato had been charming above all else.

He crossed the atrium and met his mother in the garden. "We are going to have a dinner party, Mother." He brushed at some loose stones on the atrium half wall. "How soon can the house be made ready?"

Octavia's eyebrows shot upward. "You must be jesting, Quintus! The house is musty from disuse and in desperate need of repainting and tiling! A dinner party is out of the question!"

Cato shrugged at his mother's outrage. "So we shall tell the guests to bring their rags and tools."

"You most certainly will not—"

He wrapped an arm around his mother's shoulder. "Be at ease, Mother. I shall not embarrass the Catonii."

A voice from the entry hall turned mother and son toward the door. "Is Quintus defiling the family name again?"

Portia's question was asked in jest, but he winced at the bite of truth.

His sister entered hand in hand with her husband, Lucius, and Octavia pulled away to embrace them both. "Your brother wants to host a dinner party already."

"Does he?" Portia did not share her mother's indignation, and instead her narrowed eyes spoke suspicion of his motives. As usual, Lucius remained quiet, content to let his wife speak.

"We're going to prove to the town that we have something to offer that Nigidius Maius does not."

"And what is that?"

Cato shrugged. "Choice. Integrity. Change."

Lucius's eyebrows rose. "Sounds more like a political party than a dinner party."

Cato rolled his shoulders, tension sparking down his spine. "Only a social gathering, brother, I assure you." He turned away, but not before he saw Lucius's head bent to Portia's, the two sharing a secret smile between them.

He tossed off the chill at Lucius's words and instead focused on the love between the two of them, but even that left him cold. He was keenly aware that the house was spacious enough for a large family, and that he was just as childless as his sister. At least she had someone to love. "Call a slave, Mother. I want to start writing the invitations."

Despite his mother's objections, he had messages sent through the city before the day was out, inviting the nobility to a party to be held in his home, three nights hence. There would be no overlap with the scheduled arena games, but with his party the following night, would his guests still be in a celebratory mood?

But the next morning slaves began appearing at the front door, responses in hand or mouth. Cato had underestimated his opponent.

"My master regrets that he is unable to attend." The latest messenger seemed to recite from a theater script given to each of the slaves before they arrived in his courtyard.

"That is all?" Cato scowled. "No reason given?"

A flicker of something in the slave's eyes. Amusement? Did the slave think Cato a fool? The look disappeared, and the man bowed low and backed out.

In the end, only two of his sixteen invitations were accepted. Hardly the stuff of a successful dinner party. He stood fuming in the courtyard as the last slave slunk away, and Portia and Octavia joined him.

"I *am* a fool." He slapped a nearby marble column. It answered with a puff of stone dust that settled to the ground. "I was trying to buy them all, but they've already sold themselves." He brushed the powder from his hands. "I am no better than Maius. No, I am worse. I have even failed to be sordid."

Portia patted his back. "You will find another way." Her voice was soft.

"Is this about the wine alone, Quintus?" His mother's tone accused, though he knew her heart.

"Of course not! The man believes he can control the money, the business, the people of this town. He should not be allow—" Cato sighed. He had fallen into their trap once more.

"Why can you not see it, Quintus?" Portia plucked at his tunic. "You have been here less than a week, and already you have made an enemy of an evil man. Already your purpose has become to undo him. Can you not see that you are destined for government?"

In truth, he did see it. And that was why his sister, beautiful and sweet as she was, was making him nauseated. Cato rubbed at his forehead, a bit sweaty and out of breath.

It was going to take more than the grapes to distract him.

9

"Get in there, Ari. You stink."

The lanista's words stung her femininity, but were more treacherous to her safety.

She had avoided it thus far.

In the field, on the journey she'd joined from Rome to Napoli, and then farther south to Pompeii, it had been challenging to dress alone, bathe alone, be alone. But she found ways.

The gladiator barracks in the center of the city was a different matter.

For four days she had drilled and trained and sweated, but had not bathed. She knew the odor clung to her, yet could find no options.

Drusus's stubby fingers jabbed into her back and pushed her into the dank confines of the barracks surrounding their training field. "I should send you to the Forum Baths, but this'll have to do."

Ariella turned to him, faint hope surging at the thought of being sent out of the barracks, to the public baths, but common sense took over and sealed her lips.

Which baths would she enter? The men's or the women's?

A half-dozen men clustered around the fountain built in the outermost room of the barracks, where fresh water from the city's aqueduct flowed from the stone mouth of a goddess into a shallow basin. A luxury built in the days when the quadriporticus had been the city's main recreation palaestra, not placed here for the gladiators. But from the looks of the men, they were taking full advantage. Paris plunged his head under the gush of water, then flipped it backward, laughing and sending a stream in an arc over his head, his rippled chest gleaming with water. His comrades jested with each other in voices that bounced from the stone walls.

But it was not the water nor the gladiators' amusement that flooded Ariella with fear. It was the fact that they were naked, each one of them.

And she was expected to join them.

Floronius cupped his hand in the standing water in the basin and flung water at Ariella as she approached. "Ah, look, men. It would seem Ari has put his shyness behind him." He was an ugly one, with an even meaner spirit than that of Paris.

Ariella inhaled, and the odor of sweaty men and the pungent oils they used before scraping themselves filled her nostrils and left her queasy.

They turned their attention to her, and she felt her face flush with the heat of a thousand oil lamps.

Paris guffawed. "By the looks of his face, I'd say he's still a bit bashful. Come, Ari, we promise not to ridicule your puny body. Don't we, men?" He threw the question out to the others, and of course received loud laughter in response. He stepped to her and reached for the straps of her leather vest. "Here, I'll even help you."

Ariella shoved aside the intimate gesture, sickened. "I will do it myself."

"Ho, ho!" Paris backed away, palms held outward. "He does have a spine, men. And now we shall see what else he has!"

Ariella felt as though she could not breathe and turned to the wall to brace herself against it with one hand. She bent to pry apart the laces of her sandals with the other.

They were not all Roman, the gladiators. In fact, most were not. But they reminded her of those who had sacked her beloved Jerusalem nine years earlier. A lust for entertainment that did not know boundaries and would not be denied. Ironic, since it was this city's same lust that might be the death of some of them.

They lost interest in her for a moment, so slow was she in removing her sandals. She unbuckled the leather cuff at her waist, with its pocket for her *pugio*, the short sword, and was soon down to only her tunic. Their amusement must have run its course, for they turned back to her.

"You take longer to undress than a maiden on her wedding night!" Floronius pushed his way through the others and shoved three sharp fingers into the flesh of her shoulder. She swatted at him, and he returned with a blow to the side of the head, knocking her to the ground.

They circled her and she lay there, a mortal at the foot of the gods, vulnerable and helpless in the face of their wrath.

This was it, then. There was no more escape. She could rise and run, refuse to bathe. But she knew what would happen. One of them, probably Paris, would chase her down, haul her back, and force her to undress for the amusement of them all.

Her stomach churned once again. She put a hand to her belly to quell the upheaval and stood on shaky legs. Her breath came short and shallow, and a metallic taste filled her mouth. She cursed her weakness, felt her breathing become rapid and shallow, and then she was retching. On the floor, on her own feet. Over and over while the men roared with laughter.

Another pair of feet appeared beside her own. A warm hand on the small of her back, a rag pushed into her hands. She wiped at her mouth and lifted her head.

The old slave who had attended her a few nights earlier, her countryman, watched with compassionate eyes.

"You should lie down." His voice rose to carry to the others. "Come."

He led her from the fountain room until the laughter and horse-play of the men was only a distant rumble and took her to one of the small cells that had become her home since arriving.

A bare mat lay in the corner, and she lowered herself to it, grateful to have escaped for the moment.

But there would be other moments.

"Thank you," she whispered to the old man. "You are very kind."

"Hmm." He nodded, then retrieved a bucket of water from the corner and began, for the second time, to wash Ariella's legs.

She reached for the rag. "You do not need—"

"Hush, child." He pushed her hand away. "It has been many years since I took care of my own. And you remind me of her."

Ariella leaned back on the mat, and only then was struck by the import of his words. She pushed up on her elbows. *Her?*

He smiled at her whisper but did not look up. "You are not such a good actor, my dear. It is only that your audience are fools."

Ariella closed her eyes, willing her stomach to settle.

"You have nothing to fear from me, Ari." His voice was warm, reassuring. "I will keep your secret."

"What is your name?"

"Jeremiah. Jeremiah ben Joseph."

"Thank you, Jeremiah ben Joseph. You have my gratitude."

He finished washing her and stood. "It will take more than my silence to keep you safe. This cannot go on."

She nodded. "I know. I will find a way."

He stared at her for another moment. "I shall pray for your safety." He nodded and left the cell.

She lay back on the mat and threw her arm over her face. Jeremiah was right. It could not go on.

When she had run from Valerius and fallen in with this troupe, it had seemed an answer to her prayers, if she had prayed any. Safe passage away from Rome through the fields of Italy to a sunny, seaside vacation town. But now she had arrived, the troupe had served its purpose, and it was time to make a change.

She could live here in Pompeii. Find work as a servant girl in some rich patrician's house. Like the man who had spoken to her in the training yard. The idea pleased her. If she could escape the barracks and transform herself back into a woman, perhaps she would not be recognized. Drusus would assume she had fled the city. He would not think to search through the female servants of Pompeii for his lost gladiator-in-training.

She sat up on her mat, hope coursing through her for the first time since she had escaped Rome. A shuffle at the cell doorway forced her attention upward.

"You had better not be sick." Drusus scowled at her in the dim light. "Not right before the games."

She shook her head and pushed herself to standing. "I am well."

He grunted. "We'll have a crowd tomorrow, for certain. The duovir Nigidius Maius is sponsoring a grand show."

Ariella blanched. Maius? Was he not the politician who had killed Valerius's slave the night she fled? She forced her heart to slow.

He would not recognize her. She had been a slave girl in Rome—a far cry from her present state.

Drusus was still muttering. "Going to send Jeremiah to paint advertisements in the Forum now, before the parade and speeches start."

Ariella took an eager step forward. "I'll do it." Too eager.

Drusus's eyes narrowed. "Why?"

She tried to level out her voice. "It's been too long since I held a brush."

"You're a painter, then?" He smirked and pointed to her small hands. "Could've guessed. You've got that look about you." He tilted his head as though considering the risks. "Fine. Paint us the best signs this city's ever seen. Something to talk about, eh?"

She nodded. "I have no paint, though. No brushes."

"Come."

Minutes later Ariella was headed for the Forum, three sestertii jingling in a pouch at her waist. Money to buy supplies, but a better plan was already forming in her mind.

The city was a maze of houses and shops, but she kept to the widest streets, knowing one would lead her to the Forum. Clearly, the privately owned shops had become competition for the official market. Doorways that once led to grand private homes now served as shop fronts, with the families living above and behind their source of income. She kept an eye on each as she passed, willing to stop if she found what she sought, but intending to reach the Forum first.

The three sestertii would not pay for paint and brushes. Rather, they would supply her with clothing. Something befitting a Jewish woman, for she also needed to have a head covering to hide her shorn hair. She would find a place to hide, change her clothes, and then head out into the city to seek work.

She reached the Forum at last and drew up to survey the long stretch of white paving stones, bordered on both sides by columned porticoes, ornamented with rich gold statues and white marble. The layout was orderly and pleasing, a well-built grid, busy and thriving.

A good place to disappear.

The left side of the Forum was undergoing construction, it would seem. She had heard about the earthquake that had toppled Pompeii's finest structures years earlier.

At the far end of the Forum lay the *Capitolium*, temple of the gods, with great arches on either side. And beyond and above the temple, the lovely mountain loomed over them. She could climb that mountain today, if it meant achieving freedom.

Ariella hurried along the right side of the Forum in the shade of the portico. The richness of the public square surprised her. So far from Rome, and yet excess seemed as commonplace here as in the mother city. Along with all the greed, hatred, and evil of the Empire's capital.

The first building she passed must have been the Fullers' Guild, for the urine pots at the doorway gave off an unmistakable odor. They'd been placed there for the convenience of citizens and the necessity of the fullers, who used the urine in their wool processing. The building was grand, with a broad entrance of marble flanked by niches containing idolatrous statues of gods and emperors. The fullers were an influential guild in any city.

She passed another temple, and yet another, her sandals slapping the limestone paving now. The colonnade grew clogged with shoppers and she pushed through, willing to shove away any who blocked her. Such a foul race, these Romans. More than once she flushed at the lewd paintings of male anatomy on the paving stones pointing the way to the nearest brothel. The vulgarity of the city angered her. How could the Creator allow these barbarous people to have conquered His holy city?

Finally she reached the market, passed through the shrine to Emperor Vespasian, and entered the teeming world of sights and smells, with its stalls selling meat and fish.

Wine, grain, olives . . . the market had everything. But she had need of something very specific. She strolled the perimeter, attempting to look like a casual shopper, but tasting the grit of fear. The market was jammed with people this morning, no doubt trying to make their purchases before the events of the day began in the Forum. The animals brought for the games tomorrow were to be paraded through the city today, and there would be speeches by politicians wanting to capitalize on the morale of the people in anticipation of the games. Drusus had been wise to send her to paint signs today. Never mind the flicker of guilt at her betrayal.

There. A shop with fabrics. Not traditional Jewish clothing of course, but she could make it work.

A woman worked the table of fabric, and as Ariella offered a low price on what she needed, the woman's sharp eyes took her in and seemed to guess her secret. But she shook her head. "The fabric is too fine." She held it out for Ariella to touch and named a higher price.

Ariella inhaled and closed her eyes at the softness. How long had it been since she had felt like a woman? She pulled two coins from her pouch and reached across the table with them. Her hands shook as she dropped the coins into the shopkeeper's palm, and again that look of suspicion crossed the woman's face.

"Thank you." Before any questions could be asked, Ariella hurried away with her purchases.

Now to find a hidden place to change her clothes. She glanced down at the gladiator tunic and belt. It would be lovely to burn the wretched things, but abandoning them in an alley would have to suffice. In contrast, the fabric in her training-callused hands felt like silk from the East.

She pushed back the way she had come, remembering some quieter streets she had passed. All she needed was a few moments alone.

And then she would be free.

10

The morning had already annoyed Cato by the time he left the house and headed into the city. Every glance from his mother seemed to accuse, and even his younger sister, Isabella, had been conscripted to disapprove of him.

They knew why he came here. Why did they insist on turning it into something else? It was difficult enough to be frustrated in his goal of successful wine-making. He didn't need the women to stand against him.

His head ached and the glaring summer sun felt like a knife at his temples.

The city was thronged with shoppers and diversion-seekers this morning, and he fell in with them easily, for he sought diversion himself. The speeches and animal parade scheduled for the afternoon in the Forum interested him. He was curious to hear the local politicians, to understand them better. Only so that he could better comprehend how to succeed in his new wine business in Pompeii, of course.

That was what he had told Octavia. Her mouth had twitched in amusement and she had turned away, further aggravating him.

He grew impatient with the press of crowds on the sidewalks and stepped down into the street, watching where he stepped as he followed a horse-drawn cart that raced ahead, its driver straddling the stepping-stones at the top of the street with the ease of much practice.

He crisscrossed through several streets, still a bit unfamiliar with the city, but always keeping the mountain to his right. A woman in a doorway called out to him with a howl like a she-wolf, earning her establishment its nickname of *lupanaria*. He shook his head at her offer and passed the brothel, restraining himself from looking inside. That was not the sort of distraction he sought. Unlike most Romans, he kept himself away from that type of entertainment. His mother's longstanding work in Rome to help such women lead a better life had trained him to look on these women with compassion, and though compassion battled daily with his natural tendencies as a man, he managed to mostly control his behavior, if not his thoughts.

He reached the Forum soon enough, but ignored the long stretch of shops and temples in favor of an exploration of the municipal buildings at the end closest to him, opposite the Capitolium temple and the mountain. Here, three large halls clad in shining marble housed the administrative life of the city. The two duoviri, Maius and Balbus, governed from these halls, as well as the younger aediles who also served. The city council, the *ordo decurionum*, also met here. In front of the halls stood a *suggestum*, a platform from which orators could make their appeals. Would Maius stand here later today?

A commotion at the road leading toward the Marina Gate caught his attention. A half-naked man, his hair stringy and eyes feral, shrieked like a wild monkey and danced in a circle across the stones, bent at the waist and arms dangling. A small crowd gathered to watch, but most hurried past, as though insanity were contagious.

Cato had seen this sort of thing several times in Rome and it fascinated him. He drew closer until he could see the man's wide, white eyes and broken teeth. Another man, older and heavyset, approached the animal-man slowly, hand outstretched as though soothing a vicious dog. And indeed, the crazed man ceased his agitated dance. But his eyes spewed hatred and his lips drew back from his teeth at the other's approach. Cato shuddered.

There was evil here.

The crowd wandered away now that the frantic movements had ended, but Cato still watched.

The wild man hissed, "What have I to do with you?" The words, low and rasping, issued from his broken teeth, but sounded more like a growl from the underworld.

The older man's hand still reached for him and he swatted it away, only to have the man step closer.

As Cato watched, the simple presence of the man seemed to both infuriate and bind the madman. The older man glanced at Cato, measured him with that glance, then turned back and began to whisper to his captive.

Cato stepped closer. He heard only snatches of the whispered words—*Evil . . . Freedom . . . Messiah*—and then the older man's hand was on the dirty forehead of the animal-man and he gave a mighty shout of, *"Come out!"*

At this, the madman screamed as though being burned. Cato started forward, then stopped when the man dropped to the stones and lay still. Cato looked at the heavyset man. "What have you done?"

But the one on the ground stirred, then crawled on hands and knees to the other's feet and clung to his ankles as though rescued from drowning. "Thank you." These words were spoken in a different voice than Cato had yet heard, one that sounded hoarse from disuse.

A rushing sound filled Cato's ears, as though something evil were fleeing the Forum even as he watched.

"Ah, Portius Cato, eyeing his future seat of power." The voice behind him held only a trace of amusement.

Cato turned to find Taurus, the spokesman for the group who had approached him in the gladiator barracks the night of the theater performance. He glanced back at the two, but the older man was helping the younger to his feet, leading him away. He returned his attention to Taurus and bowed his head. "Merely curious to see where the power lies, that is all."

Taurus pressed his fingertips together. "And that is where it begins, my friend."

Cato bristled a bit at the familiar reference. "And where it ends."

Taurus shrugged. "Are you engaged this morning? I could introduce you to some of the leading merchants."

Cato's shoulders tightened. "As one of their own, correct?"

"As you wish, Portius Cato. As you wish."

"Lead the way, then."

Taurus led him to the first large building off the Forum, the Eumachia that housed the guild of fullers. A statue of the priestess Eumachia, who had commissioned and dedicated the building, graced the corridor at the back, beneath a roofed portico.

Inside, the business of manufacturing wool cloth was at peak activity, with raw wool being washed, stretched, and dyed using the pots of urine that filled daily at the door. The smell was typical, if not pleasant.

Taurus led him to the side of the central room, where an elegant man directed slaves. "Emeritus, I have someone for you to meet." He pulled at Cato's arm, which bothered him.

Emeritus's eyes flicked to Taurus and then to Cato, and he drew up his chin.

"Emeritus is the top wool merchant in the city." Taurus indicated the building. "And head of the Fullers' Guild."

Cato understood the implication. A powerful man stood before him. He held out an arm and his grip was returned with a solemn nod. Emeritus had the look of intensity about him, and his eyes were night-dark. Had a life among the dyes somehow given them their unnatural color?

The eyes focused on him. "Taurus tells me you are newly arrived from Rome."

Ah, and what else had Taurus told him? Cato bowed. "Yes, come to follow in your footsteps and make my fortune in this pleasant city."

"Come." Emeritus turned away. "Have some wine. We will talk."

Cato eyed Taurus, who urged him with a nod. He followed with hesitation, knowing where this conversation would lead.

In the back of the Eumachia, Emeritus snapped his fingers at a slave who fled into the interior of the back rooms.

Cato eyed the front arch of the building, past the slaves who toiled in the center. He should have declined. "I have some business to take care of. I'm afraid I cannot stay—"

Emeritus turned to him, eyes flashing. "And you will not get far in that business without the alliances of those who can assist you."

Indeed. "Then a cup of wine would seem to be what I need."

The slave brought wine for all three, and Cato's first sniff and sip impressed him. Green apples and pears on the palate. "This is made here?" Surely his own rich soil was ready to produce something this fine.

Emeritus half smiled. "'Vesuvinum,' he calls it. A clever salute to our fine mountain and the vines that grow on its slopes."

Cato frowned into the cup. "Maius." From their shared look, he'd been manipulated. Did they intend to convince him he would fail as a winemaker?

"Hmm." Emeritus sniffed his own cup. "Pleasing bouquet, but wicked headache the morning after a feast."

Cato handed his cup to Emeritus. "Perhaps I shall improve upon even this." He bowed slightly. "It has been a pleasure meeting you, Emeritus, and I am sure we will meet again."

Emeritus thrust his cup and Cato's into the hands of the nearby slave and reached out to clutch Cato's arm with a grip like a dark-eyed tiger seizing a choice piece of meat. He stepped close enough to hiss into Cato's ear, "You are either *with* us, or you are against us, Portius Cato. And those who are with us will do whatever it takes to rid this city of its governmental stain."

Cato yanked his arm away and readjusted his toga. "I am no friend of Nigidius Maius, I assure you. But my days of public office are over." He eyed them both and dropped his voice, matching Emeritus's intensity. "Do not ask me again."

He escaped then, out of the Eumachia and into the Forum, a cage of temples, shops, and public buildings. The desire to occupy himself with its goings-on had left him and he only wanted to return home.

A young man pushed past him, his hands full of something and his head down. Cato blinked and watched the man as he retreated out of the Forum, noted the leather cuff that belted the coarse tunic. Had that been the young gladiator, Ari?

Cato followed him, curious, but questioning his own curiosity. What was it about the boy that intrigued him? Plenty of politicians in Rome had kept boys such as this, delicately featured and not yet masters of themselves, for their own pleasure. Cato had no interest in that type of thing. So what was it that directed his feet in the footsteps of the young fighter?

He may be vulnerable physically, but he has a strong heart.

Cato's own spirit accused him with the observation. The boy

was everything he was not. Courage and determination in the face of insurmountable obstacles, while Cato had fled from his failure and weakness.

The boy kept his head down and walked quickly, as though he had an important destination. Cato continued to follow, past shops and homes, around a stone fountain at an intersection and into a narrower alley, void of shoppers.

Cato watched, fascinated, as the boy seemed to cast furtive looks about him halfway down the alley. Cato pressed himself against a wall and studied the ground, hoping the boy would not recognize him. A moment later Ari ducked into a doorway.

Still curious, and glad for a diversion at last, Cato hurried up the alley to see where the gladiator had disappeared. He drew up short to find another lupanaria, and his eyebrows shot up. He had not expected this.

Amused, he decided to cross the alley and wait in a doorway for the boy to emerge from the brothel after his tryst, to have a bit of fun with him.

A minute or two later a woman emerged, but it was not a prostitute, for she was modestly dressed as a respectable foreign servant woman. Cato straightened, curiosity again a pull. What was this place?

His movement gained the woman's attention and she lifted her chin to look across the alley. Only five cubits from him, she met his eyes. He saw the flicker of recognition there at the same moment that he felt it himself.

"Ari?" What kind of transformation was this?

"What are you doing here?" The boy glanced behind himself to the brothel and flushed.

Cato shook his head. "I was following you." He felt flustered and off-balance somehow. The boy dressed as a woman looked more like a woman than a boy.

"Why?" The word was harsh, angry. The boy's face had drained of color.

Cato crossed the street, suddenly understanding. "You are trying to escape the lanista."

"It is none of your concern!" Ari started down the alley before Cato could reach him.

Again, that strange protectiveness he had felt in the barracks urged him to speak. "Wait." He followed the disguised boy, but Ari did not stop. Cato trotted up behind him and grabbed his shoulder.

Ari swung around and pushed Cato away from him, the way Cato himself had pushed Emeritus away only moments ago.

But Cato would not be put off. He only wanted to speak to Ari, but the boy was being foolish. Cato put his hands to Ari's chest and shoved him against the wall.

Ari's eyes went wide as his back hit the stone.

And suddenly, Cato knew.

11

Ariella slammed against the stone wall but its impact was lost on her. Her attention was on Portius Cato, on the way he yanked his hands away from her chest as though he had been burned. The way the whites of his eyes seemed to grow larger, his lips parted in stunned silence.

They stood there for a moment, like two carved marble pieces, and then Cato exhaled and dropped his shoulders.

"You *are* a woman."

"And you are a meddling nuisance!" She turned to slide away from him, but he shifted and blocked her way. She should shove him aside, but stood her ground and looked into his green-flecked eyes instead. "Will you take me prisoner, then?"

"I—I only want to know . . ." Cato licked his lips and shook his head.

"Ask it. Ask your questions." Ariella wished to be away, but she also wished to stay beside him. Her emotions tumbled like a mountain rockslide. Anger at being followed, at being found out, and yet a sweet sense of relief that this man who had occupied too many of her thoughts since she first met him knew that she was not a boy. The stone wall behind her seemed to radiate its sun-warmed heat into her body. She pulled away from it.

Cato began again, "They do not—the gladiator troupe—please tell me they do not keep you for their whore?"

His eyes accused and she felt the injustice of it. She wanted to see him laugh again, the way he had when they first spoke in the barracks field. "You know nothing of it."

"So tell me."

The simple words, spoken with compassion, nearly undid her. She swallowed against the emotion. *He is a Roman* . . . But his eyes, his smile, they were not Roman. They were only human and trained on her in a way no one had looked at her in years. She felt a flush begin at her neck and travel to her face.

A sudden awareness of her unwashed condition, her hacked-off hair, her peasant clothes, backed her against the wall again, though it only put another handsbreadth between them. His perfectly draped toga was brilliant white, his dark hair oiled and combed, his jaw clean-shaven. Everything about him spoke wealth and refinement.

He mistook her movement for fear. "I will not hurt you, Ari." He touched her arm, but then pulled away again, clearly unsure.

She believed him.

"Do they know?"

Ariella shook her head, then looked away, down the alley, to avoid those eyes.

It was not enough. She needed to get away. She shoved him aside and began to run down the alley.

He followed.

She could hear the slap of his sandals, but he did not call out. She reached the end of the alley, to the intersection with the main street, and fell into the crowd. It would not do to run here, to draw attention to herself. Especially with a Roman nobleman chasing her. She weaved through townspeople, wanting only to be lost in the crowd.

But he was behind her in a moment, speaking into her ear as she moved.

"You are escaping?"

She said nothing, only bit down on her lip to steel her heart.

"What is your name? Tell me that at least."

Ariella would not slow. How could she be rid of him?

She reached the Forum and looked both ways. The biggest crowds. The only way to lose him.

But then he was in front of her, blocking her way again, then pulling her into a doorway. She was vaguely aware they had entered a temple, but the building was quiet and dim.

Cato seemed to have relinquished his notion of not touching her, for he had both her arms now and nudged her against the inner wall of the temple. "Stop running from me. I only want to know more about you."

"Why?" She shot the word at his face, too close to hers, too perfect. Her neck grew damp, reminding her again of her shameful hair.

"Tell me your name."

"Ariella." In that moment she hated herself for the weakness.

"Ariella." He said it softly, and she nearly wept. "How did you join the gladiators, Ari?"

She closed her eyes, unable to stop her words now, like warm water flowing over her. "I needed to get away from my . . . situation. It seemed a good idea at the time."

"What situation?"

She turned her attention on him again, with a bit of the old fire. "An arrogant Roman who thought he could control me." The implication should be clear.

But he did not release her. "And now you are running away?"

"You've seen me train. I will not last a month in the arena."

"You will not last a month on your own."

She bristled. "I can find work—"

"There are very few who would take on an unknown foreign woman, possibly an escaped slave." His eyes narrowed. "Though your Latin is too developed for the slave class."

Ariella lifted her chin. "Not all slaves began their lives as such."

"Nor all noblemen."

She sighed, felt herself lean into him a bit. "I cannot go back."

"The lanista will scour the town for you."

"He will be looking for a young boy."

Cato cocked his head to the side. "Are you truly sixteen, as you told me in the barracks?"

Visions of the Temple of Jerusalem in flames appeared behind her eyes. "I once was."

His lips twitched into a smile. "You do not like to answer any question directly, do you?"

"No more than you like to leave your questions unanswered."

"Ari, this is foolishness. An escaped slave woman has only one place to go, and I do not wish to see you in the brothel." Cato's own face flushed. "I mean that I do not want you to be forced into that life. No one should be."

She saw something different in him in that moment. Since their first conversation, he had seemed a rushing river, all swift speech and sharp retorts, charming as he was. But she saw something else in his eyes now. A deep loathing for evil and for injustice, a desire to right all wrongs, as much a part of him as all the witty sarcasm.

It was too much for her, this quiet conversation with a good man. A priest moved about the back of the temple, and Ariella used Cato's momentary distraction to pull away from his hold and rush back into the colonnade of the Forum.

But she had only fled one problem to face another. She emerged from the temple and found herself facing Drusus, the lanista.

Her sudden emergence drew his attention, and one look at her brought recognition. She would never have fooled him by simply changing her clothing.

He looked her up and down, taking in her clothes, and scowled. Then stepped toward her. "What is this? I send you to paint signs for the games, and . . ." He trailed off, as though unable to form the words around his discovery.

She felt Cato at her back, solid and strong.

Drusus's eyes moved above her head and his brow furrowed.

"Drusus, is it?"

Ariella watched as the lanista straightened a bit to be known by a man such as the one behind her.

"What can I do for you, my lord?"

"You can accept my apologies for . . . detaining your young warrior here."

Drusus looked back and forth between Cato and her, and she felt a sweat break out on her forehead as a light of understanding came into Drusus's eyes.

"Ah, I see." He jabbed a finger at the temple. "All kinds of ways to worship the gods, of course. Who am I to say what is right?" He grinned at Ariella. "Besides, he makes a better woman than he does a man, eh?" To Cato, he added, "But I suppose you already know that."

His implication sickened her and cast an unfair light on Cato, but she could not defend him.

"Yes, well, I appreciate your willingness to share him."

Drusus bowed. "We are here to serve, my lord." He winked. "In any way that we can."

Drusus spoke out of a hope of being reimbursed for his trouble, and Cato did not disappoint him. She could not see how much money the nobleman slipped to the older man. Did not want to see.

"So get to your painting, then, boy." Drusus jabbed at her side. "*After* you retrieve your own clothing."

Ariella nodded.

Drusus continued across the Forum, soon engaged in conversation with someone, but continuing his glances in their direction.

"I am sorry." She could not look up at him.

"Listen, Ari. You should make it known that you are a woman. I saw a few female gladiators in Rome, and they were much revered and valued. Your life would no doubt be spared, if only to bring the crowds out to see you again."

She shook her head, unable to even consider going back. And yet the lanista watched her still and she could not run now. Her mind felt sluggish. "I must paint the signs."

"Where is your paint?" Cato spoke to her as though she were a child, and so she felt.

"I have none. I used the money for the fabric."

"Come." He led her down the colonnade, away from Drusus's watching eyes, his gentle hand on her elbow, guiding her. In the Macellum, she followed as he purchased supplies for her, then led her again out the back of the market, into the street. They retraced their steps to the brothel.

He held the paint and brush and steered her toward the door. "Find your clothing. Put it on."

She obeyed, because it was the only way.

Her tunic and belt still lay on the floor where she had dropped them, and she grieved for the hope that had been part of her in that moment before she left this house.

She changed quickly, refusing to look at the paintings on the walls that detailed the services offered within, but her movements drew a prostitute to where she stood inside the doorway. The woman looked over the young gladiator, amused, then beckoned to the interior of the house. Ariella shook her head and stalked from the building, courage finding its way back into her heart.

She found Cato still outside and yanked the paint and brush from his hands.

He laughed. "I cannot decide which is the real Ariella. The quiet woman being led, or the foolhardy fighter ready to oppose the world."

She turned to leave. "I would not have survived this long without being who I am." She felt him watching her as she left him. Would she see him again? She slowed and faced him one last time. "Thank you. For everything. I am in your debt."

He bowed his head. "I will look forward to being repaid."

Of course.

She chose the outer wall of the Eumachia, where the prominent fullers and their many customers would pass, for her first advertisement.

Thirty pairs of gladiators provided by Gnaeus Nigidius Maius, quinquennial duovir, together with their substitutes will fight at Pompeii

Her hands brushed the strokes without thought, and her mind grasped for answers to her new crisis.

Meanwhile her heart retreated, following the Roman who today had saved her life.

12

Cato had no heart for the speeches or the parade, and wandered home before the politicians had finished. His encounter with the madman had troubled him, though he could not say why. Only that there was something not right here in Pompeii. He could feel it. And the run-in with Ari, now Ariella, had disturbed him further. What interest should he have in a slave? He had plenty of his own.

By the next morning he had convinced himself that it was the curiosity of a female gladiator that intrigued him.

The games that Maius had so generously sponsored for the amusement of the city were scheduled for tonight. Would Ariella be there, in the arena? What would happen when she took to the ring? Would she be hurt?

Cato lounged in his gardens, trying to amuse himself with Cicero's writings and urging the sun to track across the sky at a faster pace. By midmorning he grew restless and even Octavia noticed.

"You are like a little boy, pacing as you wait." She patted his cheek. "Find something to keep you busy."

He shrugged her off. "I am only anxious to see what sort of display can purchase the silence of an entire town."

Octavia frowned. "Nigidius Maius has not stopped boasting all week."

Isabella entered the garden in time to hear her mother's comment. "The slaves are saying that he has even brought dwarves."

Octavia clucked at her daughter. "Isabella, I do not like you gossiping among the slaves. It is most inappropriate."

Isabella grinned and shrugged.

"What do they know of the gladiators?" Cato asked.

Octavia gave an exasperated sigh and lifted her hands. "You two are exactly alike. I shall leave you to your gossip."

But before Cato could question Isabella further, a shout from the street startled all three.

Remus burst through the doorway, into the atrium, skidding to a stop before the dancing faun. "The vines!" His breath came in short gasps. "The vines are burning!"

Cato pushed past his sister and mother and crossed the mosaic floor to grab Remus by the shoulders. "My vines? How?"

The servant shook his head. "You must come!"

Cato nodded, and the two ran from the house. He was aware that Isabella followed, amidst his mother's protestations, but he soon outpaced her.

It took too long to cross the city, to the outskirts where his vineyard lay next to the arena. As he rounded the corner of the last street of houses and ran through the grassy area alongside the new palaestra, he could see the black smoke rising from behind his fence.

How could this have happened? He had sent Remus to do a little pruning, after showing him how to carefully trim and crop the vines. The man should not have been using any kind of flame.

As though he read Cato's mind, Remus huffed as they ran. "I finished with the vines an hour ago. A friend found me to tell me about the fire."

They reached the gate, and Cato fumbled at the latch, then tumbled into the enclosure.

He could see no farther than the several rows in front of him, so consumed with flames and smoke were they. He started forward, as though to rescue them, then backed away from the furious heat. The blackened posts Remus had criticized were a ready fuel, enough to overwhelm the green vines and moist soil. The still-green grapes sizzled and burst like fruit cooked for a sweet meal.

"What shall we do?" Remus stood behind him, ready to help.

The orange and black flames and the thick smoke obscured Cato's view of the entire vineyard. He ran the length of the rows, assessing the damage, desperation and grief building.

Of the eighty rows, nearly half burned. But the fires had begun at the head of the vineyard and had not yet spread the length of each row. Vines still clung to their trellises at the ends of rows, with the peaceful mountain looking on.

"Bring water!"

Remus looked confused. He knew there was no way they could douse the widespread flames.

"We will make a break in the rows!"

Remus nodded at that and grabbed the two-handled cart they used for bringing water from the nearest fountain. He disappeared through the gate.

Cato's nostrils burned with the heat and stench, but he snatched up a hoe used for aerating the soil and plunged between two burning rows. He ran to the last vine that burned and hacked at the disintegrating trellis, breaking its connection with the one beside. The heat was near to melting his face, but anger spurred him on, and he used the long tool to pull the burning vines away from those that still lived.

Breathless and sweating, he finished with one plant and turned to the row behind him to repeat the attack. He felt the fire singe the hair on his arms but tore the two plants apart, then ran through the gap to attend to the next row.

Remus appeared, trundling his cart full of water pots down the first row. Isabella was with him. "There!" Cato directed with a shout and raised hand. "Soak the ground in the gap. Soak the live plants."

Remus obeyed at once, with Isabella assisting.

"It is not safe for you here, sister. Go home!" He spent only a moment seeing that Isabella, of course, ignored him. He turned back to his task. Remus would follow with the water as long as it held.

Some time later, after Remus had disappeared to retrieve more water and returned to soak more plants, Cato reached the last burning row, hacked a break between the vines, helped Remus and Isabella pour the last of the water, and then collapsed onto the grass to watch vines at the heads of the rows burn themselves out. The fiery orange turned to red embers, glowing like rows of evil eyes staring at him.

His vineyard.

His eyes burned with more than the smoke and heat. He swiped at his cheeks, streaking black soot from his hands across his face.

Isabella lay against him, crying. "I am so sorry, Quintus. So sorry."

His own grief burrowed deep into his heart. The lifeblood seemed to drain out of him, into the field. It had been his dream to make a success of the wine-making business here. Now what would become of his dream?

"There are still many vines left." Remus sat with his hands stretched out behind him, as though he might fall over with fatigue. "You still have more than half the crop, I believe."

Cato inhaled and nodded. "We will make the best of it, then. As we always do."

Isabella clutched his hand and he returned the pressure.

"Come." He pulled his sister to standing, and Remus followed. "Let us get clean. Mother will be anxious to hear news."

They trudged back through the city, and Cato was heedless of any stares that might have greeted his appearance. His mind was full of the ruined vines, the ruined dreams.

He took himself to the Forum Baths and let the soot and sweat soak from his body in the *tepidarium*. A slave assisted by scraping his skin with a strigil, until all traces of the afternoon's disaster had been removed. Despite the heat, Cato felt numb.

At home, he found his midday meal laid out in the courtyard, and he ate in silence, alone.

Octavia appeared and came to stand behind him, her hands on his shoulders. He sighed and patted her hand with his own.

"The games are to begin soon." Her voice was low, sympathetic. Like the mother of a boy who'd lost his favorite pet. "Will you go?"

He nodded, swallowed the last of his wine, and wiped his mouth. "I will go."

In truth, he had lost his excitement for the games altogether, and not only because of the fire. A fear of seeing Ariella at the edge of a sword lay like a stone in his belly.

They went together, Octavia, Isabella, and Cato. For all her protestations about the games, Octavia chose not to miss them either. Cato held his tongue. He was not in the mood for teasing today. They joined the steady stream of townspeople heading east. The arena had been built to contain the whole city, and it would seem that today it would. Only slaves remained in the city's homes, protecting their valuables.

He refused to even look at the vineyard as they passed it on their left, approaching the arena. The dark stone of the circular structure rose out of the field at the end of the street like a walled city. Huge arches allowed access into the lower level from various points around the arena, and outside stairs led to the tiered seating. The press of the crowd threatened to separate him from the women, and he threaded his arms through each of theirs. The contact comforted him somehow.

Thousands of tickets had been on sale for days, with others thrown to the poor by Maius's men. Those not fortunate enough to secure a ticket had lined up before the various entrances hours ago, hoping to find standing room. They had brought their food with them and were being entertained by dancers, musicians, and acrobats who hoped for one or two tossed copper coins.

Cato and the women emerged into the seating to the beat of drums and were shown to their seats by the *locarii* hired to usher. They were among the last ticket holders to arrive, for minutes later the soldiers guarding the entrances stepped aside and the crowds held at bay flooded into the arena, in a rush for the standing room in the top tier, where sailors manned the rigging for the arena's awning.

Isabella covered her ears to block the frenzied screams of the peasantry as women were knocked aside and children trampled in the passageways that led upward.

Hawkers selling programs for betting, chilled drinks, and cushions for the hard marble forced their way through jammed aisles.

Cato took it all in, from the teeming crowd shouting odds and placing bets, to the background noise of howling wolves and trumpeting elephants from the cages beneath the arena.

The national institution of the games employed millions of people across the Empire, from animal trappers and breeders, to gladiators and trainers, and the entire supply chain that kept the men and beasts flowing into the arena. And in a sense, the games occupied them all, a narcotic that soothed and distracted a people whose slaves and plebeians did the work of the Empire, leaving them free to pursue nothing but leisure. And it kept them out of the affairs of government.

From outside the arena, the sound of drumbeats brought on a mighty cheer from the spectators. The procession approached. Cato forgot his vineyard and craned his neck toward the arched entrance, the Gate of Life. Slaves in golden armor led the procession, blowing on long trumpets, and a chariot came behind, carrying Maius and pulled by black-and white-striped tiger horses.

A group of supporters in white togas surrounded Maius's chariot, holding up placards declaring his candidacy for duovir, as if anyone did not know who sponsored the games and why.

Cato sneered at the display, but soon forgot even Maius at the sight of the floats—a long series of wheeled platforms with young men and girls posing to reenact stories of the gods.

The crowd settled and quieted as Maius reached his place of honor and stood to speak. His voice was as big as his body and it carried across the stone ring of tiered seats to every hushed spectator.

"It is my pleasure to present these many hours of entertainment for my fine citizens today. Remember that it is Gnaeus Nigidius Maius who cares enough about the people to bring the hunt, as well as the gladiators!"

The crowd erupted in cheers for the diversions to come. There were some other political and civil announcements, and then the entertainment began with lesser attractions, namely a few public executions of some criminals.

Cato had been anticipating this day for a week, and he fought to forget the vineyard for now, but the thoughts intruded and he ignored the condemned as they were brought out to the wood set for their fires. Someone shouted their offenses, impiety and treason, but Cato cared little for any of it.

It was only when he heard the word *Christian* added to their list of crimes that he straightened and peered into the sand below. Beside him, he felt his mother's tension.

The accused were not a crime-hardened string of scruffy men. Instead, a man and woman emerged from the corridors below the arena, hand in hand. Several more, including a few women, followed. Octavia clutched his hand.

In Rome, it had been fifteen years since charges of arson were brought against Christians, in Emperor Nero's rampage across Rome. The intervening years had brought spotty accusations, intermittent executions. But the sect grew and thrived in secret. And his uncle Servius, his mother's brother, was one of them.

Octavia turned wide eyes on him. "They are executing them?"

"Perhaps it is only here in the south, Mother. Perhaps they are not yet as tolerant here as those in Rome. Your brother is wise. He will not bring danger upon himself."

She nodded quickly, as though willing herself to believe Cato's words.

He wanted to search for the man he had seen in the Forum yesterday, but it was difficult to watch. Though the crowd seemed to enjoy the reinforcement of governmental authority, Cato could see only his uncle's kind face among the flames. They did not resist. They did not cry out. They perished with a dignity befitting nobility. No emperor would have died so well.

Cato's heart troubled him. They were justly accused of their crimes, true, but had a great evil been done here tonight? The flames consumed their bodies, like his grapes burning. Fire purged and purified. Did it do so in his vineyard? Did it do so here today? He had always cherished a curiosity about his uncle's secret religion, meeting behind closed doors and partaking of mysterious rituals. But he had chosen to pursue a more standard version of religion, seeking favor of the gods on behalf of his family.

There were more executions, and if the crimes of thievery and murder were ordinary, the execution methods were not. Men were bound to rotting corpses and dragged around the ring. Women tied naked to rampaging bulls.

Cato had to look away. What was happening to him? He had never been bothered by the arena before. The faces that had become known to him, his uncle Servius and the disguised Ari, were ruining his enjoyment. And beneath that realization, he felt . . . tarnished somehow. There was something so . . . so *enslaved*—about all of it— the people's obsessions with death and sex. It reminded him of the madman in the Forum.

Soon enough, prisoners lay mangled in the sand, flames had burned out, and a flood of slaves poured from the corridors to clear away the debris. The crowd began to hum with anticipation of what would come next.

It would be the hunt. He would not see Ariella for some time. Hopefully not in the sand at all. To see her fall today as well would be too much to bear.

The hunt began with the release of a dozen tigers, imported from the dark lands below Egypt. They slunk out of opposite iron grills below the seating level, heads low and backs arched as they circled each other. The crowd shouted as one, and the noise confused the animals and set them running across the sand. Those in charge of this first act would let them play it out until each tiger fed on another. Then the hunters would charge.

Cato watched the tigers, mentally cataloguing strength and

tenacity, betting himself which one would be the victor in each alter-cation. Focused on the animals, he did not see Maius approach until his mother elbowed him and cocked her head.

Accompanying Maius was one Cato never would have expected. Portia.

13

His sister's face was drawn, her lips tight.

Cato stood and moved into the aisle. "Portia." He indicated his own seat.

"You shall not have the pleasure tonight, Cato." Maius put an arm around Portia's waist. "Your sister is my guest for the evening, I'm afraid."

Cato flicked a glance at Portia. She shook her head so slightly he nearly missed it. "Then you are more fortunate than you deserve, Maius. And where is my sister's husband?"

Portia cleared her throat. "He is ill at home."

Maius smiled. "Nothing serious, she assures me. But his illness is my good fortune, I suppose."

Cato's vision went dark for a moment and his gut clenched. "Let us hope the situation reverses itself soon."

A city council member approached from a lower tier and begged a moment of Maius's time. The duovir nodded to Cato and Portia. "If you will pardon me, I shall return shortly." He pulled the council member down a few steps to continue their conversation.

Cato grabbed his sister's arm. "What is going on? Why are you with him?"

Octavia joined them, waiting for Portia's answer.

She inhaled and glanced at Maius. "He—he has been pursuing me."

"You have said nothing!"

"I thought I could rid myself of him. I did not want you to get involved in a personal clash with him."

Cato nodded. Portia had other, more public plans for him. "And Lucius's illness?"

"It is as Maius says. Not serious. But Maius made it clear that there would be consequences if I did not accompany him tonight. I dared not refuse." She put a hand on Cato's arm. "Please do not tell Lucius. I fear for him."

Maius moved upward again. "Come, dear. The hunters will be out soon. Let us return to our seats." He held out a hand.

His lustful expression nearly brought Cato down on him.

Portia turned her stricken face to Cato, her eyes pleading for his inaction, then reached out to clasp Maius's hand and descended the steps.

Octavia seethed, and Cato could feel the heat. "That man." She spoke through clenched teeth and her voice was like the growl of a mother bear protecting its cub.

Cato pulled her back to their own seats and said nothing. His own heart burned with fury and his mind raced. Portia must be extricated from the sticky fingers of Nigidius Maius before the situation grew worse.

He barely noted the hunters on horseback when they were released to take down the remaining tigers. The first hunt was followed by charging elephants and a mob of wild cats with white fur that Cato had never seen. An extensive trade in exotic animals brought from the frontier provinces had sprung up through the Empire for just this purpose, and Maius had spared no expense. The *bestiarii* who fought the animals were as trained as any gladiator, and the crowd laughed and hissed around Cato with great amusement. The arena filled with the stink of blood and entrails, and perfumed fountains shot colored water into the air, cooling the spectators and saturating the air.

A musical interlude came after the hunt, with one musician playing the *cornu*, its conical bronze circle wrapped round his head, and another a water organ, with an attendant to pump the air. The crowd paid little attention, using the time to stretch their legs or exit the arena to relieve themselves. Cato did not move.

Octavia gave him some bread she had brought, then she and Isabella left him to his thoughts.

He tore into the salty bread as though he had not eaten in weeks.

A dog race, with monkeys as jockeys, was followed by a fight between big cranes and African pygmies. Men fought pythons with bare hands, and equestrians flew at each other with sharpened lances. Through the long afternoon the frenzy of the crowd built.

But as the sun dropped beneath the upper lip of the arena, and the sailors were sent aloft to retract the awning, a gust of enthusiasm blew in with the cool breeze. The braziers of incense were removed and the patricians put away their scented sachets. But on the heels of the cool relief came a hot anticipation. The gladiators were announced.

The crowd exploded. Feet stomped the stone tiers. Shouts and applause drowned out the announcer's words. Cato strained to hear above the screaming crowd, to learn who would fight first. But the declaration was lost in the chaos.

A lone figure stalked from the far arch, down through the center of the sand. A moment later laughter greeted the gladiator's entrance as the crowd took in the diminutive size of the fighter. Cato searched his memory. Had any other fighter been as small as Ariella? No, this must be her.

The gladiator fought as a Retiarius, with a net and trident. The Retiarius typically fought a Murmillo, one who sported a fish-crested iron helmet, an oblong shield, and a short sword. But Ariella also wore a helmet. Cato waited, breath held, for her opponent.

When he emerged, it was to another howl of laughter—and delighted applause—from the crowd. Ariella's opponent was even smaller than she—Maius's promised dwarf.

They circled each other in the sand, and even from this distance Cato could sense a fierce anger in the dwarf's stance. The laughter of the crowd no doubt had coupled with his fear and the injustice of his plight, and it would spew out with violence. He may have been shorter than Ariella, but he was thick and powerful. And he was a man.

This was madness. Cato raked his fingers through his hair. How could he have allowed this? He should have done something to prevent it. His heart beat with guilt as much as fear, and he did not stop to analyze why he cared what happened to this slave girl. He stood, wavered, then sat again. What could he do now? Run into the arena? It was too late. He had failed to put a stop to something evil once again.

Octavia watched him with narrowed eyes. "What is it?"

Cato shook his head. His throat was dry and tight and he had no words. He fixed his eyes on the fight once more and prayed that the gods would spare her.

This was the light entertainment, the precursor to the serious bloodshed, and the crowd lapped it up. But there was no promise it would not turn deadly. Would the lanista allow his youngest trainee to be killed so early in his career?

Ariella and the dwarf circled for only a few moments, and then the pitched battle began. Any hope that this was not Ariella fled as he watched her move. The dwarf could only strike when close because of the shortness of his sword. She poked at him from a distance with her longer trident, then ran at him and swept her net of knotted rope toward his lower legs. He jumped it lightly and landed on flat feet, then took advantage of her proximity to slash at her net arm. She backed away and the dance began again.

She fought with a fearlessness that surprised Cato, even though he had seen it earlier, in the street and the Forum. She was a warrior, through and through, and envy stabbed him, oddly.

But even warriors could be defeated by brute strength, and the dwarf was well-muscled and skilled. The fight favored one, then the other. The people screamed and pounded the seats. Maius must be already pleased with his investment, so enraptured was the crowd with this first battle.

But then at last the dwarf made a critical error, getting in too close.

Ariella jumped and twisted, the dwarf's feet tangled in her net, and he went down. Ariella was on him in an instant, one knee in the sand, and a short dagger appeared at his throat.

The people shrieked with delight. The match had been lengthy and nearly even, the best kind. Ariella looked to where she had been instructed to look, to the place of honor where Nigidius Maius sat. She waited for him to indicate death or mercy. Cato's blood surged. He cared not whether the dwarf lived or died tonight. But Ariella had won! It sickened him to think that if the fight had gone the other way, it would have been Maius who could have ended Ariella's life.

But the crowd was pleased with the little man, and Maius read them well. He signaled Ariella to release the dwarf. She grabbed her opponent's hand and helped him to his feet, and the two ran for the arch at the end of the arena.

Cato sat back, his relief palpable.

Isabella nudged him. "That was only the first fight, brother." She laughed. "You're not going to reach the end of the night if you take each one so seriously."

But he reached the end of the night with ease, because he cared little about all the fights that followed. Even Paris failed to gain his interest. His mind was taken with his sister Portia, with Ariella, with Nigidius Maius, and with his burned vineyard. Darkness fell and the games continued. Dozens of smoking torches were lit and flamed around the oval of the uppermost tier, casting flickering shadowed stripes across the masses and burning incense in hues of red, yellow, blue, and green. Catapults flung dates and nuts and cakes into the crowd, and free wine was passed.

The games concluded with a chariot of beautiful nude girls circling the arena, chanting songs. Cato averted his eyes for his mother's sake, difficult as it was to ignore.

He did not expect to see Maius again, but it seemed as though the man was drawn to him somehow, for as the final display ended, he was there again, Portia at his side.

"I have come to return your sister, Cato." He allowed Portia to pass him on the steps, and she came to huddle close to their mother. "I hope the next time I shall have her even longer."

Cato stepped into the aisle to meet him once more. To Octavia he said, "I will join you three outside." His mother's face registered concern, but he nodded. "Outside." The women filed out and up to the highest tier to access the outer stairway, and Cato turned back to Maius.

"It is enough, Maius. My sister is a married woman."

"Come, Cato." Maius laughed and spread his hands. "We are both Romans, not pious Jews or peasant Arabs. There is freedom among Romans, you know this. I can do as I please, without fear of reprobation."

As much as the energy had drained from him after the vineyard fire, it stoked again as he faced Maius.

Cato stepped closer, his fists clenched at his sides and his jaw tight. "You shall not have her, Maius."

Maius's eyes flickered, the casual light replaced with something darker. "I do what I like in this town, Portius Cato. It is past time that you learned that."

"Not with me. Not with my family."

The older man's full lips pursed. "No? It would seem that I already have done what I wanted today. An unfortunate fire, I'm told."

Cato had suspected as much. He stepped down to stand next to Maius on the narrow stone tier, chest to chest, heedless of the small crowd that had tarried to hear the two exchange words.

The day's events crowded Cato's thoughts, like bright frescoes in a story tableau. Christians standing firm in the face of flames. Ariella, unafraid against great odds. And Maius, sending slaves to burn his vineyard.

He saw in that moment that Maius would always have the upper hand, regardless of Cato's efforts, because he was willing to cheat to get it. And something broke in him then. The fear that had pushed him out of Rome fell away. A reignited desire for justice flared in its place. He brought his face close to the other man's, his chest expanding.

"Listen to me, Nigidius Maius. Your days of using this town to satisfy your own greed are over. And that includes my sister."

Maius did not back away, and the dark fire in his own eyes deepened. "You are entering an arena yourself, Cato. And your record of success is not good." He leaned in. "I had thought to take you down simply because you are far too arrogant. Now I shall destroy you, and your family, because it will please me very much."

He turned and descended the steps, and Cato let him go. There was no need to have the last word tonight. For Cato would have the last word in the end.

Of that he was determined.

14

Maius left the arena escorted by slaves and was helped into his gold-leafed chariot by two others. The arena on the southeast outskirts of town was as far from his northwest villa as it could be, and he had no desire to make the journey on foot.

Pedestrians kept to the sidewalks as they made their way home in the torch-lit darkness, and his two-wheeled chariot, pulled by a handsome matched pair of black horses, sped through the noisy streets with Maius lifting one hand in greeting to his grateful townspeople and holding his toga at his waist with the other. This left nothing with which to grip the side of the chariot, and a bump against stepping-stones sent him reeling. He cursed the slave who held the reins and righted himself.

The evening had gone as planned, and he attempted to savor the event, in spite of the bitter aftertaste of his encounter with the haughty Portius Cato. The crowd had been enthralled with the hunt, with the music, with the gladiators. All in all, a complete success.

Added to the fiery blow he had dealt Cato's wine-making business, and the delightful hours spent with Portia at his side, he should have been gloating over the day's triumphs.

By the time the chariot reached his villa, he had thrust away all discontent and entered the massive doorway flanked by lofty columns determined to enjoy the rest of his evening. The beauty of his villa always soothed him. While urban houses were forced to look only inward, his villa opened to expansive views of the countryside and sea. Large windows were placed strategically, and walls were replaced with colonnades to open the space. The house sprawled outward in all directions and boasted over sixty rooms. But more than soothing, his villa housed his secret pursuit, the mystery rites that only a select few shared, in ceremonies held late into the night, when inhibitions were chased away by the urging, pulsing voices of the gods.

Inside the peristyle, slaves unburdened Maius of his weighty wool toga, leaving him in only a short tunic better suited to relaxation, and led him deeper into the villa, to the courtyard where he often enjoyed outdoor dining amidst the flowers and fountains.

The garden was quiet this evening, save for the gentle trickle of the fountain in the center, a whimsical representation of the wine god Bacchus riding a bloated wineskin, with the water pouring like wine from the skin's mouth. Maius lowered himself to a couch and lifted his legs with a heavy sigh, grateful that Nigidia and his extensive staff of slaves were all occupied elsewhere. The scent of night flowers weighted the air and the red silks that covered his couch seemed to embrace him.

The silence pleased him because he wanted to recollect his evening with the luscious Portia. Slaves brought honeyed dormice and snails in silence, placing the food on a low table beside his couch. Maius ate, musing over his plan to make the woman his mistress.

That she was married meant nothing. A small inconvenience that could be dealt with. His own marriage had been for property only, and even while his wife lived he had been expected to make use of his own slave women and of the brothels. Why should a mistress be any different?

He summoned a slave to play a lyre for him. The man was still young, though his undernourished body, rotted teeth, and multiple scars from beatings and branding spoke of a life too long lived. As he played, the bright-colored birds Maius kept at the edge of the atrium joined the melody. Maius continued to eat, then clapped his hands for more food.

There was still the tickle of discontent beneath it all, however. Foolish that he could allow one insignificant character such as Cato to disturb him. He dismissed the musician with instructions to fetch his chief slave, in charge of his business dealings. The man was a Greek scholar, purchased in Athens and brought to Pompeii with a mind for numbers and analysis.

Primus entered soon after.

"I have need to hear that all is well in my enterprises."

The Greek, only a few years older than Maius, nodded once and then sat cross-legged on the floor of the atrium, near the couch where Maius still reclined. "Then I shall tell you all is well."

"The wine business, specifically?"

Primus shrugged. "What do you have to fear, in any of your undertakings?"

Indeed. "And there have been no rumblings from the people? Talk of another candidate, that sort of thing?"

Primus shook his head.

But the slave was too pensive for Maius's liking. "What is it?"

"There is only some business with the brothels." He shrugged. "Nothing serious."

Most of the town's many brothels were occupied by slave women owned by Maius, and the profits funneled back to him on a regular basis, thanks to the insatiable lust that enslaved the idle and rich Pompeiians.

Maius jutted his chin toward Primus. "Speak."

"There is a noblewoman who is purported to move among the women, urging them to find a different life."

"How would they do such a thing?"

Primus shrugged. "Save their money. Purchase their freedom, perhaps. I do not know."

Maius waved a hand at the absurdity. Primus was right, it was nothing to be concerned about. "Who is this generous noblewoman?"

"Her name is Octavia. Of the Catonii."

Maius felt his lips part. He swung his legs over the side of the couch, striking Primus. The Greek skittered backward.

"Cato again!" The cursed boy was everywhere he turned. He rounded on Primus. "Get out."

The slave only stared.

"Get out!"

Primus obeyed, but Maius was not content to remain where he was, even alone. He paced the garden, then strode from it and took to his veranda that overlooked the city.

Torches still burned across Pompeii, mirroring the starry night. Maius gripped the curved stone wall and stared across the city, as though his vision could travel down street and alley, through the doorway of the house of Portius Cato, and straight into the man's heart like a knife.

Cato was a danger. He could see that now. For all Maius's posturing, he would admit, to himself alone, a latent fear that the ex-politician from Rome could damage him. More than damage. If Maius lost his position as duovir, he could be prosecuted for any charges that the ordo chose to bring against him. Most of which involved execution if he were found guilty. And he was not so naïve to think that once out of office, he would have enough friends to keep him safe. He slapped his hands against the stone wall and pushed away to pace the veranda.

No, he must move against Cato, and he must do it strongly, show him who controlled this city and its resources. It was not about wine anymore.

What would it take to frighten the young man back to Rome? Clearly, the burning of his vines had not intimidated him. But he must have a weakness. He conjured up Cato's image in his mind, held it there like a magician with a spell, seeing Cato's fiery indignation at the plight of his sister.

Yes . . . his sister. There was weakness there. Like his mother, apparently, Cato suffered from a disadvantage ill suited to political life—compassion. And that weakness could be exploited. Maius's heart quickened with a beat of anticipation.

If nothing else, Maius was an expert in finding ways to bend others to his will, and the plan came easily now that he had seen Cato's frailty. It would have to be about the sister. How easy it would be to spread rumors that Portia was being unfaithful to her husband. Poor woman, desperate to bear a child and convinced her barrenness was the fault of her girlish husband, she had turned to a man whose very essence was virility. Flattered by her attention and never one to turn away an admirer, Maius had succumbed to her charms.

Maius stroked his full lips. Yes. It was good.

Maius could have the city council press for Portia's divorce. Her husband had the right to divorce her for infertility already. Adultery would be another strike against her, and Maius could wield the mighty weapon of influence. She would be disgraced, stripped of her property, and unable to remarry. It was the perfect threat to use against Cato. And perhaps also against Portia. Who knew what she would be willing to do to avoid such charges?

His belly was full of the night's sumptuous food, but tonight he also gorged on revenge.

There came a mighty shift, deep within the earth beneath Vesuvius.

The massive, broken plates of continents that rubbed shoulders snagged and tried to break loose. They floated on a fiery sea of melted rock, carrying oceans and continents, ever so slowly. Sometimes these plates merely passed each other without incident. Sometimes they drifted apart. But at other times—at other times they were not so tame.

It was then that they pushed against each other, each plate insisting on its own passage, the pressure building and building and building until finally—with a force to shake the nations—one plate would dive under the other. Rock liquefied, fissures widened, and a channel burrowed up, upward to the surface where it could find release.

The mountain had found this release many times in ages past, and under the heavy vegetation, its slopes bore the scars of countless lava flows. But did the people who sheltered in its shadow, who farmed its fertile soil—did they remember its power?

No, they saw it as beneficent, always. As though it could not destroy, as though it did not hold sway over their very lives.

Foolish. They had been foolish. And they would soon know their folly.

15

When Ariella left the sand that afternoon, followed by the dwarf whose life she had nearly been required to take, her veins were on fire and her senses more acute than they had ever been.

She strode under the stone arch that led out of the arena, then down the vaulted corridor behind the seating to the holding room where ten other pairs of fighters waited for their turn at glory.

She couldn't help a raised fist when she entered the room. There were shouts of acclamation, if half-amused. The dwarf had gone elsewhere, to wherever they were kept.

Celadus slapped her back and knocked her off balance, then laughed. She laughed with him.

"Knew you could do it, boy. Never a doubt."

She chose not to argue, instead basking in the moment. She was invincible, unbeatable. The chants of the crowd rose again on the other side of the stone wall, recalling her own moments before them, all white and gold, gasping and cheering at each move she made, their thunderous applause when she had the dwarf on the ground.

Hours later the glow had not worn off, and she joined her fellow gladiators in the dark courtyard as the lanista brought jugs of wine to be passed among them. They had lost only a few of their near-hundred men. It had been a good night. The purple wine slid down her throat cool, then hot, and no wine had ever tasted better.

There were more shouts, more laughter, and back-slapping from those who had not seen her in the holding room. Strange, to feel herself a favorite. She straightened and nodded, warmed from the commendation and from the wine. Spectators, ardent fans who lived for the games, milled through the training yard, wanting to get closer to their heroes. They were mostly women, and Ariella watched, fascinated, as they clustered around their favorites. Celadus, with his big smile and missing front teeth, seemed to draw the nurturing types, while Paris and his friend Floronius, haughty and proud, had the young ones fawning over them. Ariella drew some attention as well, but fled from the strangeness.

They fell onto their mats eventually, and most of the men snored within moments. Ariella propped her hands behind her head and stared at the roof of the cell, reliving the fight once again.

She could do this. She had seen that running away would be fruitless. But why could she not stay, train hard, and win real battles? Not battles against dwarves, but real matches with some of the men here. She could survive. She had seen that tonight. Especially if she could win the favor of the crowd.

She must create a nickname for herself. Something to make her known among the townspeople . . . An idea came to her, bringing a small smile in its irony.

Scorpion Fish. Venomous, hidden, and masters of disguise and deception, the bright fish could blend in with its surroundings, unnoticed by its prey. She had already worn the fish-crested helmet of a Murmillo.

Yes, it was perfect.

She fell asleep at last, confident in her plan.

The next day it took only a small amount of persuasion to get the lanista to let her paint more signs for the next fights, ten days hence. She did have artistic ability, and her first advertisements had done their job well. But she did not expect the metal collar he locked around her neck before allowing her to leave.

"Not taking any chances," Drusus said.

She touched the bronze at her throat. There would be no escaping now, with the clear indication of her status bolted to her body. No matter. She had found another route to freedom.

Once out in the city, paint in hand, it was a simple matter to work her own publicity into the task.

See Paris, the favorite of Rome, together with Scorpion Fish, slayer
of dwarves, and twenty other pairs of fighters

Never mind that she hadn't killed the dwarf, which in truth she was very glad about. It was enough to identify her, and if she knew this town, they would seize on her nickname and make it an object of fascinated conversation.

She continued through the city, painting her placards outside bakeries and brothels, taverns and *thermopolia*, where hot foods waited in bowls set in the marble counters for those who preferred not to cook their own.

When she returned to the barracks, the old slave, Jeremiah, met her in the training yard. "You have been given new quarters." He took her paint supplies and indicated that she should follow. "I am to take you."

Confused, she followed Jeremiah into the shaded portico that bordered the field, past the cells she had shared with the others. "Why?"

He did not answer until they had ducked under a doorway into a small room with a mat, some rough bedding, and two pots. It smelled of urine and waste, but it was hers alone. "Perhaps *HaShem* has heard my prayers, to keep you safe from those who would harm you." He patted her back, a touch soft enough to comfort.

Ariella turned to study him, watched his faint smile and then the downcast eyes. How had he accomplished this? She surveyed the tiny chamber. To have her own cell, a private place to dress and bathe—the blessing of it brought tears. She swiped at them and patted Jeremiah's arm. "Thank you, Jeremiah."

He shook his head. "Thank HaShem, dear child. He is the giver of all good things."

She smiled sadly. Her childhood faith had long ago been trampled by Roman boots, replaced by nothing but cold anger. "You thank Him for me, Jeremiah. He has not heard from me in many years."

Jeremiah came to touch her face, like a rabbi's blessing. "Do not let them conquer your spirit, child. The evil one toils to keep these people oppressed, obsessed with violence and lust. Do not let him pull you into the gutter."

In the morning, when she was able to prepare for the day alone, in her private cell, she nearly did give thanks to the Creator, so grateful was she for the respite.

But the break was short-lived, for she was expected on the training field by sunup. Remembering her renewed plan yesterday, she determined to train hard today, to better prepare for the next fighter she would face.

Today's partner, however, could not have been more daunting. When Drusus called out the pairs and she found herself faced with Paris, her heart pounded in a rhythm that matched the fighters who beat against the wooden palus.

She expected amusement, mockery from Paris as he circled her and strapped leather around his hands, his perfect body gleaming with oil. Instead, he appeared angry.

"What did I tell you about stealing my glory, runt?"

Ariella swallowed and readjusted the sword in her hand.

"Did you think I would not find out that you've been running around the city, painting your name next to mine?"

What a fool she was! He had warned her already that an attempt to draw attention to her status as the smallest fighter would not be welcomed. She licked her lips. "There is room on the walls of Pompeii for two fighters, Paris."

"Not when you are one of them." He slashed at her with his wooden sword, and she jumped back.

The fight was quick and dirty. Paris had her on the ground in seconds. Ariella sensed the other fighters break off their training to watch. Paris grabbed her by the leather vest and yanked her upward, off balance and held upright only by his hand wrapped around her buckles.

Ariella's breath came quick. She took in with sharp clarity the tan leather of his own vest, the acrid smell of his body, the roughness of his hands.

He used the flat side of his sword to swat at the side of her head, as though she were an annoying insect.

Shouts erupted from the rest of the fighters, but Ariella could not tell if they encouraged Paris to free her or to beat her until she was dead. Another slap with his sword. Her face stung and her eyes watered. She tasted blood in her mouth. He jabbed his sword into her side. The wood was too dull to pierce skin, but would her ribs give way?

She fought to pull away and regain her footing. Fear coursed through her and made her desperate. She dropped her own sword and reached to claw at his eyes. Her fear merged into hatred and anger.

A shout from the side of the training yard turned Paris's attention away from her. She used the moment to break his hold and shuffle backward.

"Is this the kind of training I have instructed?" The lanista's eyes flashed as he stalked across the grass. He came up close to Paris, jutting a finger into the fighter's chest. "You have a chance to run your own school someday, Paris. But not if you let your emotions rule. Understand?"

Paris grunted and turned away.

Ariella leaned over, her hands on her knees, and tried to catch her breath.

Drusus flicked a hand at her. "Take a break, little boy."

She stumbled back to her private cell and was unsurprised to find Jeremiah waiting for her. He probed her ribs with gentle fingers, but she winced with even the slight pressure. "No breaks." He took her face in his hands and turned her head left and right. "You will live. This time."

His disapproval angered her.

He laid her down on her mat. "You are like a strong horse, but one with no leads. You run wild."

"And I will continue to do so!"

He shook his head in silence.

She tried to soften her harsh words. "I must."

"You are a mighty warrior, Ari. Ah, what the Lord could do with that fighter's heart."

He left her then, left her to her thoughts, which at once grew dark.

She had been a fool. It did not matter how hard she trained, how skilled she grew. She could never survive a match with a fighter like

Paris. She was destined always to be a prelude to the real entertainment, always to fight dwarves and animals. Or else she would be pitted against real gladiators and she would lose. Would the crowd have mercy? Would the editores of the games let her live?

The dwarf had gained the crowd yesterday and saved his own life. Dwarves were a curiosity, and no one wished to see them dead. Were not women gladiators also a curiosity?

How long would it take for Scorpion Fish to make a name well known amongst the townspeople? And when Scorpion Fish revealed that he was in fact a woman . . . She smiled at the plan. Paris had said that he would win his freedom by earning the favor of the people. If a stupid beast like him could do it, then so could she.

A few more fights, a little more attention, and then she would be ready to amaze the town of Pompeii with something they had never seen.

A woman in the sand of the arena.

16

Cato's declaration at the games, though made only to himself, still occupied his thoughts in the new day. He *would* bring Maius down.

Taurus would have him run for election as duovir against Maius, since the other duovir, Balbus, would not face an election for a while, but running was only a fraction of the battle. It was winning that meant something. And winning was far from guaranteed, with Maius owning most of the town's loyalty for one fraudulent reason or another.

And so he entered the Forum once more, to put a finger to the political winds and see if they might blow favorably in his direction.

His first stop was the Eumachia, where Emeritus, head of the Fullers' Guild, had dealt unspoken threats the other day. He would rather have avoided the beak-nosed man, but it would seem that strong support could come from this group, and it would be invaluable.

Emeritus was deep in conversation at the back of the building under the roofed colonnade when Cato entered, so he strolled through the working slaves, as though interested in their work. The chalk they used to whiten the togas given to them for washing smelled as foul as the urine, but some of the slaves hummed or sang while they worked and seemed immune to the odor. He lifted the corner of a silk, half-submerged in a dye pot, then replaced it at the look of a slave who frowned at him like he was a meddling child.

Emeritus turned his dark eyes on Cato, arrested his conversation seemingly in mid-thought, and stared. Cato dipped his head, and Emeritus indicated that he should approach.

"I did not wish to interrupt—"

Emeritus brushed away his apology. "You are not interrupting. You are the very subject of our discourse."

Cato inclined his head. "I am sorry, then, that you do not have more interesting topics to discuss."

"On the contrary, your arrival makes the topic that much more interesting. You are reconsidering?"

Cato sniffed and looked out over the slaves in the courtyard once more. "I am asking questions, that is all."

Emeritus seemed to remember himself and introduced his associate. "Otho, another of the city's fullers."

The man was as young as Cato and looked as though he had worked his way into the upper class from a poorer beginning. Cato bowed in acknowledgment. "And are the fullers united in their . . . dissatisfaction with the current leadership?"

Otho snorted. "The man is a—"

Emeritus laid a hand on the younger man's arm. "Careful, Otho. We are, above all things, discreet." He turned back to Cato. "You can be assured that the Fullers' Guild would support a change." He leaned in close, confidentially. "Especially one that would place a man of integrity on the seat of duovir."

Cato pulled back and lifted an eyebrow. "And where would you find such a man?"

Emeritus smiled. "Your modesty becomes you, but is unnecessary. Rome is not so far away."

"Then you have heard of more than my integrity."

"We must not expect to always be successful in our attempts to quash corruption, Portius Cato. Failure is part of the battle. We are looking for a man who will fight. That is enough."

The commendation was like soothing oil on an old wound, and Cato bowed in appreciation. "I thank you for your wisdom. I shall inform you of my decision." He turned to leave, but Emeritus called him back.

"Do not tarry too long, Cato. Evil has a way of multiplying when left unchecked."

Cato returned to the Forum's main square, fortified that at least there was support from somewhere. But it would take more, much more, to make him believe he could be successful.

Were there others he could approach and try to read? The danger was in Maius's loyal supporters getting word back to him about Cato's inquiries. He mused over the possibilities of the fruitsellers, the goldsmiths, the carpenters. Each industry had its own guild, not so powerful as the fullers, but still able to deliver votes in a block that would be important.

He decided to search out the jewelers, as Taurus, who had worked so hard to convince him to run, was part of that guild. He crossed the Forum's central pavement at a diagonal to the opposite corner where the shops might yield the man.

Indeed, he had not even reached the other side when Taurus appeared, spotted him, and strode toward him, his face pinched. "What is this, Cato? Do you attempt to disqualify yourself before you have even begun?"

Cato held up his palms and grinned. "I did not think a visit to the jewelers would be such a black mark—"

"Cato, be serious for once. I am speaking of your sister! It is all over the city."

Cato waved away Taurus's concerns. "She has done nothing to welcome his advances—"

"*His* advances? It is everywhere that she is after Maius to give her the son that her husband cannot."

Cato's blood surged. "You cannot believe—"

"It matters not what I believe! Perception is everything, my boy, and right now your family is cast in a very ill light. Adultery by a woman of standing is nothing to be ignored."

"She has done nothing!"

Taurus shook his head and held up his hands. "Understand me, Cato. I do not care if your sister is as pure as lamb's wool or as tainted as the foul sewage that runs the streets. I only care about your reputation, and how this situation makes you look."

"And I care more for my sister than your cursed election!"

Taurus opened his mouth to reply, then closed it again and snorted. When he spoke, it was quieter, the tone soothing. "Listen, Cato. You could do much good in this town, and that includes helping your sister, and your mother with her endeavors, and any other women you wish to help." His voice held amusement, but Cato's thoughts jumped to Ariella. He had already done a bit of good for her in the past day, but she was still in danger.

"You must be reasonable about your priorities," Taurus was saying. "First things first."

Cato looked off to the mountain, so solid. Unlike the wavering allegiances of a town that put its own needs above all else. "Do I have the support of the jewelers, or is it only you?"

A slow smile spread across Taurus's face, like a satisfied cat after a bowl of milk. "The jewelers are united behind me. You will be our man for duovir."

Cato nodded, pivoted, and left before he could say something about the man's "priorities" that would not be favorable.

Enough politicking for one day, however quiet it had been. He headed home, past the thermopolium where the smell of onions and garlic made his mouth water, and he stopped to purchase a bowl of meaty stew. He stood at the marble slab with others enjoying hot food from the sunken pots and scooped the stew with two fingers, savoring the flavors and thinking over the two encounters and the rumors that were spreading about his sister. A beggar came to the counter, asking for food, and Cato started to chase him off, but the shop owner held out a bowl to the man with a few quiet words—"in the name of Jesus." A chill ran over him at the statement, the third time in as many days he had heard that name. In Rome and now Pompeii, they seemed to be everywhere, these mysterious followers.

He crossed the threshold of his house some time later, still debating whether to tell Octavia and Portia about the gossip, but one look through the atrium answered his question. Portia clung to her mother, her face buried in Octavia's shoulder.

Cato hesitated, but Octavia waved him in. "They are saying awful things about your sister." She patted Portia's back.

"I have heard."

At the sight of him, Portia pulled away from her mother and came to grip Cato's toga. The fabric fell away in her hands, but she seemed not to notice. "Lucius is furious." Her face was tear-streaked. "He had already heard about my being at the games with Maius, and now he says he is unsure whether to trust me. Can you believe that?"

Cato wiped her tears with his thumbs, then held her face. "Give him a little time, sister. He knows you, knows your love for him. He will come around."

"I hate him!" She sobbed once. "Maius! Not Lucius." And then more tears. Cato returned her to their mother, unwrapped his toga, and tossed it across the stone half wall of the atrium. "There is nothing to be done except to stand and insist upon your innocence. He has no proof, and everyone in this town knows what he is. They have no reason to doubt you."

Her temper flared. "You are a fool, Quintus! Even Lucius doubts me! How can I expect—"

Octavia intervened. "Lucius is hurt, dear. His emotions cloud his judgment. Others will not be so harsh."

Portia's hands fisted at her sides. "Oh, you two. You are both naïve." She spun and ran for the interior of the house.

Octavia watched her go in silence, then spoke without turning back to Cato. "She may be right. There may be no recovery from this."

"There is only one way for this town, for us all, to recover. It is for Gnaeus Nigidius Maius to be no more."

Octavia's eyes slid to his face and she read him well. "You have decided, then."

He rocked forward on his toes. "I am still considering."

She nodded, as though content to give him the time he needed. They both knew her expectations.

17

It had taken less effort than even Maius expected to begin the campaign of untruth against the sister of Portius Cato. He had more in his employ than he sometimes remembered, and a few well-placed whispers soon spread to jokes told in the baths, to glances in the market. Within a day Maius saw the fruit of his efforts himself when he conversed with several in the Forum, and the dalliance was referred to by more than one acquaintance.

He smiled and looked away from the merchant, as though embarrassed. "Ah, well." He shrugged one shoulder. "I am a fool for beauty, I will admit."

That evening he again reclined in his atrium, satisfied that the time was right for him to bring his threats against Cato. The moon rose and still he lay there, thinking through his plan and the way in which he would bring Portia to his house. His eyelids grew heavy with scheming, and though the dampness of the night fell on him, he was too weighted to move.

A scratching beside his couch half roused him, and he opened one eye, thinking to have a slave assist him to his bedchamber. But the flames in the brazier nearby did not illuminate a slave.

He must be dreaming, and the lovely Portia had come to him in his dreams as she sometimes did, leaning over him with whispered words of admiration.

But this was no dream, and though Portia did lean over him, it was with the deadly glint of a silver dagger.

He scrambled backward on the couch and propped his hands behind him. "What? What is this—"

The dagger was at his throat in an instant. "Do not scream." Portia's voice rasped at his ear. "Or I swear by the gods I will slit your throat and not care who finds your blood on me."

Maius pressed his lips together and swallowed. Her eyes were wide with fury and a cold sweat formed across his neck and dampened his hands. "You cannot harm me without retribution."

"No one saw me enter."

Maius began to shake, and he held his hands in front of his face. "Please. What do you want?"

She advanced the dagger. "I want my life to return to what it once was."

Her hand shook. Maius saw the tremor and gained confidence. This act of defiance was outside her ability to carry off. She was bred to days of refinement and luxury, not knife-wielding in the night.

Summoning his own courage, Maius jumped from the couch, grabbed her wrist, and twisted the knife from her grasp.

Portia cried out and went down on her knees.

Maius held the knife in his right hand and still bent her wrist with the other.

She raised white eyes to him.

Anger surged through him. Anger at showing fear in front of a woman, anger at how near she had come to taking vengeance. He reached out with the knife, jabbed it close to her ear.

She yelped and squeezed her eyes shut.

With a flick of his wrist, he sliced a lock of her dark hair from her head and let it fall to the atrium floor.

She breathed again, opened her eyes, and went limp in his grasp, then sank to the floor, her face in her hands.

Maius gazed at her there at his feet and felt himself spent and satisfied. For good measure, he kicked her in the ribs.

She made no sound.

"Take yourself back to your husband and your brother." His voice was a hiss only a whisper above the fountain's murmur. "Give them a message from me. Nigidius Maius owns Pompeii." He poked at her with his toe again.

This time she roused, pulled herself to standing, then fled the atrium without a word.

Maius bent to the floor when she had gone, lifted the single dark curl, and let it wind itself around his forefinger. And then he shifted his eyes to the doorway where she'd disappeared and smiled.

18

Portia had remained in Cato's house for the day and stayed the night, saying she was not yet ready to face Lucius again. When the morning meal was served in the triclinium, she joined them looking haggard, as though she had not slept. Octavia fussed over her, but Portia sank to a couch without speaking, almost without seeming to hear.

With his father gone, Cato was now the *pater familias*, and he performed his duties to the gods on behalf of his family today, taking a portion of the meal and tossing it onto the flames of the brazier, and setting aside a small offering of salt and fruits.

Isabella did her best to charm a better mood from her sister, but it was almost as though Portia had seen some dark specter in the night and could not shake it from her. She took no food.

Before they had finished their pastries and wine, however, the darkness seemed to spread into the house. A commotion in the front of the home made its way to the triclinium, where the four had already risen to their feet.

Portia hung back, clinging to Cato's tunic.

Cato took in the three soldiers. "What is this?"

"We are under instruction to take Portia of the Catonii into our custody to await trial."

Portia gasped behind him, and Octavia and Isabella both stepped forward.

"Who brings a charge against my sister?" Cato's palms grew sweaty and he shifted to block Portia from their view.

"Nigidius Maius. On the charge of assault."

Cato reeled back as though he had been struck. Adultery, he had expected. But assault? "This is ludicrous. My sister has assaulted no one."

Behind him, Portia's fingers twisted his tunic until he felt her knuckles dig into his back.

"She has been accused of stealing into the home of Nigidius Maius and attempting to murder him with a knife."

Cato turned enough to see Portia's bowed head, then pulled away from her grasp. "Portia?" She raised fearful eyes to him, and he read the truth at once. "When?"

She leaned in, until they were cheek to cheek. "I am sorry, brother. I do not know what came over me. Last night—"

Cato put two fingers over her lips. "Say no more." He turned to the soldiers. "This situation should be treated as a civil offense, not a criminal one. I will discuss the matter with Maius, and we will come to a financial agreement—"

"Maius has indicated that she will be tried."

Cato's mind raced. The Roman judicial system allowed much leniency in these types of cases, and a sufficient payment should cover the offense. That Maius would insist on making it a criminal case could only be for revenge.

Was it not enough for Maius that he burned Cato's fields?

He remembered his words to Portia last night, that the people would believe her innocence. What would they believe now?

The soldiers would brook no more delay, and they shoved Cato aside to grasp both of Portia's arms.

Octavia and Isabella cried out as if they'd been seized themselves.

"Do something, Quintus!" His mother's eyes on him were like twin fires.

A soldier jerked Portia away from her family, breaking the hold Octavia had retained on Portia's robes.

Cato was powerless to change this, she had to know that. Not now, not today.

He pulled his mother back. "We must let her go." He caught Portia's eye before they pulled her from the room. "Be strong, sister. We will have you home before you know it."

At the mention of her home, Portia crumpled, no doubt remembering the angry husband who awaited her there. The soldiers dragged her from the room.

And then she was gone, leaving Cato and the two women staring through the triclinium doorway in stunned silence.

But Cato could not keep silent for long. No jesting comment, no irreverent sarcasm could mitigate this disaster. Instead, a deep and furious anger boiled up from within and spewed out with flaming curses. He kicked at the couches, knocked over the tables of food, sent pastries scattering across the mosaic floor.

His mother tried to calm him, cool hands on his arms, but he shook her off. He despised injustice of any sort, and this was the worst kind, the kind that threatened those he loved.

In the stillness that followed his rampage, a terra-cotta jug teetered on its side on the floor, the only sound in the room save Cato's panting outrage. He lifted a sandaled foot above the jug and smashed it down, welcoming the pain of jagged edges.

Perhaps there had never been a doubt. Perhaps since that first meeting in the wine shop, when Maius had looked at Portia with greedy eyes and smirked through his subtle threats against Cato, perhaps he had made his decision in that very moment, though he had not known it until today.

Whatever the case, there was no longer any question. Cato would run for duovir.

And he would win.

19

Ariella measured the hours by the bruises she received in training and counted the days until her next fight. Only a flamboyant performance in the arena would gain her the attention necessary to make a name for herself and win her freedom. Time passed in a blur of tears and sweat, a hardening of her muscles, a growing confidence, and a sense of what it would take to entertain the populace. She was ready.

Her increased commitment did not go unnoticed by her fellow gladiators, and they left her alone to beat against the palus and showed more respect when paired with her.

On a sun-hammered afternoon, when most of the fighters had retreated to shade and sleep in their cells, Ariella still thrust at the palus, feeling herself watched by the always-smiling Jeremiah from his smoking cookfire at the edge of the training yard, and by the ugly Floronius, who also pushed through the customary afternoon rest.

Jeremiah brought her a dipperful of cool water and she stopped to guzzle it, then to squeeze his arm. He smelled of the boiled fish he was cooking.

"Where is my water, slave?" Floronius stood near the palus, leaning on his wooden sword jabbed into the dirt.

Jeremiah bowed slightly, then retreated to his bucket, refilled the ladle, and turned to trek across the grass.

"You are as slow as an old turtle, slave. I'm likely to die of my thirst before you reach me."

Ariella bristled. "Take a few steps yourself then, Floronius."

Floronius bared his teeth at her. "I've seen the way he takes care of you, runt. You think he belongs to you? The runt gets his own personal slave, eh?"

Jeremiah's slow gait at last reached Floronius where he stood at the palus, and the larger man grabbed the ladle, sloshing water onto his feet. "Arrgh! Fool!" He slapped Jeremiah across the face.

Ariella approached, alarmed. She did not expect Jeremiah to retaliate, but almost she believed he offered Floronius the other cheek. "This is what you've come to, great Floronius?" She tipped her chin toward Jeremiah. "Choosing old men for opponents? What will Drusus say?"

Floronius's eyes went dark. "And you would tell your tales to Drusus like the child you are, rather than fight your own battles like a man."

Ariella took a step toward him, sword arm raised, but Jeremiah stepped between them, his palms up. "No need for this, men. Floronius, my apologies for both my speed and my clumsiness. Forgive an old man who has served too long."

But Floronius had his eyes on Ariella, and it would not end with Jeremiah's undeserved humiliation. "If you have served too long, then, old man, perhaps it is time you were relieved of your duties." He shoved the dull end of his sword against Jeremiah's shoulder, pushing him back.

"Stop." Ariella tried to push Jeremiah behind her, but Floronius seemed to seize on her weakness for the old man and use it as a deadlier weapon than a sword. He shoved Jeremiah again before Ariella could intervene.

She saw the man stumble, saw his feet catch under him, but could do nothing to stop the fall.

His eyes widened and his arms spread wide, and then he pitched backward and fell against the palus.

Ariella felt more than heard a horrifying crack, like the snapping of a brittle tree branch. Torn between a blinding haze of fury at Floronius that prompted her to rush at the brute with her fists and a flush of concern for Jeremiah, she chose to race to the older man's side where he lay in the dirt, panting.

"What is it, Jeremiah? Where is the pain?"

Jeremiah's face paled, and he reached to grip her arm with a strength that belied his age. She tried to absorb his pain through that grip, but he looked faint.

He licked dry lips and rasped out, "My hip."

Floronius's derisive laughter echoed. "So we shall be looking for a new slave after all."

Ariella ignored him. For now. There would be time for retribution later. She ran a hand over the man's hip but could feel no disjoint. Broken, then, most likely. "Do not move, Jeremiah. I will get Drusus."

He nodded slightly, eyes closed.

Ariella found Drusus in the portico at the end of the barracks' large training yard, sharpening a *lancea*. She pointed to the distant figure of Jeremiah, still on the ground. Floronius had vanished.

Drusus huffed in annoyance. "Well, I did not pay much for him, so the loss is not too great. It was time for a younger man anyway."

"He needs a physician, Drusus! His hip is out of place, or broken. It must be set."

Drusus shrugged and returned to his sharpening. "A slave his age? He will not live to recover. Why bother?"

Ariella kicked at the lancea, knocking it from Drusus's hand.

"Because he is a good man! Unlike the rest of the monsters in this place, including yourself."

Drusus stood, fire in his eyes, but Ariella did not care. "Prove me wrong, then, Drusus. Let me care for him."

"Take him to your own cell, then, if you wish. I care not what you do with him."

Ariella fumed at the cruelty but said nothing more. She returned to Jeremiah with a few comforting words, then sought out Celadus to help her move Jeremiah as gently as they could manage. Once in her cell, she bathed his forehead with cool water and promised to find a way to relieve his pain.

But Jeremiah shook his gray head. "If it is my time, then I am only glad I have you to ease the passage."

Ariella's heart warmed with the words of affection, but she would not give him so quickly to the afterlife. "Do you have family here, Jeremiah? Anyone I can find to help you?" Why had she never asked him such a question?

His eyes misted. "Family, yes. I have family here."

"I will take you to them."

With whispered instructions he told her where his family lived. She would bide her time until nightfall, then somehow get him out.

Through the evening meal, while the other fighters laughed and told their ribald stories as usual, with no thought to the faithful slave suffering in her cell, Ariella choked down Jeremiah's fish stew and waited for her chance. When the time came for her nightly chains, she convinced Drusus to leave her free for the night, to care for Jeremiah. Her earlier words must have penetrated to some degree, for he said nothing but left without locking her in shackles.

She sat beside Jeremiah on the ground, singing soft songs from home, while he dozed in snatches and groaned in his sleep. When the chill convinced her that night had fallen, Ariella slipped from the cell, found the wobbly wooden cart Jeremiah used to bring his purchases from the Macellum, and rolled it through the damp grass, as near to her cell as possible.

It would not do to involve Celadus in this effort. She did not trust him so fully.

She gave Jeremiah a rag to bite down on, then half carried, half dragged him to the cart. He collapsed in relief.

A few quick turns took them through the bumpy streets of Pompeii, each rut another injury to the dear man. The night air wrapped chilly fingers around her and squeezed. The shadowy streets quickened her pace.

"Are you certain they will be awake?" She rolled the cart to a stop in front of a large set of double doors.

"They will come."

Ariella took in the size of the doors. This was no poor relation. "Your family lives here?"

He smiled, his head against the side of the wagon. "They will come."

And so she knocked with trembling fingers on the door of this wealthy home and waited for a servant to answer the late-night summons.

When the door opened, a bulky Persian stared down on her with dark and suspicious eyes. She stepped aside to reveal her cargo. "He is hurt. I have brought him to his family."

The Persian flicked a glance over the wagon, then his eyebrows shot up. "Rabbi!" He pulled the door wide. "Can he walk?"

Ariella shook her head. *Rabbi?*

The servant opened the other wide door, then helped her navigate the cart over the threshold and into the entry hall of the grand house. Ariella caught a glimpse of the expansive courtyard in the center, with moonlight playing over flowering bushes. And somewhere, deep within the house, she heard the sound of singing.

The house still hummed with activity, even at this late hour. The Persian left them in the atrium to fetch someone else, and she eyed the comings and goings of the staff, carrying platters of food and bulky cushions toward one of the entertaining chambers off the central garden. So taken was she with the evidence of a late-night party that she missed the entrance of a woman until the matron of the house was upon them, her worried voice calling out to Jeremiah where he still lay in the cart.

Her hand was on his forehead at once, and she looked Ariella over, a question in her eyes. She was dressed in a scarlet stola and heavily jeweled, but there was no arrogance in her look, only a concern that seemed to extend to them both.

"I am one of the gladiators." Ariella dropped her eyes. "It is his hip. I fear it is broken. He—he told me to bring him here." Uncertainty at her course faltered her voice, but the woman patted her arm and smiled. Ariella found herself drawn to her warmth.

Within moments, others had been summoned, and Jeremiah had been carried to the triclinium where a large group assembled and lay on cushions.

Ariella stood beside him at the wall, uncertain of whether she should stay. But Jeremiah's hand found hers and did not let go.

She could make no sense of this family of his. The size of the house, its abundant statuary and elaborate frescoes, spoke of great wealth. People of all ages filled the room, men and women, peasant and noble, even foreigners. Fires burned in braziers at the corners of the warm room, and the table was laden with an abundance of food and drink. Her muscles relaxed, as though she were coming untied within, and she sank to the cushion beside Jeremiah. "You are a rabbi?"

She felt her face flame with embarrassment. She had thought of him as only a slave, but of course he had another life, before. Just as she did.

He smiled sadly. "I once was. In happier days."

A physician had been summoned, but while they waited, the group focused its concern on the two newcomers. The noblewoman, Europa, brought her a dish heaped with lentils and urged her to eat. Ariella shook her head, embarrassed further to be treated thus, but Europa took Ariella's hands and wrapped them around the warm bowl. "You are Jeremiah's friend"—she put an arm around Ariella's shoulder—"and so you are also our friend."

The light touch of the woman, so like a mother, dissolved her, and she bent to the dish of lentils to hide her misty eyes. She should be getting back to the barracks before her absence was noted. Instead, she inhaled the spicy scent of the food, her eyes closed in pleasure.

Jeremiah whispered to Europa, "Do not let me keep you from your meeting. Please, go on."

Europa started to object, but then seemed to sense something unspoken from Jeremiah and nodded. She circled the benches set before the three tables and bent to speak into the ear of a man, presumably her husband.

A young girl leaned against him and looked to Europa with the devotion of a daughter. She stood and crossed the room to bring Jeremiah a woolen blanket. Her foot was deformed and twisted inward, and she had an impossibly loping gait, as though she struggled to maintain her balance.

All of this Ariella watched with great interest, even as the comfort of the room and the warmth of the people seemed to woo her into a kind of stupor. She ate the lentils, only half-aware that the food was richer than any she'd tasted since leaving the frightful home of Valerius in Rome.

Europa's husband stood and began to speak, and Ariella's attention was captured at once, for he spoke like a rabbi himself, quoting from the Torah, of the wickedness of man becoming great in the earth, with every imagination of his heart becoming evil continually. It shocked her, to hear this Roman speak of HaShem, quote from her Torah, even to condemn the evil so rampant in his world. He spoke with heaviness of their fallen friends.

And then, as though the very room had lifted from this place and floated to the heart of Jerusalem itself, someone in the flickering shadows of the corner began to speak in her native tongue, her beloved Hebrew.

Ariella's jaw slackened to hear it, and she hung on each word as the young man spoke from the prophet Isaiah's writings. "The Creator's hand is not shortened, that it cannot save. His ear is not heavy, that it cannot hear."

He paused and someone else across the room repeated his words in Latin, translating for the rest of the crowd. And then he spoke again, wrapping Ariella in the rhythm of his words, carrying her backward to home and family: "But your iniquities have separated you from your God, and your sins have hidden His face from you so that He will not hear."

Again someone translated, and when he had finished, Ariella slumped against the cushions, drained as though she had faced an opponent in the arena.

"This was for you," Jeremiah whispered.

"Where is he from?" Perhaps she had known him as a child in Judea.

But Jeremiah shook his head. "He is Roman. He does not know Hebrew."

Ariella frowned. "He speaks with the tongue of a native."

"A gift. A sign for you."

She understood none of this. "For me?"

The teaching seemed to have ended, and as the people conversed, Jeremiah spoke to her alone. He nodded toward the girl with the deformed foot. "Flora was born in Rome, to parents who believed themselves cursed."

Ariella studied the woman, Europa. "She is not their daughter?"

Jeremiah's eyes on the girl held fondness. "They found her beside the river. Her father had exercised his right to expose her. Deformed children are seen as useless or cursed, and are rarely spared."

Ariella gritted her teeth. More evidence that the Roman conquerors were swine.

"But as the prophet Isaiah says, we are all twisted, deformed by sin, destined for destruction."

Ariella shifted, uncomfortable on the couch. "But for this, we have the Day of Atonement." Yet even as she said it, the memory of the burning Temple filled her mind.

"No sacrifice, no altar. No Temple." Jeremiah shook his head. "And the Law and Prophets tell us that HaShem will not hear the prayers without the atonement."

"What are we to do, then?" She did not know why she asked. She had given up caring what HaShem thought of her many angry years ago.

Jeremiah patted her hand and smiled at Flora. "Thank the Creator for making *our* adoption possible."

The man spoke in riddles. She opened her mouth to question, but the room had quieted, and attention had turned to a slave at the doorway.

"The physician?" Europa asked.

The slave shook his head. "Two noblemen. Unknown to me. They are asking for you."

At this a hush fell over the group, as though they feared this intrusion, and even Jeremiah's grip tightened on hers.

Ariella cursed her thoughtlessness. She had risked much in coming here and had stayed too long. And now, perhaps, she would have to pay for such foolishness.

20

Thirty days until the election. Thirty days until Cato could see Maius's smug face tossed into a cell to await trial for his crimes. Thirty days until he could free Portia from her bonds.

Too short to mount a successful campaign, and too unbearably long to leave Portia locked in a cell beneath the magisterial offices. Before he could begin meeting with the guilds, before he would even declare himself a candidate, he must find a way to ensure Portia was well.

In the early morning hours, the coolness of his bedchamber drove him to the atrium to seek the uncertain warmth of the watery sunlight that filtered past the Cyprus trees in patches on the walkways. He took his meal of bread and grapes in the garden, nodding acknowledgment to one of the newly acquired slaves.

Octavia soon appeared, and it seemed to Cato that she had aged a decade overnight.

"Any word?" She twisted her hands together at her waist.

Cato shook his head. "I have sent inquiries. But no one knows exactly where she is, nor do we have any disloyal to Maius who have access to the cells."

From the doorway, a steely voice joined the conversation. "I know of some."

Portia's husband, Lucius, stood framed in the still-shadowed double doors to the street. His tight jaw and dark-circled eyes spoke of a sleepless night.

Octavia held out welcoming hands, and Lucius strode across the atrium and embraced her, his voice muffled against Octavia's dark hair. "She thinks I disbelieved her."

"She knows your love. It will sustain her."

Cato clapped his sister's husband on the back. "You know some who could help?"

He pulled away, raked a hand through his hair, and nodded. "There is a group of people who care for those in prison. They've been given special permission to enter the cells, to bring food, clothing. Perhaps messages." His voice broke on the last word.

Cato reached across to squeeze his upper arm in sympathy. "Who are they?"

"I do not know. I have heard tell of them over the years, but they seem to be a mysterious sect of some kind."

Cato eyed Octavia. Did her thoughts travel in the same direction, to her brother in Rome?

She glanced sideways at him but said nothing.

"You can find them?"

Lucius nodded. "I will make inquiries. I will find them."

By nightfall, Lucius had made good on his promise. He returned to the house, where Cato had stationed himself in the *tablinum*, the reading room off the courtyard, poring over some public records of Pompeii he had borrowed and trying to find an answer to the riddle of unseating Nigidius Maius. At Lucius's footfall he jumped to his feet. "Yes?"

Lucius nodded, breathing heavily. "If we go now, we will perhaps find them meeting together."

Cato rolled the records and secured them with a string, then tossed them to the table. "Then let us go."

They crossed the city in silence, Lucius leading the way. The night held a damp chill, and Cato shivered a bit at both the night air and the mystery of the errand. Soon enough they reached a home across the town from his own, but matched in affluence, if the ornate carving of the doorway spoke truth.

A dark-skinned, muscled slave answered their summons, then bid them wait while he carried their message. He returned a moment later and bid them enter, then glided through the courtyard.

Lucius looked at Cato and shrugged, and the two followed the bulky slave to the doorway of a large triclinium.

Cato stood in the door, taking in the crowded room, the faces upturned with wide, frightened eyes. Were these truly the fearless people who ventured beneath the Forum into the cells?

Lucius spoke first, uncharacteristically. "A friend, Septimus, sent me." His words were for the room at large, for no one had yet stepped forward to greet them. "He said you could help my wife."

Movement then, from the back of the room, and a large woman pushed through the group to stand before them.

Cato took her measure. She was wealthy, but also interested in their message.

"Who is your wife? And how do you think we can be of help?"

Lucius opened his mouth to speak, but emotion choked his words.

Cato stepped to his side. "My sister." The woman nodded for him to continue. "She has been falsely accused by a powerful man and committed to the cells until her trial. We fear for her safety and her health. We were told—are hoping—that there are some here who might help."

He surveyed the group again, making eye contact with many. Young and old, rich and peasant. His eyes widened when he saw the large man who had subdued the madman in the Forum sitting in the back of the room. And was that the wild man himself, seated nearby, dressed and clean-shaven?

To the man's right, an old man lay outstretched on a cushion, and beside him, head bent and face hidden, a familiar shorn head and gladiator's leather. A strange mixture of feeling rushed through Cato, concern and fear, surprise and pleasure.

"Ari?" He was careful not to use her real name, and she lifted stricken eyes without raising her head. He longed to ask if she was again trying to escape, taking refuge with this compassionate group, but dared not endanger her by revealing anything.

Their hostess seemed unsurprised that Cato had spoken to Ariella. "I am Europa." She patted Lucius's arm. "Please, you must sit and take food or drink." She indicated the cushions and several guests slipped from their places to make room.

Cato crossed the dining chamber to squeeze into a space beside Ariella. She did not meet his gaze.

Lucius spoke with Europa now, earnest and intense, leaving Cato to address the gladiator beside him. It was the first he had seen Ariella this close since discovering her escaping in the streets near the Forum, when the shock of her gender was still fresh. Now he had the chance to study her as the woman she was. To see the stunning beauty, despite the brutally chopped hair. How had he been so blind when they had first spoken in the training barracks?

She shivered beside him, though the room was warm.

He leaned in to speak into her ear. "You are safe?"

She nodded once, a brief, clipped movement as though she feared to speak with him.

The chamber soon filled with the quiet buzz of conversation, and with Lucius and Europa too far to hear, Cato was free to draw her out. She held the hand of the old man who lay beside her, and he began there.

"Is he injured?"

She swallowed and still did not meet his eyes. "Yes. His hip is out of joint, or perhaps broken. I have brought him here, to his—to his family . . ." She trailed off, as if aware that the word did not seem to fit. But Cato had already formed an opinion of the strange and varied group that reclined around the dining tables.

"You broke away from the barracks?"

"Yes. I must return soon, though. Before I am missed."

The old man patted her leg and nodded, then closed his eyes.

What would she look like dressed in silk robes, draped with jewels? The thought danced across his mind unbidden, and Cato shook his head to clear it. He would speak of other things, more ordinary things, with her, but his tongue seemed thick, the way it sometimes did before he had to speak in a council meeting in Rome.

Neither did she speak, and they sat that way for some minutes, as though strangers. And yet Cato was fiercely aware of her closeness, as though he had measured every breath of air between them. When she reached for her cup, her arm brushed his own and set it on fire.

Not good, Quintus. Not good at all.

He played the fool. But it could not be helped. The flickering warmth of the brazier fires and the heavy air scented with honey seemed to root him to the cushions despite his misgiving.

Lucius stood at last and approached him. His face had lost some of its weariness. "They will help." He held out a hand to lift Cato from the cushions. "In the morning they will find her and see that she is well."

Cato grasped his brother-in-law's hand and hefted himself to standing.

Lucius inhaled deeply. "It is all we can do for now."

Cato nodded. "That is good. For now it is good. Tomorrow we can begin to find a way to free her." He glanced down at Ariella, still on the couch, then turned to Lucius. "Go ahead home without me, Lucius. I have . . . some business to attend."

Lucius took in Ariella. Clearly Cato had betrayed his interest, and he could only imagine what Lucius was thinking about his sudden attention toward the young man. Or perhaps her identity was as obvious to Lucius as it was now to him.

But Lucius only nodded, eyes narrowed. "We will speak tomorrow, then."

"Tomorrow."

Cato sank to the cushions once more, but when Lucius was well away from the house, he whispered to Ariella. "You should return to the barracks. Let me walk you there. The streets are not always safe."

She half smiled. "For a gladiator?"

He laughed quietly. "For certain gladiators."

He had expected her to refuse, in the stubbornness he had already sensed in her, but she did not. Instead, with a kiss to the forehead of her old friend, she stood and bowed toward Europa, then followed him from the chamber.

They walked in silence through the darkened courtyard, past the Persian slave who stood with bulky arms crossed against his bare chest. Cato slowed inside the doorway before the street and ran his fingers over a mosaic design embedded in the wall.

"What is it?" Ariella tilted her head to examine the colored stones.

"A fish. It is the sign of the fish."

"Perhaps they have made their fortune on the sea."

But Cato had seen this symbol before. In Rome. Inside the home of his uncle Servius. A chill shuddered through him.

It would seem that at every turn he aligned himself with those who could do his political career more harm than good. First the rumors of Portia, then this strange and haunted gladiator beside him, and now a sect of people who took care of prisoners, fed the poor, and banished evil and madness from the souls of men, and yet were highly disfavored by Rome.

He led Ariella into the night, now black as silk, and walked at her side toward the theater and the barracks. Their arms brushed together, and he did not move away.

She spoke first. "Your sister—she is in prison?"

"Yes. Unjustly."

"She was the woman with you in the training yard that—that day?"

Cato smiled into the darkness. "The day we met? Yes."

She was silent then. He told himself she was relieved to hear Portia was not his wife, nor his mistress.

"Do you have family? In Judea?"

She tensed. "You killed most of them."

"I—?"

"You Romans. My parents, my sister. All killed when Titus took Jerusalem. Only my brother, Micah, escaped, but I do not know if he still lives." Her voice fluttered over the last few words.

"I am so sorry, Ari." Did she see only murdering tyrants when she looked at him?

The few minutes' walk with her was too short. All too soon they reached the edge of the quadriporticus, where she should be able to sneak back into her cell without notice. He looked across the shadowy field to the series of darkened doorways under the colonnade. "You are left alone in your cell now?"

Behind him, her voice grew wary. "How did you know that I was given a private cell?"

He shrugged. "I thought it would be best—"

But she pushed past him. "I do not need your help—"

He pulled her to face him before she disappeared under the stone arch. "I watched you fight."

Her expression was still haughty, but after a moment she exhaled and grinned. "Not bad?'"

He laughed. "I was sick the entire time."

Her smile faded, replaced by a vulnerability he had not seen before. He longed to touch her, to feel that fascinating hair, to see if her lips were as soft as they appeared. His mouth went dry with the thought, and his heart thudded against his chest.

You are such a fool, Quintus Portius Cato.

Ariella was not a woman he could ever marry, clearly. And without doubt she would never consent to be his mistress, even if he asked.

What then was left for them? Only a gentle squeeze of her fingers and a quick farewell. "Be safe, Ari the fighter." His words were a whisper in the darkness.

She said nothing, only watched him as he backed away.

When he finally turned toward home, it seemed to him that she watched him still, warming his back with her dark eyes.

21

Ariella watched Cato walk toward the street, away from her. What could she say to bring him back?

Nothing, silly girl.

The night had been fearful, then baffling, then as near to wonderful as she had come in many years.

Before he reached the street, before he could look back and find her watching, she slipped under the stone arch into the barracks, then stepped aside and leaned against the wall. She was not ready to trade the beauty of the night for her ugly cell.

Moonlight played over the dark green grass and striped the portico around the field with bands of white and black. She could smell the damp grass, and it recalled to her mind the way Cato smelled, of grapes and fertile soil. Her shoulders dropped and she leaned her head against the stone. The night was hushed, with no sound but the trill of unfamiliar night birds, wrapping her in their sleepy song and loosening the tightness she strove to retain around her heart.

When Cato had first appeared in the doorway of Europa's triclinium, Ariella's heart had leaped with the ridiculous thought that he had come for her. After that initial foolishness, she had struggled to find sense in the coincidence. But when Cato called her name, and Jeremiah realized who stood in the door, the old man squeezed her hand until she looked into his pained eyes.

"This meeting is of HaShem." His smile competed with her scowl. "He watches over you, dear girl, and He has something for you in this man. I know not what. But you must be ready."

She had listened to the words spoken in Hebrew, words for her, Jeremiah had said. She had felt the hand of the Creator on her, as she had not felt in many years, since she had turned her back on Him and His holy city and fled from both.

And now, alone in the grassy training field, Ariella still had only questions.

That Cato had some interest in her was clear. He had paid Drusus for her private cell! She had thought it was Jeremiah who had some-how arranged the luxury, but saw now that only money crossing his palm would have induced Drusus to agree.

Her breathing shallowed as she thought of Cato beside her on the cushions, his skin brushing against her own. Of his eyes on her in the street only moments ago. He was a man with the beauty and money to have any woman he wanted. What was she to make of a Roman nobleman who looked at her thus?

True, in Jerusalem she was not a slave. But that was many years ago, and she had fallen a great distance. Cato was as sophisticated and smooth as the fine wine he smelled of, and though it flowed over her, warming her, he could want nothing honorable. She should not be sur-prised. From the moment they had first spoken she had seen that he wore the role of jester, of the carefree rich who sought only to amuse them-selves. She was the latest amusing thing to capture his interest, a woman disguised as a man pretending to be a fighter. An oddity, nothing more.

She pulled away from the wall. Jeremiah's injuries would be cared for, and she must forget the rest of the night's events. Forget the Romans who quoted from the Torah and spoke of her God as though He was their own and showed her love despite her status. Forget the single fascinating Roman who drew her to himself like no one ever had.

She must train, and train well. Only ten days until the next fight, and she had much to prove.

And so she returned to the field, returned to her leather and sweat, to her wooden rudis and the palus and to sparring with men twice her size and of even greater strength. She laced up her heart even as she wrapped the leather around her hands and swore that she would think of nothing but the arena.

And for several days, she found success. She fought with the fierceness of a trapped and hunted animal. The taunts grew fainter, and the occasional word of praise from Drusus reached her ears and strengthened her arm. She *could* achieve her goal of making a name for herself in the arena, then reveal her gender to win the crowd's acclaim.

Perhaps it was the lull of temporary success, perhaps it was only fatigue that lowered her defenses and made her foolish. She had always taken great care to dress and bathe in the dark hours of the late night and early morning, when a stray glance into her cell would reveal little to the passerby. But one evening while the light still found its way between columns and stone and gate, she stripped the sweaty armor from her body and sought relief from a rag dipped in a bucketful of cool water.

A scrape of sandal on stone was followed by a sharp intake of breath. Ariella snatched up her tunic and covered herself, then lifted her eyes to the bars.

Celadus stood before her, the whites of his eyes impossibly large. He reached out to grip the bar, as if to steady himself, and his voice was a harsh whisper. "How could I have not seen it?"

Ariella's stomach heaved. "Celadus—"

He shook his head, held up a palm, and strode away, back to the quadriporticus.

Cursing her stupidity, Ariella dressed quickly, with shaky hands, then hurried out. He stood across the field with three or four others, and Ariella slowed her frantic rush and bit her lip. Was he revealing her secret already? Dare she approach?

But though the fighters laughed over some shared humor, they did not look at her any differently when she neared.

"Celadus." She kept her voice low. "I must speak with you."

He did not look at her. "Not now. *Ari*." He spat her distorted name as though it were distasteful.

She pinched his elbow. "Please, Celadus."

But he yanked away and brought the laughter of the group.

"It seems it is more than the women who are your fans, eh, Celadus?" Floronius punched his arm and winked. "Even the girlish boys have their eye on you."

Celadus's face flushed, but he would not look at Ariella.

"Ari!"

Her name was shouted from across the field, and she jumped, her nerves tight.

Drusus crossed the grass. He carried her painting supplies. "Need more signs. For the next fight." He reached the men and pushed the paints and brushes into her hands. "Something that will make people stop and read, understand?"

Ariella glanced at Celadus, but his back had turned. "I understand." She backed away from the men, hoping Celadus would at least give her a look of compassion, of continued friendship. Of forgiveness. But it was as if she did not exist.

She moved into the city on wooden legs, unsure of whether her ruse had finally come to an end or if Celadus would keep her secret.

The evening sun had dipped behind many of the walls in the tight streets she crossed, but the crowds had not diminished. Delivery carts rattled over the rutty stone streets, their drivers shouting at animals and people alike. The offending horses and donkeys snorted and clicked an uneven rhythm across the cobbled stones and the people responded with matching shouts and rude gestures. Ariella bumped along, a piece of wood caught in the human tide, toward the Forum. The city passed in a blur of tans and reds and oranges until she reached the white stone of the Forum, lit like gold by the setting sun.

She found a space of wall without any notices painted on it, outside the Eumachia, and began to paint. The outline of the arena took shape under her brush, and it would capture attention.

Inside the painted arena she wrote the first words that came to her.

Celadus the Thracian makes all the girls swoon.

She smiled. He would like that. But would she get the chance to tell him?

All too soon the twilight fell, and she made her way back to the barracks. The lanista met her inside the entrance, his face grim. Her stomach dropped.

"Need to speak to you, boy."

She breathed. There was the *boy* at least. "You will like the signs." Her voice sounded feeble. Girlish.

"I hope you painted something about yourself." He turned and crossed the grass, and she followed.

"Myself?" In truth, she had. Still clutching at her hopes to win her freedom, she had not passed up the opportunity to promote Scorpion Fish on the city walls.

His voice barely reached over his shoulder to her. "I've been watching you. I think you're ready for more."

Ariella's hands tightened around her brushes and paint. Yes.

"I'm putting you against Floronius." He turned at last in the shadow of a carved column. "You will be third." She must have betrayed her excitement because he chuckled.

"Yes, Ari. A real fight for Scorpion Fish."

She flushed, then nodded. Drusus disappeared into his own chambers, leaving Ariella in the courtyard to contemplate the rise and fall of her fortune.

Could Jeremiah be right? Was she indeed watched over by the God of her fathers?

22

Cato shoved aside all thoughts of gladiators and focused on his own fight for the position of duovir. There was much to be done, beginning with taking the temperature of the city's rich and powerful. As there was no better place for such a thing than the baths, Cato headed there early one morning. He carried his small potbellied jug of oils in his palm, but his mind was occupied with neither luxury nor cleanliness. His campaign did not have much time, and it might be the same for his sister.

While there were a number of baths located throughout the city, drawing their patrons from the surrounding neighborhoods, Cato chose the Forum Baths for the patronage of those with whom he needed most to mingle. The lavish bath complex had been generously supplied by Emperor Augustus some time ago, and the dedicatory inscription chiseled into the marble lintel above the door proclaimed that the baths had been furnished *ex pequnia publica*, without the public's money.

Cato passed under the doorway and into the outer room, which was already warmer than the morning air. The effect of luxury was immediate, with soft music strummed somewhere within, the sound of running water, and the scent of perfumed oils. Ordinarily, Cato would have succumbed to relaxation, to joining others in this cult of luxury, this worship of the body. Today his muscles remained knotted. He had work to accomplish.

He crossed the mosaic floor and entered the *apodyterium*, the changing room for the men. The room was a celebration of the male physique, surrounded on three sides by sculptured pillars of impossibly muscled men with their arms raised above their heads, holding up the wall above them that curved upward into a domed roof. Even the fantastical frescoes painted on every wall and across the dome chronicled the male gods of old in their feats of glory. The pillars, half-flush with the wall, left cubicles between for personal belongings, and Cato stripped off his toga and tunic and placed them in one of the empty niches, then sat on a bench to remove his sandals and scan the room for any whose conversation he might seek. There was no one.

Perhaps the tepidarium would yield better results. He crossed into the warm room, with its blazing brazier and benches around the perimeter, and found several of the city's prominent men already lounging. A few heads turned his way, and nods signified his welcome.

In the days since deciding he would run for duovir, Cato had mapped out his main obstacles. The city was owned by Maius, and this would cause many to remain loyal despite the man's character and his crimes. Cato would need to inspire them with a fresh hope for something different, for change they had not yet seen. And for this he would need money, something lacking since his flight from Rome and purchase of Saturninus's vineyard, home, and wine shop.

He slid to a bench beside Oceanus, another native of the mother city who had retreated to Pompeii on a holiday and stayed ten years. The older man's graying head leaned against the warmed wall, and he opened only one eye to Cato, then closed it again.

"Good morning, Oceanus."

The man grunted.

In the corner near a brazier's heat, a seated lute player piped a slow tune and two naked women danced seductively. Cato watched for a moment, then dropped his gaze, fighting the usual battle and failing, as usual. He searched for an opening to the conversation he must have with Oceanus. "I can see why you chose to stay here in Pompeii all these years. The luxury rivals even Rome, and the weather is perfection."

Oceanus nodded, eyes still closed. "Yes, this town gets into your blood, I'm afraid. For all its grandness of size and architecture, Rome begins to lose its luster from this distance."

"It's only a pity that all this beauty is not reflected in its leadership." It was a bold statement, but necessary.

Oceanus lifted his head now, glanced around the tepidarium, and looked sideways at Cato. "Ready for the *calidarium*?"

It was an invitation for more dialogue. Cato nodded and followed Oceanus into another elaborate room, the hottest of the complex, where the hot plunge pool at the end of the room already held several men seated within a cloud of steam.

The calidarium showcased the finest in Roman engineering, with water that started its journey through the massive aqueduct that fed the city from the port of Misenum, to the huge tank at Pompeii's highest gate, to one of over a dozen secondary tanks situated throughout the city, then through piping into the baths. The floor of the entire complex was built of thick stone over a shallow chamber of brick columns. A furnace outside the baths was fueled faithfully, pushing super-heated air into the subfloor chamber, heating the brick columns that supported the floor, and in turn heating the room above. Other channels pushed hot air beneath the pool, keeping the water heated enough that Cato was forced to step in slowly, letting the water scald him by degrees.

But the heat seemed to loosen tongues as well as muscles, and before many minutes Oceanus had resumed their conversation, including the others in the bath. "Our newest citizen, Portius Cato, seems dissatisfied with the city's current leadership."

Curious eyes shifted toward him, then away, ever casual. Silence followed, so still that Cato could hear the condensation on the vaulted ceiling run down its ribbed channels into the narrow gutter at the floor. He tried to relax in the steamy heat, but his nerves were strung taut.

"Perhaps a change is called for." This from a man unknown to Cato.

With that, the conversation opened, and serious talk of the election began. Cato found himself the center of their attention and used the opportunity to expound on his developing ideas for the city, for the changes he would enact, for the fresh breeze of integrity that needed to blow through the corrupt streets.

"You will need something big to announce your candidacy." Oceanus wiped condensation from his brow. "Something that will show people who you really are."

Cato gripped the side of the pool where they sat. "I have a plan."

Some time later, after they had been oiled and scraped by slaves and had moved to the *frigidarium* for the cold plunge, Cato dried off and dressed, anxious to get to his next destination, where he would begin to put the plan into action that his new friends in the baths had endorsed.

Stepping from the bath complex into the mucky street was like a descent from the heavens into the unclean world of mortals, but Cato took little notice. He strode through the street that ran parallel to the Forum, not wanting to be waylaid by anyone, and reached the theater and the barracks behind it in a few minutes. So occupied was he with his plan that he didn't slow as he entered the training field and found himself in the center of a dozen men pitched in mock battles.

"Whoa!" One of the men held up a hand, and the others lowered theirs to let him pass.

He glanced at each, but Ariella was not among them. This close, they were huge, most of them. How did Ariella even train against them? He turned to watch them, his eyes following every memorized move, his mind naming each tactic as it was executed. But he had other business.

There, at the end of the field, training alone against the wooden post. She looked so small down there, so isolated.

He tracked through the green grass to reach her. If she saw him, she gave no indication until he was upon her. Her dark hair was growing out a bit since the first time he'd seen her here. If it were up to him, she would not need to chop it again.

"Ari." He said it quietly, but still she jumped and twirled, her wooden sword at the ready.

He grinned and held up a palm. "Friend, not foe."

She jabbed her sword into the grass. "What do you want?"

He exhaled. "I—I have an idea. I need your help."

"How could I possibly help *you*?"

"I am going to run for duovir."

She shrugged and lifted her sword as if to go on practicing. "Some kind of city official, right?"

Cato bit the inside of his cheek. She was not Roman, nor Pompeiian. Why should she care about the city's governing bodies? He needed to reframe his proposal. "I have a way to help you that will also coincide with the announcement of my candidacy."

She narrowed her dark eyes, and her lips tightened with suspicion. "Help me?"

"The upcoming games. I know they are scheduled to be small, more of an exhibition, since no one has yet offered to sponsor something larger. But I am going to sponsor a grand display, and the centerpiece of it will be to show the people something they have never seen."

She straightened and stared him down. "A woman in the arena?" Her voice was low, but it carried the tone of fury, not conspiracy.

"It will be perfect. I am trying to show the city that I am the man to bring something new, to make changes. Giving them this extraordinary thing will set them talking, and it will keep you safe. Once they know, you will never be killed by an opponent."

She advanced on him, her eyes twin fires, dark and furious. "You will ruin everything!"

Cato tried to touch her arm, but she stepped back. "No, don't you see—"

Her chest rose and fell under her brown leather, her anger barely harnessed. "Stop trying to help me, Portius Cato. You think you can save the world, but you cannot save me. I will make my own way!"

His own anger sparked in response. "And you know nothing but the fight. Are you too proud to see that you have need of someone to save you?"

She came at him again, shoving against him, her face turned up so that her full lips were just beneath his chin. "Drusus has scheduled me to fight Floronius. I am on the verge of making myself known as a fighter. To reveal myself now, before the city knows my name, would destine me to fighting dwarves and animals forever. A onetime surprise, soon forgotten. And then where will your help be?"

He grabbed her arms, but she yanked them away. She was like an injured animal, so quick to retreat. The sun seemed to flush him with heat suddenly, and he rubbed at the back of his neck, then paced a few steps away and back.

"You are too stubborn, Ari. It will get you killed."

"And what is that to you, Cato?"

He stopped before her. What, indeed?

"I will tell you." She poked at his chest with her forefinger. "You cannot pass by someone in trouble without playing the savior. It's the only thing that makes you feel like a man, isn't it? Righting the wrongs of the world? Saving the women? Your sister, me. Well, you can keep your supposed *help* and find some other way to win your precious election. I want none of it."

The lanista approached, preventing Cato from barking a response. The aging fighter peeled an orange as he walked, tossing sections between yellowed teeth. "Portius Cato." His words were muffled by the mouthful of orange. "You favor us yet again. I see you have found your little pet."

The leer and wink made the man's meaning clear. Cato had paid far too much attention, and too much money, for Drusus to believe his interest in the young fighter was merely as an athlete. Beside him he sensed Ariella's tension, even her contempt—for him as much as Drusus.

"I am thinking of sponsoring your next exhibition, Drusus. And I will want it to be spectacular."

The man's bushy eyebrows shot upward, and then his head tilted back to the blue sky, as if he lifted a prayer of thanks to the gods above. "Shall we go somewhere to speak, then?"

Cato bowed and followed the man. He looked back once to Ariella, where she remained motionless, watching him with those dark and furious eyes.

23

It was done. He was committed. A quick appearance before the tribunes in the Forum offices to register his intention to run as duovir, then a couple of days of circulating through the city's elite and the heads of guilds, and the name of Portius Cato was soon on the lips of every Pompeiian. Already his slogan of "Something you've never seen before" had been painted on city walls and repeated in meetings both public and clandestine. Cato moved through the churning tide pool of the Forum, gripping arms and greeting town leaders, and forced back anxious thoughts over what he planned for Ariella and the anger he had seen in her eyes.

The extent of Maius's hold on the town became more evident, giving Cato cause for worry. Numerous men had expressed a desire for new leadership, but also let him know that they would not, could not, support him publicly. Maius either controlled their source of income or held something over them they could not see revealed. Many had been muscled into submission by Maius's enforcers, and these could be swayed to vote for Cato, but there still remained a large block that would not be moved.

But at least the money had ceased to be an issue. Along with the Fullers' Guild, support from both the Fruitsellers' Guild and the Jewelers' Guild had flowed toward him, enabling him to announce his extravagant offer of games and a hunt in the arena, and ensuring that he would have the funds needed for his campaign. He began to taste success already, though there was still much to do. Within a few days the city had begun to buzz with talk of Cato's "something new" and the games where he would surprise them all.

But the taste of success was soured by worry over his sister. Every day Lucius brought scraps of news, and Octavia and Isabella hung on each word, wringing meaning from every phrase until Lucius would hold up his hands and plead for them to cease. But for Cato, it was not enough, and he longed to see for himself that Portia was still well, as the Christians claimed.

And so his feet took him to the house of Europa and her husband, Seneca, the night before the big event, and his heart told him it was only for Portia, that it had nothing to do with the chance of seeing Ariella there, in that place where race and class seemed of little import.

The doors of the house were closed, and when the large Persian answered his knock, he shook his head at Cato's inquiry. "They do not meet here this night."

"Elsewhere, then?"

But the slave seemed reluctant to part with secrets. He left Cato standing inside the doors and retreated into the house. Europa's husband appeared moments later, trailing the Persian.

Cato cleared his throat. "I'd like to meet with them again. For news of my sister. I want to see her."

The man cocked his head to the side, studied Cato, then nodded. "Come."

Through dark streets Cato followed the man, studying the "cat's eyes," the diamond-shaped white stones embedded in the sidewalk to catch the moonlight and guide the traveler. They reached a narrow doorway, where Seneca pushed into the house and beckoned Cato to join him.

The house was one of a poor man, only a few rooms and these small. Could the whole group be meeting here? Cato worried that he would not encounter those who had helped his sister. The front room was empty, but Cato could hear the group in the secondary room, and when they crossed the threshold, it seemed that they *were* all here, crowded and packed into the dingy room like slaves transported in the hull of a ship.

The room had gone silent at their arrival, and Cato found a slice of space against the wall and leaned one shoulder against it, his body touching those on either side. He scanned faces for a short-haired woman, but she was not present. A girl about Isabella's age caught his eye, familiar for some reason, but she looked away, as if wanting to remain unseen. Cato studied her for several moments. Where had he seen her before?

"Portius Cato joins us for news of his sister." Seneca nodded in his direction.

Smiles lit the faces of a few, and reports were given that Portia somehow thrived in the cells, and that good food and clean water had been brought for her daily.

Cato bowed his head, emotion tightening his throat. "You are good people. Thank you."

Seneca spoke from beside his wife. "Cato, I believe I speak for the group when I say that you are supported here in your bid for election."

Cato lifted his head, surprised. Christians were often accused of being enemies of Rome, of seeking to subvert all that was good about the Empire. "I will have your votes?"

"Our votes and whatever else we can give." There were murmurs of agreement around the room, and Cato noticed the old man, Ariella's friend, on a mat near Seneca. He bent to the prone man, who appeared to be speaking to him. "Will you stay for our meeting, Cato? We would be glad to have you."

Cato did not miss the looks of surprise that traveled the room. "I would be honored."

And this was truth. He *was* honored to be invited. They were a mystery sect, and their rites were closed to outsiders. He was fascinated and curious, but even more than that, his heart was being drawn to these people. Discreet inquiries around town had uncovered more than concern for those possessed by evil, trapped in prison, or hungry. It seemed they also cared for orphans and widows, shared their wealth with the poor, performed healings, and welcomed prostitutes into their midst.

This last particularly interested him, given his mother's activities. Octavia had her own reasons for helping, but she could never seem to make a permanent change. Yet Cato saw clear evidence that women once enslaved to the brothel now joined the sect, somehow free. And above all this humanitarian effort, or perhaps behind it, was something even more. It was the look he had seen on the faces of those who had perished in the games of the arena. Their willingness to die for what they believed made him ache for something so powerful, so important, something to live for.

Despite his insistence on standing like so many others, Cato was placed on a seat near the old Jeremiah. "How do you fare?" he asked, thinking to carry a message to Ariella.

Jeremiah smiled and patted his hip with a wrinkled hand. "Better. I am healing. Have you seen her?"

So the old man also knew her secret. The realization bothered him. The knowledge did not belong to him alone. "She is well also. But determined to fight those who outmatch her."

Jeremiah chuckled. "Outmatched in size only. She has the heart of a mighty warrior."

That she did.

"I sense you also have been called to fight a battle." Jeremiah's hand reached up to grasp Cato's with surprising strength. "And that is why you are here."

"I did not think I would be permitted to stay. I have heard you are a secretive people."

Jeremiah studied him, head cocked. "It does no good to force answers on those who do not yet ask questions."

Perceptive man. Cato's questions had begun in Rome, in the home of his uncle, and had carried him here, to this house. A young man at the other side of the room began to speak, and Cato turned his attention there.

Strange religion, this was, with no temple, no incense, no sacrifices. They had come from the wealth of Europa and Seneca's home to the cramped poverty of this one, but did not seem to notice. In fact, the house seemed like a pool of still water in the midst of the city.

Cato listened first with curiosity, interested to learn more about this strange sect that had captured his uncle's allegiance. But as the evening wore on, and the words of the speaker took on fuller meaning, he began to see that this new religion that had begun as a splinter of Judaism was not a Jewish religion any longer, and that the invitation it extended was for all people. Something about the way the man described their prophet, the Messiah, appealed to more than his mind, but also his heart. There was a sense of belonging in this community that he had never before encountered.

Too soon the meeting ended, concluding with a song sung by the group, a deep and haunting melody that left Cato with a profound sense of emptiness, and yet was wonderful to hear.

They would try to slip him into a cell tomorrow, they told him. After the games had ended. Cato gripped hands in gratitude once more and returned to his home, full of the teachings of the Way, of this Jesus they claimed had been a god-turned-flesh, not in the fantastical stories of the Roman pantheon, but in a true and real way, walking here among men only fifty years ago. And with some who knew him still able to testify to his death, to his burial. To his resurrection.

But it was too much to puzzle through tonight, and Cato found his bed and fell asleep thinking more of tomorrow's performance than yesterday's prophets.

The morning dawned with a red sky in the east, an ill omen for a sea town. Cato dressed hurriedly, kissed his mother and Isabella, and headed for the arena. The muscles between his shoulders had already grown tight before he crossed half the city, like an icy hand gripping his neck. Today's event weighted him. It was critical that he impress the citizens with the chance for something new. All the while, Ariella's anger nipped at his conscience, making his head spin.

A quick stop in his vineyard found Remus supervising his field slaves in the pruning, trying to make the most of the vines he had left. Cato stopped out of guilt and duty rather than desire, then left the vineyard to cross to the arena's massive circular wall. He was a man of a single passion, and he had already set aside his grapes to pursue a different harvest, sweet wine for a city too accustomed to bitter.

He passed the outer steps that led to tiered seating and crossed under the massive tan-and-black stone arch where the fighters and principals entered. Inside, wide corridors led in either direction, circling the arena under a series of arches. The amphitheater at Pompeii was the oldest in the Empire, built over one hundred fifty years ago, and it held a timeworn charm. Though Vespasian's colossal Flavian Amphitheater was nearly completed in Rome, with massive underground tunnels and even a water flow that could flood the arena for mock naval battles, Cato found this smaller arena a better forum for winning a town.

He passed the corridors with only a glance, for ahead in the yellowish sand he could see that the fighters had already arrived. Dozens of pairs spread out over the elliptical sand, surrounded by all that marble seating, blinding white without the thousands of spectators. Tapestries were draped over the sides of the seating, down toward the sand. Slaves hung garlands of woven leaves along the ledge.

He stood under the arched stone, half shadowed and half sunlit, and watched the fighters as they warmed their muscles in preparation for the event. Across the sand, Drusus paced and screamed instructions, but the clash of their swords drowned his words.

It was like a dance, these pairs of men, thrusting and parrying in rhythm, and for a moment all their movements seemed to synchronize, as though the dance had been choreographed. It was beautiful to watch.

But then the spell broke and the fighters drew apart. Cato inhaled, hardening his determination, and crossed the sand to Drusus to work out the final details of when he would speak to the crowd. He forced himself to ignore Ariella, though he was well aware of her place in the sand. And did she watch him as he walked?

Indeed, when he had finished with Drusus and turned back toward the end of the arena, Ariella stalked over to him, her lips tight and her cheeks a mottled red.

"What are you going to do?"

Cato looked sideways, knowing they drew attention. "It is for your own good—"

"Do not dare to speak to me of my good!" Her nostrils flared and her voice was a low growl. "I have been taking care of myself for many years before you came along, Portius Cato. I know what is best for me, and I do not want your help!" The last few words were spat on him.

Cato rubbed at his clenched jaw. He had nothing to say, and so pushed past her and tried to walk away.

She trotted backward alongside him, then blocked his exit. "So that is it? The great Cato will do what he wants?" She shoved a fist at his chest. "Then do not speak to me of doing it for my good. We both know this is about your own glory, about making a name for yourself and using me to do it. But know this, Cato. By tomorrow I will be nothing more than the plaything of this troupe, and I will lay the blame at your feet."

He searched her eyes for any sign of weakness. "What are you talking about?"

"I told you days ago. If you reveal me this day, before I have won the crowd's loyalty, you will have your surprise, and then they shall forget me. But the rest of the fighters"—she waved her sword around the arena where the matched pairs loitered or sparred—"they will not forget. And what do you think will happen to one small woman housed with a hundred men?"

Cato swallowed, his stomach rebelling. He had not thought of that. Perhaps he had not thought. "I promised the people something they'd never seen . . ."

She drew herself up until she seemed as tall as he. "Then do what you must." She turned her back and headed for the corridors on the far side of the arena.

Cato watched her go, his heart beating with heaviness, seeming to have lost its right rhythm. The tightness in his jaw and shoulders spread to every muscle. He had made a mistake.

He had set everything on this event today, funneling funds into it and making claims that he would impress the people. He had fooled himself into thinking he did it for Ariella's protection.

He saw now that she was right. He was exploiting her for his own purpose. The vileness of his action churned in his stomach and climbed up into his chest, then plummeted. He stood in the center of the sand, with the well-trained fighters ranging around him . . .

And felt as though he were being torn apart.

24

Ariella watched Floronius from under the arch at the end of the arena. The baffling nobleman Portius Cato had retreated, thankfully, so that she had nothing to distract her from her study of her opponent. She would fight today as a Retiarius, and had been practicing with the net since Drusus had told her. Floronius was a Secutor, heavily armed and relying on strength. Matches were often arranged thus, with strength and armor pitted against speed and mobility.

She had planned more than the movement of her feet and net, however. It would take every trick she could devise to win the crowd today. Drusus approached and she reached a hand out to slow him. "I will go out before Floronius, yes?"

It was the third or fourth time she had asked, and from his scowl it was once too many. "Yes, yes. Now worry about your fight, not your pride!"

She nodded and let him pass, then inhaled deeply and returned to her study of those still warming up.

She had done all she could to prepare, painting signs all over the city of Scorpion Fish, hoping they would come, eager to see this new favorite. She would appear outmatched because of her size, but that was not enough to win their favor. She would need to be amusing, to capture their imagination, to make them laugh and to make them watch.

And Floronius—she had memorized every one of his standard tactics, studied his weaknesses until she knew them well. He was slow on the turn and heavy on his feet.

She braced a hand against the stone arch and felt her breath quicken. Could she kill him? He might die at the end of her trident in the heat of the battle, or she might pin him and look to the games' sponsor for his indication of death or mercy. It would be Cato in that box today. Would he want her to claim her victory, or would he want to spare her the unpleasantness of Floronius's execution?

She saw in her mind Floronius's grinning face as he stood over Jeremiah's fallen body. Heard his derisive laughter. Oh yes, she could kill him.

But there was a greater question she dared not ask herself. When she fought today, would she fight as Scorpion Fish, or revealed to the crowd as a woman? Had she convinced Cato to keep her secret, or would his infuriating need to interfere ruin her plans before she'd been given a chance?

All too soon the stands began to fill with excited townspeople, eager for the early entertainment. A few mock duels were staged to warm up the crowd, but before long the animals, kept starving and tortured under the arena floor, were released. The iron grills that barred their cells were swung open, slaves set fire to straw behind them, and terrified by flames and smoke, they ran up the ramps into the sun.

Ariella paced the corridor, only occasionally glancing out at the menagerie of exotic animals that snarled and attacked each other in the

ring—bears and bulls, antelopes and jackals, hyenas and leopards—
the entire arena seemed covered with skins and fur. Ethiopian bowmen
in ostrich-plume headdresses let arrows loose from upper tiers, and the
roar of fallen beasts mingled with the screams of the crowd. And still
they wanted more.

Though she was part of it now, still it sickened her. Boredom had
brought them to this—a whole society that could feel nothing anymore but death and sex. Their common criminals were sentenced to
the arena simply to fill demand, and still they wanted more.

More novelty. More cruelty.

What had been a blood sport had become a bloodbath. Horsemen
would hunt down armed men on foot. Terrified prisoners were tortured. Pubescent girls raped.

More!

Ignoring the boiling heat and putrid stench, the crowds shrieked
with pleasure. Women in the stands tore long gashes in their cheeks.
Men beat their fists against the marble seating. "Kill! Kill! Kill!" Their
tedious, purposeless existence found vent only here, intoxicated on
blood and making use of prostitutes in passageways to satisfy their lust.

Ariella braced a hand against the wall. Her stomach plunged then
surged. What had she become?

Slaves ran past her with baskets of fresh sand and jars of perfume
to pour on the arena.

It was time for the main event. Ariella noted the shift in the sound
of the crowd. Her time was short.

Celadus and Bestia fought first, with the women nearly faint-
ing over Celadus, and still Ariella paced. Both returned to the wide
corridor under the seats, and Ariella did not even ask who had won.
She could not see Celadus's eyes through his protective visor, and the
scimitar he carried at his side made her fear approach. He had thus

far kept her secret, but also kept his distance, and she had let him have it.

One more fight, Papus and Flaccus, and then it was her turn. She snatched up her net and trident and ran to the entrance. Floronius stood there already, about to enter, but Drusus held him back with one hand and jerked his head toward Ariella. She nodded once in acknowledgment, then ran past the two, under the stone arch and into the hazy sun.

She stood at the edge of the sand, awaiting the sponsor's announcement, her breathing measured and controlled even while her heart raced.

And then his voice was there, carried across the vast arena, lifted to the red pennants that waved and snapped in the breeze at the upper lip of the stone circle.

"Scorpion Fish, the Retiarius!"

The crowd responded with a rush of noise, and the sound took her backward in the odd way memories sometimes surge, to a Passover day in her childhood, when the crowds around the Temple had shouted thus—but with religious fervor, not bloodlust.

Forcing back the memory, Ariella strode forward and shot her trident into the air to receive the acclaim. She took another four steps and pivoted, saluting the crowd behind her. A scream of, "Scorpion Fish!" returned to her, an ardent female voice, causing the adjacent crowd to laugh.

Ariella bowed toward her admirer, then trotted backward toward the center of the arena, swishing her net about her feet and her head until the crowd applauded.

But she was not yet finished. Years ago, as a child, she and her younger brother had played with a shepherd's rod out in the fields, practicing twirls and tosses until they would fall exhausted to the grass, laughing and dizzy.

Her hands still remembered the skill, and she dropped her net now and twirled the trident once, twice, three times, faster and faster until it grew blurry, then tossed it up, up into the cloudy sky. The crowd seemed not to know what to make of this display, and it was as if they held their collective breath until the trident fell from the sky into her waiting hand.

And then, as she had hoped, as she had needed, they erupted into screams of acclaim. She hefted the trident above her head once more, snatched up her net, and turned just in time to face Floronius running toward her across the sand.

She lowered her trident to the level of his midsection and let him come.

Floronius paused, still a dozen cubits from her, and waited for his turn to be announced. Cato's voice rang over the sand.

Was that concern for her in his voice?

And then a bell rang, and it began. Her first real fight.

Ariella circled Floronius, flexed at the knees, loose and ready to leap away from his sword. Floronius was heavily defended, with a large shield, a heavy helmet with eyeholes, a protective arm sleeve, and a leather greave for his forward leg. In contrast, she had only her net and trident, and her only defense was a shoulder piece to protect her net arm. The match was about brute force versus trickery and speed.

Ariella placed the image of Floronius laughing at Jeremiah before her mind's eye again, let it build her hatred for him, called on that hatred to strengthen her arm and sharpen her wits.

It began well. She spun around him, counting on his slowness to come at him from the next position, to jab him with the three prongs of her trident, all the while keeping her nets moving around his feet, throwing off his balance.

But this must be more than Retiarius versus Secutor. This must be a *show*.

She backed away, then pointed to Floronius with her trident and began to lumber around him, slow and heavy, in an obvious pantomime of the larger fighter. The crowd recognized her farce at once, and howls of laughter rewarded her.

Floronius seemed baffled by her antics and turned a slow circle to watch as she pranced around him. Then, angered at the way she appeared to have amused the spectators, he rushed her.

She let him come, counted the beats, forced herself to hold, hold—even as he hefted his sword above her head and she saw the iron cutting a path through the thick air toward her skull. Then a leap and a dart, and she was clear of him, leaving him to stumble over the place where she had stood.

She pantomimed again, this time clasping a hand over her heart as though mortally frightened and bending the knee to beg for her life. Given her clear superiority thus far, the townspeople shrieked with delight at her mockery.

But it could not be all farce for long. Floronius's rage built and narrowed his focus, and Ariella was forced to engage him with all her strength, dodging and sweeping until her arms grew shaky and sweat ran down her forehead, burning her eyes and salting her tongue.

Still Floronius did not weaken. How would she ever bring him down? True, he was slow on the turn, but his eyes were sharp, and she could not sweep the net without his being ready to leap it. They came together and then apart, together and apart, in a kind of sickening death-dance, and then Ariella saw it.

The look of hatred in his eye.

Her former confidence in Cato's mercy had been misplaced.

Floronius need not wait for Cato's decision . . . not if he killed her during the match.

Her mouth was as dry as the arena sand, and in fact tasted of its grit, and the muscles of her thighs trembled. A moment of inattention and she felt a sharp burn on her upper arm. Floronius's sword had sliced her, twice perhaps, before she had even seen it. She backed away as warm, sticky blood ran down her arm onto her hand. The trident grew slick in her palm and her arm weakened.

Still thrashing with the net, the first tickle of true fear swept her. Did Floronius see it in her eyes?

She managed to swing the trident in an arc above her head, to remind the crowd of her earlier performance with the long piece of iron. The applause still favored her, surely, but the sound wavered, like heat rising from pavement, or perhaps it was her hearing that wavered, for the sand also seemed to ripple and swell, and even Floronius's face blurred.

I am going down.

The thought came only a moment before she felt the sand smack her cheek. Every muscle seemed paralyzed and tears came unbidden, for which she cursed herself without mercy.

Floronius stood above her now, one foot on the small of her back and his sword pricking at the base of her neck.

She waited, unsure if her rival's hatred would outpace her sponsor's mercy—

And unsure if she even cared.

25

⸙

Cato watched Ariella swagger into the arena, her trident lofted above her head, from the box reserved for the editores, the sponsor of the games, and his stomach churned over what was to come. Whether it was betraying Ariella or seeing her fight, he could not say.

Isabella tugged on his arm and offered him salted fish she had wrapped in fabric before leaving home.

The odor of it further aggravated his stomach. He pushed it away and kept his eyes on the sand.

The crowd loved her. Of course they did. This was her plan, the plan he was about to ruin. But even as the thought accused, he knew he would not do it. The gods help him, he could not betray her. So his first public appearance since declaring himself Maius's rival would end in ridicule, and his chances of defeating the monster would be slaughtered before he had begun.

Octavia was clucking her tongue beside him. "These fighters these days. They believe it's all about them and not the fight. We are subjected to more personality than performance."

Cato barely heard his mother. Down below, in the section reserved for the elite, Nigidius Maius had turned in his seat to look at Cato, as if he could read Cato's dilemma from twenty rows away and was even now glorying in his victory. Cato saw each detail of the arena in sharp relief, senses heightened. Maius's bushy eyebrows, the heads of his sycophants in a pack around him, even the details of sand and sword, of the next two fighters waiting in the wings for their own moment of glory.

But the fight was beginning, and all thoughts of campaign promises and rival candidates fled as Cato focused on Ariella, on her dark hair and muscled arms, on every thrust of her trident and swish of her nets. He stood and gripped the low stone wall. Isabella was pulling on his arm again, but he shrugged her off, and his vision narrowed until he saw nothing but the battle in the center of the yellow sand and felt nothing but the stone ledge cutting into his hands.

She was quick, that was certain. But Floronius had the advantage of size and strength. Wide in the chest, powerful arms. Cato felt each blow to her as though it were his own body, and his muscles jerked and twitched as if he were in the sand himself.

His earlier thoughts of the dance returned, and Ariella indeed could have been a dancer, so fluid and graceful were her movements as she leaped and twirled around Floronius, nets flying about her head.

The shouts of the crowd rose and fell with each blow, with each strike of trident and sword. When they were silent, the heavy grunts of the fighters pushed through the weighted air, reaching Cato and reminding him that it was not a dance, but a fight to the death.

His arms grew fatigued by the tight grip on the stone wall. How could Ariella still push on with her trident and nets?

But it could not last. He saw that now. Saw her weakening, slowing. She had only speed as an asset, and without it she would fall. He watched her face for signs of defeat, but he was too far to read her expression.

Floronius delivered a kick to her ribs and Ariella bent over the blow. Cato started forward, as though he could put a stop to this madness. Heat sparked along his fingertips and he felt himself flush with panic and indecision. Torn between a desire to save her and a desire to honor her wishes, he shuffled his feet in the stone box.

Octavia smacked his arm. "Sit down, Quintus. You are making me nervous."

Beside her, Isabella chimed in, "Isn't he the same little fighter who had you so agitated at the last games, Quintus?"

The crowd sent up a gasp and then a shout.

Cato watched in terror as Ariella backed away, her upper left arm blooming with the spread of purple-red blood.

She used her other forearm to wipe sweat from her head and gave only a glance to the injury.

Cato had known before the fight began that should Ariella go down before Floronius, he would certainly declare mercy for her. But the blood began to run down her arm to the hand that held the trident, and Floronius circled her like a lion preparing for the kill. It was likely this brute would make an end of her before Cato had the chance to intervene.

Gods have mercy, she was going down.

He felt it in his own body even before the crowd sensed her wavering on her feet. A moment later and she was facedown in the sand, Floronius standing over her . . .

Somehow, impossibly, Cato found himself leaping the stone wall and running down through the tiered seating toward the arena wall.

The drop from the edge of the seating to the sand was no more than his own height, and it jolted but did not slow him. He ran past the arched entrance to the arena where Paris and another fighter waited.

Paris watched him come, eyes wide.

Cato spotted the scimitar in the fighter's hand and pointed as he ran. "Give me that!"

The gladiator looked down, held out the weapon, frowning.

Cato snatched the curved blade, turned, and ran to the two fighters in the center.

Floronius had put his foot onto Ari's back and his sword at the base of her neck. His back was to Cato.

The crowd had gone deadly silent at Cato's leap into the arena, and Floronius searched the stands to see why he was not cheered.

Cato yelled. It came deep from his chest and exploded as he ran, sword raised, across the sand at Floronius.

The fighter spun, his own weapon held out at his waist.

Cato did not slow.

The crowd screamed their delight.

Their swords met in a deafening clash of metal. They pushed apart and Cato gained his balance for another charge. A quick sideways glance revealed Ariella scrambling to her feet and pulling back.

Good.

He ran at Floronius once more, and their swords met again, the sound lost in the frenzied screams of the spectators.

Somehow he held his own. Calling on everything he'd learned by years of watching the gladiators, he thrust and jumped back before Floronius could strike. Some part of his mind evaluated the situation, aware that this was something he had dreamed of since he was a boy.

Aware that it was ludicrous and he was soon to die.

Just as he had known that Ariella could not have victory here, it did not surprise him when it was his own back in the sand, with Floronius's angry and confused face above him.

"What is this?" Floronius's voice was the growl of an abused animal. "Did you wish me to let you win?"

Cato inhaled, fighting the tightness in his chest.

Floronius seemed to sense his chance to perform. He lifted his voice into the air. "What shall it be, sponsor? Death or mercy?"

The crowd laughed at the irony, then waited for Cato's response.

Before he could speak, a flash of leather and rope, flesh and blood, flew across the sand. Ariella's nets whipped around Floronius's feet, and with a practiced yank, she toppled the bulky fighter. A moment later the prongs of her trident were balanced across Floronius's chest.

Again the townspeople went wild. It had been a fight to talk about for years.

And Cato saw his moment.

He scrambled to his feet, crossed to Ariella, and lifted her good arm into the air, signaling her as the victor. To Floronius he whispered harshly, "Get up. Get out of here."

The fighter performed his duty, retrieving his shield and sword and running from the sand.

Cato shouted into the heavy air, and the crowd seemed to perch on their seats to hear every word. "I promised you something you had never seen before!"

Beside him, he sensed Ariella's tension, even her anger.

The moment hung, suspended, and he let them wait, then turned a circle, arms out, and made good his promise. "When have you ever seen a politician in the arena?"

Thousands of cheers lifted from the seats.

"There are some who say that I cannot win. That I do not have the strength, the power, to take on my rival." He was warming to his speech now, and he had them. "That may be true. But like Scorpion Fish here, I will fight with everything I have. I stepped into this ring today to show you who I am." He paused again for effect. "I am a *fighter*!"

The crowd screamed.

"I am a fighter who despises the odds and the risk! And I will fight for what is right, for the good of the people of Pompeii!"

The crowd was on its feet now, fists and voices raised in defiance of the city government that had too long oppressed them. Cato felt the flush of success and turned to Ariella, who still breathed heavily.

"I thank you for coming to my rescue." His words were only for her.

Her lip curled. "I did not do it for you."

"Even so." He bowed. "I am grateful."

Her eyes were narrow slits. "And I thank you for not revealing me. You have benefited me, even. They will be talking about this fight, about Scorpion Fish. The next time I fight—"

Cato took a step closer to her, close enough to smell the sweat and blood and leather. He leaned in until his lips brushed against her ear.

"Listen to me, Ariella, and listen well." All the terror and fury of the day hardened into one fierce truth. "I swear by all the gods, you will never fight in the arena again."

26

Cato was still posturing before the crowd when Ariella made her escape. She ran from the sand, grateful that her injuries were all in her upper body so that she was able to flee the arena without limping, or worse—being carried out.

In the corridor beyond the arena, Floronius waited, fuming. "What was *that*? Do you suppose I am going to allow you to be declared the victor—"

But Ariella did not want to hear it. Wanted none of it, this life of a gladiator, this life of slavery. She dropped her trident and net, ran past Floronius, past the other fighters waiting to be called to the sand, and up the ramped exit to the city. The arch ahead streamed light into the dingy hall and she flew toward it as though chased by demons.

Her left arm throbbed where it had been sliced open and she dared not look. Her ribs burned and every muscle seemed as though it had been stretched over a fire.

Still, she ran.

And as she ran, the truth pounded up through her sandals and into her heart.

You will never be a true fighter.

Never make a name for herself as an opponent of anything more than dwarf or beast.

You will never be free.

There was nothing for her but to be killed in the arena. Or to run away, be found, and be executed.

And Portius Cato, what of him and his threat? No doubt he would have her scrubbing the barracks latrine and serving porridge to her former colleagues.

At the thought of slavery in the barracks, her heart and mind turned to Jeremiah, and her feet soon followed. Through the city, drained of people by the games at the end of town, she ran, then walked, then stumbled to reach the house where she had left Jeremiah some nights earlier. She had only this one friend in Pompeii. Where else would she go?

She reached the massive doors set so close to the street, leaned a weary hand against the wood, and panted. Her arm was a bloody mess, and she had no legitimate right to be here, as she had the night Jeremiah had directed her to this door. Why would they even open the door to her?

And yet she knocked. Would Jeremiah still be here? She would beg to see him.

The house slave who greeted her that night again opened the door. She swallowed, searched for the words, but he seemed to recognize her. A glance at her bleeding arm and he pulled the door wider and yelled for someone else.

A younger woman, the adopted daughter, Flora, appeared. Ariella staggered across the threshold. Flora caught her around the waist and led her forward, into the spacious atrium, to a bench beside the impluvium, where water sparkled above the blue and green mosaics of the basin.

And then she was there, Europa, whom Ariella only now realized she had been longing to see. The woman bustled out of nowhere as though Ariella were an expected guest, directing slaves to bring water, to bring rags, to move Ariella to a front room.

Ariella let herself be led, silent and numb, to one of the rooms off the atrium, a lavish receiving room where Europa's husband would meet with business associates. The walls were frescoed in red and yellow plasters, with ceiling-high inset squares that fooled the eye into thinking they were paneled, with painted vases and sculptures and bowls of fruit on low tables, all done in the realistic style that made the room seem even bigger, grander.

Her fuzzy mind noted amazement that she would be brought here instead of one of the back rooms, unfinished and rough, where the servants and slaves spent their time.

"Bring Jeremiah," Europa was saying to Flora. "He will want to see his friend."

She guided Ariella to a couch and laid her across it, her arm extended where it could be treated.

Ariella fixed her eyes on Europa's purple-edged robe, pulled up at the shoulders over her ample bosom and fixed with gold pins. A hopelessness washed over Ariella, as though she had held the tide at bay as she crossed the city and only now it swamped her, drowned her.

The big Persian brought an orange terra-cotta basin and some pure white rags.

Europa bathed Ariella's arm with the cool water, pausing each time Ariella gasped. "It will heal." She squeezed the rag and dipped it again. "But you will have a scar."

Ariella turned her head to examine the wound and found two cuts, perpendicular, with the horizontal slice shorter than the vertical. She closed her eyes and laid her head back against the cushions.

Fitting. Her injury formed the symbol of Rome's favorite method of criminal execution: a cross. How many of her countrymen had she seen hanging, tortured, along the roads leading out of Jerusalem years ago? That she should be identified with Israel's destruction, with criminals, seemed only right.

Jeremiah hobbled through the doorway.

Ariella lifted a hand in a weak greeting.

Europa spoke over her shoulder, still tending Ariella with the soft touch of a mother that broke her heart. "She has taken a beating in the arena. She's lost some blood, and I believe a rib or two may be broken. But she will heal."

Ariella noted Europa's knowledge of her gender and looked to Jeremiah. "You told her."

Europa snorted. "Told me what? That you are a young woman?" She patted Ariella's cheek. "One does not need the gift of a prophet to see such a thing. Later, when you are ready, you can tell me what brought you to the arena dressed as a boy."

Ariella sighed, overwhelmed with a mixture of gratitude and weariness.

"Come, Jeremiah." Europa stood and gave her place to the old man. "Sit with her. Sing her songs of home until she falls asleep."

Her old friend lowered himself slowly, carefully.

"You are well?"

He smiled. "I will be ready to train with you in no time."

Ariella turned her head away from him. "I am not going back."

"Hmm. Have you always gone your own way, Ariella? With no care for HaShem's direction?"

She shifted and winced. "HaShem cares nothing for me!" It felt good to say it—to declare the truth. No more masks. She was a woman and she had set herself in opposition to the God of her fathers who had long ago abandoned her. Neither of these would she deny any longer.

Jeremiah brushed the hair from her forehead and obeyed Europa by beginning a soft song.

Ariella gripped his hand and closed her eyes, trying to recall better times. But she floated on a river of hopelessness, such as had carried her out of Jerusalem nine years earlier and deposited her at the feet of Valerius, where the true humiliation began.

Jeremiah's voice rose and fell and became a prayer over her, spilled out in her beloved Hebrew as he rocked back and forth, his chants soothing, hypnotic. He sang and prayed of the prophets, of their promise of a Messiah to save Israel. And then his songs grew unfamiliar, words of redemption, of forgiveness and love and purpose, all found in this Yeshua, this Messiah he had claimed.

But Yeshua was not her Messiah. Had the prophets even spoken truth when they promised that the Creator would one day redeem? The God of Israel was not a good God as she had been taught. How could He be, with what had happened to His city, to His temple, to His people?

The anger built within her like a solid thing, pushing impossibly against the love Jeremiah claimed that the Creator had for her. Anger and love—two immovable forces in collision in her heart, the pressure almost too great to bear.

Ariella felt the tears slide from the corners of her eyes to the cushions, and she let them fall, let herself weep for Jerusalem, for her lost family . . .

For her future.

Vesuvius had given them the gift of their wealth, and yet they credited the mountain with little.

It loomed over Herculaneum, over Pompeii, over the towns that reaped its benefits unthinkingly, and rivers of magma beneath its surface churned and boiled.

Ironic that the towns that prospered because of its rhythmic spewing could also be destroyed by it.

How much of their riches had been given by the mountain? Granite, basalt, pumice—all formed by its cooling magma. Opals and sapphires broken loose from the depths and sent upward to be discovered. Fertilized soil where oranges, lemons, and grapes thrived like nowhere else.

And yet it was not appreciated. If they knew what raged within, they would show proper respect. But they wanted only its benefits, without paying the price.

There had been some who were thankful, once. A group of slaves, escaped from tyranny and led by one of their own, a gladiator. They had hidden in one of the craters until the army had come for them, and their leader Spartacus led them down the other side to freedom.

But that had been many years ago, and there were none who even looked up from their own lives long enough to recognize the gifts of the mountain.

They would soon regret their inattention.

27

Despite the strange outcome of the arena games, and the attention that followed as Cato made his way back through the city, he did not forget his errand as the sun set. The Christians had promised to take him to his sister. Lucius wanted to come, but Cato convinced him it was better for him to wait.

He was invited into the home of Seneca and his wife, Europa, but kept in the atrium as the slave went to fetch his master.

Ariella had not been far from his thoughts since she fled the arena hours earlier. He stopped at the barracks, but Drusus shook his head, denying knowledge of her whereabouts. This seemed to be truth, as the lanista was furious over her disappearance, especially after the spectacle of the afternoon.

Could she be here, in the house of Europa? He had seen her in this home once, but would she come here after her injury? He longed to be certain that the cuts were not dangerous. Europa appeared, and almost he asked her about Ariella, but in the end held his tongue, unsure of what the woman knew of the gladiator in disguise.

"We must wait awhile." Europa indicated that he follow her

deeper into the house, around the stone half wall that bordered the gardens and into the colonnade that ran alongside it. "It must be fully dark before we attempt to get you into the prison." She looked him up and down and smiled. "And we must get you other clothes."

Cato looked down at his toga, wrapped and draped with fashionable precision. "What? Not the right attire for a prison visit?"

Europa ushered him into the triclinium where he had been that first night. "No one in your position goes there."

"You do."

She studied him for a moment. "I can see why Jeremiah speaks of you highly. I sense in your heart a strong passion for justice."

Cato lowered his head. She had seen too much. "I only want to help my sister."

"Your sister. The city. Those oppressed by evil."

Cato shrugged. Wasn't there a lighter topic?

She patted his arm and motioned for him to sit on one of the plump cushions placed on the benches around the low tables. "I believe you are still finding yourself, Portius Cato. And I believe the hand of God is on you, to use you for His purposes. We shall see."

A chill passed through Cato at her words, as though she were some sort of oracle telling his future. He said nothing.

Europa's husband, Seneca, joined him in the triclinium, and food and wine were brought to pass the time. Cato found the man fascinating and listened to his tales of fortune on the seas with delight. Ironic that Ariella had guessed correctly, though the fish symbol near the door held another meaning. But as the night fell, their mood fell with it, and the somber journey became their focus.

Cato was given a servant's tunic, and he stripped and changed.

Europa draped a heavy mantle over his shoulders, as though he were of Eastern descent, to further disguise his jawline. Another man came to the door to escort Cato through the streets, and Europa introduced him as Albus. The madman from the Forum, now in his right mind.

They crossed sidewalks and stepped over gutters in silence, moving toward the Forum and its underground cells. The city smelled of sewage at night, and the purple-green mountain that always shed such beauty over the landscape disappeared into the inky darkness. The clouds that had grown thicker through the day blotted out the moon.

Cato could not keep quiet, however. "I saw you. That day in the Forum. With Seneca."

Albus slowed. "The day I was set free."

"What held you?"

"Not what. Who. The demons took my mind and body years ago."

"And now?"

He laughed. "Once Yeshua has set you free, you are free indeed. There is nothing left but to follow Him."

Freedom. The word clashed with their prison errand—and with the bondage of his own heart.

Cato had been given a large basket to carry, and he kept his face half-hidden. They approached a darkened doorway and Cato followed the younger man past a guard and down a flight of shadowy steps that grew damper as they descended. Somewhere at the bottom a torch flickered uneasily, and an oily smoke filtered up to assault his nose.

Portia was down here.

Anger and powerlessness swept over him, as strong as he had felt earlier when Ariella faced her opponent.

Another guard sat at the bottom of the steps, and he jumped to his feet, rubbing his eyes, at their approach. Cato's escort whispered to him, as though they were acquainted. The guard stepped to Cato and rifled through the contents of the basket, clean tunics and loaves of bread.

Cato kept his head down, but the guard's attention was on his cargo. He nodded once, jerked a thumb over his shoulder, and regained his seat.

His new friend led him deeper into the underground chamber. "We are allowed to bring supplies to the prisoners several times each week. A charitable pursuit looked on with favor by the city's officials, thankfully."

And not the least of their charities.

They passed several tiny chambers, with only a narrow door to mark each one and a squat little window that looked upon the inside of the prison. The cells smelled even worse than the street.

The young man stopped before the fourth door. "She is here." He took the basket from Cato and indicated that he should step to the tiny window.

Cato peered through the square opening but could see nothing in the darkness beyond. "Portia?"

There came a shuffling, slow and deliberate. Then a pale face at the hole, eyes sunken and hair hanging in stringy clumps. "Quintus? Is that you?"

Oh, Portia.

Cato's heart fell to his feet. He beat back the tears that threatened to spill and reached cold fingers through the square. She studied his hand as though it were a novelty, then clutched at it with a desperation that broke his heart. "Portia, you are ill!" She fared even worse than he had feared.

She swallowed and leaned her forehead against his hand. "I have been ill, yes. But—but it is not the confinement." She lifted her head, and he saw her own tears streak through the dirt that clung to her pale skin. "Quintus," she whispered, "I am with child!"

Cato cursed inwardly. No. Not now. "We will get you out, Portia."

She shook her head. "I have heard things. Maius does not push for a trial yet. He uses me to blackmail you. He will tell you that you must give up the election." She tightened her hold on his hand. "Do not do it, Quintus. Not even for me. He must be stopped."

Cato's companion was at his side, pushing clean clothing through the opening, and Portia accepted it with a grateful smile. He gave her bread and a jug of something, and she disappeared from the opening to store her treasures.

When she returned, her spirits seemed lifted, but it shattered Cato again to think that such small comforts could cheer her. "I will stop him, Portia. I promise you. But I will not leave you here."

"How is Lucius?"

"Like a ship with no rudder. He mourns your absence every moment."

She bit her trembling lip at this, but then succumbed to more tears. "You will give him my love?"

Cato nodded.

"But do not tell him of my condition, Quintus. Promise me this. I want to tell him myself. And I fear what he might do if he knew. And Maius—I am afraid that Maius would claim that the child—" She seemed unable to speak the words.

Cato reached through the opening to cradle her cheek. "I will not make this promise, dear sister, because I cannot be certain what tomorrow will bring. But if I can keep your secret, I will."

She leaned into his hand, apparently content with his answer.

"We must go," Cato's guide said at his shoulder.

Cato turned to find the basket empty. The man had already distributed its contents to other prisoners. Were any of them innocent, as Portia was?

Portia brought his hand to her lips and kissed his fingers.

He leaned his forehead against the small opening, as close to her as he was able. "I will be back, Portia. Courage!"

And then they were out, back up the steps into the black night, crossing the city in silence once more. Snatches of drunken laughter and the shrill calls of brothel women echoed through the streets. The respectable citizens were behind their doors and it was the time for other pursuits. Cato followed his companion back to Europa's house, his mind and body numb, his eyes trained on the dark sidewalk and its cat's-eye stones.

Portia and Ariella. Two women with secrets. Two women in trouble.

The frustration of helplessness surged in his chest, hot and bitter. He marched on, noticed a patch of tiny yellow flowers that bloomed in a crack between sidewalk and house, a surprising bit of beauty in the grubby street. Cato ground his foot into the flowers until they were crushed into the crack. The puny show of power did nothing.

How could he make a difference in this city when he could not even save two women? He was a kitten fighting a bull and would soon be stomped on like the flowers.

Back at the house of Seneca and Europa he changed his clothes quickly, thanked the couple for their help, and headed back out into the city. Already his fury had hardened into a new goal.

The moon still hid behind the night's clouds, making it difficult to judge the time. But Cato decided he did not care if he roused the lanista from his bed. He had business with the man that he intended to conclude tonight.

Perhaps he could not help Portia immediately. But there was another woman who needed him.

And he had not lied when he promised she would never again stand in the arena.

28

Maius was displeased with the day.

He paced his lower gardens, which were angled to catch the rays of the setting sun, but took no notice of the spectacular display of purple clouds and pink light in the west. It had been frustrating enough to hear of Portius Cato's sponsorship of the games, but today's events far surpassed Maius's dour expectations in the damage done to his own position.

The younger man had been a candidate for only a few days, and already he had won the hearts of the fickle public—at least when it came to showmanship.

A cushioned chaise sat near the central fountain, and Maius forced himself to recline, for pacing showed a certain amount of weakness, of fretfulness, and he had no need for such things.

But his thoughts flowed back and forth, first assuring him that Cato was a novelty whose charm would soon wear thin, then warning him that the man was a danger to the life he had shaped here in Pompeii.

Maius focused on the trickle of fountain water and the scent of evening flowers, wanting his gardens to soothe him as they usually did. A flutter at the edge of the enclosure brought welcome distraction. His daughter's penchant for bright fabrics made her seem like one of his exotic birds.

"Nigidia, come and sit with your father."

The girl slid to his side and perched on the edge of his cushion, extending her bottom lip. "You are so glum, Father. The games always make you giddy for hours." She laughed and ran two fingers over his brow. "I believe you have new lines here since this morning."

Maius caught her fingers and kissed them. "You know me too well, my pet. I am afraid your father is not so pleased with the games today."

Nigidia's blue eyes danced. "I found today's games especially amusing. When that Cato fellow jumped over the wall and ran into the sand—"

She did not finish, perhaps because the black fury that swelled through Maius was evident on his face. He leaned forward. "That man is your father's enemy, Nigidia. Do not speak of him in my presence, nor praise him to anyone!"

She patted his arm, as though his anger were nothing to her. "I have never known you to have an enemy of any consequence, Father. Doesn't everyone soon learn that Nigidius Maius rules Pompeii with a fair hand?"

He tried to smile at his loyal daughter. "Of course you are right, Nigidia." He nudged her away from the chaise. "Run along now, and leave your father to his thoughts. You have cheered me greatly."

She pecked his cheek with a quick kiss, but before she ran off he almost believed he saw . . .

No, he was being foolish. His Nigidia would never look at him with a hint of anger or, worse, disgust.

Still restless, he pulled himself from the cushions and crossed the terrace to his birdcages. The servants were faithful in leaving scraps of meat and vegetables in a dish placed nearby for Maius to push through the bars into their eager beaks, and he chose a red-plumed warbler, whose ruffled feathers reminded him of Nigidia, to offer a bit of veal.

"That's right," he whispered to the bird who greeted him with a chirp and hopped to receive his offering. "It is Maius who feeds you, Maius who watches over you."

All of Pompeii needed to be reminded at whose hand they flourished. But how could they be reminded when they were so distracted by the juvenile antics of a young winemaker?

The gardens grew dark and servants came to light torches, but still Maius wandered, ripping leaves from plants and shredding them, kicking at dirt that had escaped its borders. The visitor he had been expecting arrived at last, ushered in by a slave to stand at the edge of the garden, under a smoky torch planted in the garden's soft soil.

Maius tossed away the flower he had been ripping apart. "Otho. I began to think you had more important business to attend."

Otho, a local fuller, was a frail man, with cheekbones that seemed almost to protrude from his skin. His sallow eyes traveled to the stone walkway. "Forgive me, Maius. There was an emergency—"

Maius held up a hand. "Spare me the inconsequential tedium. You have given Primus your payment, I assume?"

The man's expression flickered, and something akin to defiance seemed to cross his features. "Yes, of course."

"Is something wrong, Otho? The month's payment seems unfair, perhaps?" Maius baited him, both waiting for and fearing his response.

Otho straightened bony shoulders and lifted his pointed chin.

Again there was that look in his eyes. "Unfair? Payments made to you simply to keep my business going?" The sarcasm was faint but clear.

Maius spread his hands. "You wound me. Surely you realize how much more I do for you than that? Safety for your workers, peaceful and profitable transactions."

Otho looked away, shifting his weight from one foot to another, then returned his gaze to Maius. "Perhaps these things would be free in a different Pompeii."

Maius pressed his fingertips together over his ample belly. "A different Pompeii? And where should we find such a thing?"

Otho shrugged one shoulder. "There are alternatives . . ."

"Courage, Otho. Speak your mind. Portius Cato? Is that the different Pompeii of which you are dreaming?"

Otho said nothing but did not look away. The defiance Maius had sensed under the surface became plain.

The man seemed to find his courage then and spoke quietly. "They are saying that he is the man to restore the health of our city."

Maius crossed the terrace quickly, surprising Otho with his advance. "Listen to me. You can listen to talk of change and dream of a new Pompeii all you wish, but your vote belongs to me, as surely as your business belongs to me, and to give away one is to give away the other." He poked a thick finger into Otho's frail chest, pushing the man backward. "Do not believe for a moment that I cannot destroy you. And I *would* destroy you without a thought."

Otho swallowed, and the knobbiness of his throat was almost comical.

But Maius was far from amused.

"I will see you next month, then." Otho bowed.

Maius smiled and dipped his head. "Until next month."

In the moments that followed Otho's departure, Maius's thoughts went from dark to black. He crossed to the low wall that bordered his garden and faced the city, each of its lights representing to him another traitor to his leadership.

To eliminate, rather than defeat, one's opponent was also weakness. But there were times when it became necessary. This had become one of those times.

Portius Cato must die.

29

The morning after Cato's sponsored games dawned fair, and the threatened rain of the previous day was forgotten. Cato rose early and again left the tending of his vines to Remus. He made his way to the Forum, his mind full of today's goal.

Thus far he had made his candidacy known and performed a bit of theatrics for the populace. But it would take far more than such attention to win the election.

The magistrates' offices at the southern end of the Forum housed the treasury and were the main locations for justice since the basilica's unrepaired damage from the earthquake over a decade ago. And the offices' position at the bottom of the Forum, where the road from the Marina Gate led across the Forum to Market Street, made it the busiest section of town.

Not coincidentally, it was outside these offices where a suggestum had been erected.

There would be a time for climbing the suggestum. Not yet.

He crossed the Forum and entered the Temple of Apollo. His rituals were overdue. Though he had maintained the rites faithfully at home, a sacrifice here was called for. He went through the motions of paying the priest, money that would be passed to the slaughterers, and stayed for the blood sacrifice and the flute player's melody—loud notes to drown out any sounds of ill omens. The priest kept his head covered, also to guard against ill omens, and Cato said the prayers intended to make the gods favorable toward him. He had given to them. Now they must give to him.

But the ritual felt hollow and pointless. Was this all the gods offered—a trading of favors? Did not Jeremiah's God's offer of a *relationship* far outweigh such practices?

He returned to the Forum, and as the morning sun lifted over the top of the Eumachia Building on his right, Cato ascended to the suggestum and surveyed the Forum below.

Already the city churned with the early shoppers, with horse-drawn carts crisscrossing to make deliveries. Philosophers spouted ideas to small groups of intellectuals, and beggars and prostitutes made their appeals to the rest.

Cato inhaled and set his shoulders, lifting his eyes to the mountain beyond the Forum, lit by the morning sun and watching over the city as always. From this height, above the chaos of the Forum's paving stones, he felt a strange kinship with the mountain, a parental sort of feeling for Pompeii, as though the mountain were Mother and he were Father, called to protect. He shook his head at the notion.

This business with Portia had made him sentimental.

He had stood thus on platforms in Rome. Had stated his case, made his position clear. There had been powerful men there as well, men he had tried to unseat.

Tried—and failed.

The experience had shamed him, made him fearful. He saw that now. He had come to Pompeii to hide, to avoid ridicule and forget his failure. But the failure had followed him, because the failure was not the political defeat but a more personal fear.

It was time for the fear to be put away. Time to become the man he truly was, and to remove the mask of indifference.

A merchant of the Fruitsellers' Guild ambled to the base of the platform from the direction of the Marina Gate, followed by a slave pushing an aging cart of oranges and lemons, its blackened wood rotting in places. The merchant shielded his eyes from the sun and looked up at Cato. "Time for a speech?"

Well past time.

Cato nodded, and the merchant raised a fist in support and directed his slave to circle the cart and become the start of an audience for Cato.

And so it began. In the manner of the Greek philosophers, adopted and expanded by Roman politicians, Cato lifted his voice to the hurrying crowds and began to recite the crimes of his opponent, the promised benefits of his own leadership, and the dire need for change in the government of Pompeii.

Some continued on, more interested in their own affairs than the politics of the city. But many more slowed, then stopped and gathered around the fruitseller and his cart, curious to hear the first public speech by the candidate who had everyone talking.

Cato's voice took on strength as he warmed to his subject, reminding the people of Nigidius Maius's stranglehold on the economics of Pompeii, of his criminal tactics for maintaining power. Gone were the generalizations of change and new leadership. Cato had committed himself now, accusing Maius by name of everything from blackmail to treason.

"How long will you allow yourselves to be bullied into voting against your conscience, citizens? How long will you allow your livelihood to be threatened by the greed of this one man? It is time to stand!"

As he had in the arena yesterday, Cato received a shout of agreement from the men and even some women who had gathered. Upturned faces reflected confidence, passion for change.

"We will take back Pompeii, friends! I promise that fairness will become the new standard for government in this town. And we will flourish here at the base of Vesuvius, enjoying her many blessings!"

He stepped down soon after and was mobbed by supporters. Back slaps and gripped arms, eager faces and offers of campaign help.

The nagging condemnation that had plagued Cato since he fled Rome began to dissolve in the support of the people and the confidence that he was at last where he needed to be.

Cato broke free of the crowds later in the morning. His new purchase should be waiting for him at home by now, but he took the slow route back to the house, stopping to talk with several businessmen along the way.

Yes, he had crossed a line today, committed himself to a course of action.

But he was far from sure that everyone would approve.

30

Ariella woke to sunlight streaming onto the cushions from high windows in Europa's house, found Jeremiah dozing on a mat beside her, and jumped from her bed, forgetting her injuries.

Several breathless moments later, she probed her ribs with her fingers and decided that, although painful, the pain was bearable. The cuts on her upper arm were still dressed with Europa's rags. The bruises, well . . . there was nothing to be done there.

She slipped past Jeremiah, not wanting to disturb his rest, and made her way to the garden, where several servants tended the flowering bushes, stripping dead blossoms and clipping stray branches.

Flora was there as well and looked up at her approach.

"Will you give your mother my thanks? I must get back." How much did the girl know of her plight? She nodded in seeming understanding, and Ariella fled the house and headed through the morning shopping crowd, toward the theater and the gladiator barracks behind it.

The sidewalks were crowded already, and more than once she came up fast behind a strolling citizen and had to pull back, circle around, and dodge through gaps in the crowd to keep moving. Drusus and the others would have missed her by now. What would be her punishment for having been gone all night?

But when she crossed under the entrance to the barracks training field and saw Drusus under the portico at the field's edge, he held out his hands in a gesture of welcome and even relief.

She approached warily, disbelieving that he had been concerned.

"There you are at last." His voice carried across the field and drew the attention of those who lounged or trained.

"I am sorry, Drusus. I was—"

He waved away her apology. "I care not where you spent the night. Or with whom." He winked as if they were drinking comrades. "But you have turned out to have more value than I ever dreamed, and I feared I would have to return the gold if you did not show."

"The gold?"

"Oh yes." Drusus's yellow-toothed smile was one of leering amusement. "He has paid quite a sum for you. At first I said my new little gladiator had turned out to be a better entertainer than I had imagined. But in the end"—he spread his palms wide, as if to indicate his own helplessness in the face of a tempting offer—"I had to agree that gold in the hand is always worth more than the uncertain gold of the future."

Ariella shook her head several times, for a strange, warning sort of buzzing had begun between her ears. "What are you talking about, Drusus?"

He grinned. "Oh, do not act surprised, my young lad. You must have known that this would be the outcome of all the attention your benefactor has displayed. It was not enough to pay for your private lodging, to sponsor the games, to watch you fight." Drusus shook his head, his greasy hair swinging. "Ho, when he jumped into the arena to save you, I saw a hundred more games sponsored by noblemen anxious to prove their manhood. But it would seem that he must have you closer than that. In his house, where his access to you will be unrestricted." Drusus again held out innocent hands. "And who am I to prevent ardor, in whatever form it takes?"

Ariella's head throbbed now, with a sharp pain that felt like a dagger behind the eyes. "Portius Cato?" She felt her hands clench at her sides. "Are you saying that he has paid for me?"

"Oh, he has paid well, my boy. Quite well."

She staggered backward, saw the blue sky ripple above her. Drusus reached out a hand to steady her. "Come now, there are worse things than being the slave of a rich man." He laughed. "You will not likely die at the end of a sword, for one."

Unless it is the end of my own sword.

He gave her a little shove. "You must go now. I promised him I would deliver you before noon, and you have kept me waiting."

Ariella shook her head, wordless.

"What? You don't want to go?" He leaned in, his lecherous voice a rasp in her ear. "Does he do things to you? Things you do not like?"

Ariella swallowed. Drusus's question came not from concern but from some sick curiosity.

"Do not do this, Drusus. Do not sell me to him."

He brushed his hands together. "It is already done."

"I will not go."

His eyes narrowed. "Then you shall be taken there." He glanced across the field at the clustered group of fighters, passing the dipper of water. "Two of you, over here."

Ariella turned to her colleagues, hoping for pity, an ally. But it was Paris and Floronius who responded. Perhaps they sensed that the summons had something to do with her and were quick to grasp the chance to humiliate her.

"Our newest fighter is leaving us." Drusus pushed her toward them.

She stumbled, lost her balance, and was forced to brace herself against Paris's chest. She snatched her hand back as though she had been burned.

"Ari has been purchased by Portius Cato, in the Arnio Pollo block. But it would seem that our young friend will not go willingly."

He needed say no more. The two brutes grabbed her by the arms and dragged her toward the gate before she could get her feet under her body.

Her feet spun to gain ground, and she yanked at their hold on her. "I will *walk*!"

But her two nemeses would not give up the sanctioned rough handling. Neither released his grip, only their tongues as they dragged her through the city streets.

"At last." Paris's voice was gleeful. "We are rid of the runt who would steal the people's attention."

Floronius laughed. "We can be glad, at least, of the attention of one nobleman."

Ariella struggled still to get free of the tightening grasp of their iron fingers on her upper arms. Paris's grip pinched just below Europa's dressing of her wound, threatening to tear open the gash. Her ribs blazed with heat. "Please." She still scrambled to keep up with their longer pace. "Let me walk."

"Let you run, you mean." Paris chuckled. "Run away as you did last night? Not a chance."

They drew attention as they pushed through townspeople milling along the sidewalk or coming and going from various shops, and Ariella cringed at both the physical pain and the pain of humiliation. She trained her eyes on her feet and let the anger build in her like embers fanned into flame. Sweat ran down the center of her back, but the sounds and sights of the busy streets faded as she released her surroundings and gave her thoughts free rein.

That Cato had bought her like a piece of fowl hanging from a hook in the market infuriated her like nothing she could ever remember. The arrogance, the overweening conceit was like a monument built to himself, to glorify his own power.

She should have known that he was no different. These Romans did whatever they pleased, acquired whatever they desired, gorged on possessions, food, and wine, even as they consumed the world with their ever-marching military. And now she was one more thing that Portius Cato desired and would have.

No, he would not.

She had succumbed to the strength of such a man as this once, but she had been younger then. Weaker. Fresh from the loss of her beloved city and her family and unable to fight for herself.

But she had become a fighter. She thought of Jeremiah's words. *"A mighty warrior."* And though Portius Cato had seen her in the arena, he had not yet truly seen her fight.

The streets disappeared under the churn of their feet, and Ariella barely heard as Paris and Floronius asked throughout the Arnio Pollo street for the home of the Catonii. Soon enough they were at a blue-painted doorway, carved with flowers and vines in the most pompous of styles. Like the equally wealthy home of Europa and Seneca, but she would not find such kindness within these doors.

Indeed, when the door was opened by a slave and the two men explained their delivery, she was shoved into the lofty entry hall and the door slammed behind her without a good-bye from the gladiators, whom she hoped to never see again.

The hall was a wonder in itself, with carved shelves high above her head on each side, holding the most ornate of statuary, and plaster behind painted with blues and golds that seemed to light the small entryway. Before her, the impluvium with its mosaic pool and ridiculous dancing faun spoke of a man who delighted in all physical pleasures, who took no care for anything but his own enjoyment, and wanted to be certain that all who entered knew him to be such a man.

The slave left her in the impluvium, still taking in her surroundings, with a single syllable of, "Wait."

She had time, then, to reflect on this newest development in her quest for freedom. If her plans of winning the townspeople with her fighting prowess had not been crushed under the studded sandals of Floronius in the arena yesterday, then today there was nothing left but ash and dust. Cato had thwarted her from start to finish, and now he planned to use her in a new way, and she was once again without a plan to find freedom.

A rage that longed to vent itself shook her from head to foot as she waited for Cato to arrive and inspect his newest purchase. But it was a woman who bustled through the greenery of the garden in the center of the home and beckoned Ariella with an elegant hand.

"Come." She stood tall and regal at the atrium's half wall, her gold-edged robe lit by the morning sun above and her hair woven atop her head with a delicate gold chain. "Come here, where I can better see you."

Ariella ran a self-conscious hand over the back of her own short hair, circled the mosaic pool, and approached the woman. She was still beautiful, though old enough to be Ariella's mother, with well-defined cheekbones and a trim figure. Ariella's rage did not subside in the presence of this highborn beauty who had the power to command Ariella's future as though she were nothing more than the newest piece of furniture to be put to good use. She lifted her chin and met the woman's gaze.

Her defiance seemed to surprise the lady of the house, as she must be. Her eyebrows lifted, not in annoyance but more in amusement, disarming Ariella.

"So I hear that my son has purchased a slave from the gladiator school?"

Ariella tightened her lips and did not look away.

"I am Octavia. Do you know where you are, boy?" The words were not unkind, though she probably did not care.

"In the house of Portius Cato." Ariella tilted her head and looked the woman up and down. "To be used in whatever way the household wishes."

The lady frowned. "You will find us good masters here." She indicated the gardens. "The house is pleasant, and our slaves are well cared for, as you will learn."

Again Ariella said nothing.

But her silence was unnoticed, for another woman entered the courtyard from a back hall and passed through the garden toward them. "Who is this, Mother?"

The mother held out her arm to welcome the daughter.

Ariella took in the girl with a glance. She was about the same age as Ariella had been when she left Jerusalem, though far more innocent. She wore her hair much as her mother, and again Ariella's hand strayed to her leather vest and then her cropped hair, and a shame she had thought long destroyed washed over her soul. The girl's fine white robe was secured with red jewels at her shoulders, and she looked as though she were another flower in the garden she crossed. In their presence, Ariella was a caricature of a woman, like one of the stage men who dressed as women for the plays, ugly and laughable.

Octavia pulled the young girl to her side in the embrace of a mother. "A new slave Quintus has purchased, Isabella. From the gladiator school, it appears." Her inflection implied all the curiosity she must have felt.

Isabella broke away from her mother and stepped to Ariella for a closer look. She smelled of honey and flowers, the smell of wealth. "Why, it is the young boy Quintus saved yesterday!"

"Is it?" Octavia squinted at her.

"Of course it is, Mother. And the same fighter he studied at the first games."

Octavia frowned. "Why does he have such an interest in this one?"

Ariella breathed through her nose, trying to control her anger over being spoken of as though she were not present. But the young Isabella stood close, too close, peering into Ariella's eyes. All at once, she clapped her hands together and began to laugh.

"Isabella!" Octavia's rebuke was gentle.

"Can you not see it, Mother?" Isabella circled around Ariella, gleeful. "It is quite obvious once you realize!"

"What foolishness do you speak, girl?"

Ariella stood between them and flushed at their inspection.

"Look closely, Mother." Isabella touched her hair. "She is a *woman*!"

Octavia reeled backward as though struck. "A woman!"

Ariella's heart beat out her shame, and she dropped her eyes for the first time since entering the wealthy home.

The young Isabella laughed. "So Quintus has finally taken some interest in women."

"Isabella!" The reprimand was more from duty than outrage.

"You must admit it, Mother. He has never taken a mistress, takes no interest in the female slaves or the brothel. It's the first time he's shown such humanity!"

"Is it true?" Octavia reached out to touch Ariella's arm. "Are you a woman?"

Ariella jumped backward, avoiding the touch.

"Yes, Isabella." Octavia smiled a little. "I see it now. You have been masquerading as a boy?" Her eyes were sympathetic. "How difficult that must have been."

Ariella steeled her heart, clenched her hands into fists at her sides, and studied her feet.

"Mother?"

The male voice from the doorway behind them forced a pounding in Ariella's chest, but she did not turn.

"Quintus!" Isabella was all laughter and amusement. "Come and see what we have here."

She heard his footsteps behind her, the same footsteps that had accompanied her back to the barracks after Jeremiah had been hurt. She swallowed and tried to still her trembling limbs, uncertain of what emotions caused such unrest.

Cato slowed behind her, silent.

She refused to turn.

"Quintus." Octavia's voice still held curiosity. "What is this?"

"I already told you, Mother," Isabella interrupted. "Quintus has taken a woman."

Cato cleared his throat. "She told you of her disguise?"

Isabella laughed. "Do you think we are blind, Quintus?"

There was a beat of silence and then Cato spoke her name, low and quiet. "Ariella. Turn around."

She pivoted to her new master, aware that she had little choice in this or any matter.

His eyes on her were as kind as his mother's had been, but strangely the kindness only raised her ire, perhaps because she understood none of it.

He studied her. "You are angry."

217

It was not a question, so she did not answer.

Isabella and Octavia seemed to sense that they should retreat and did so.

But Cato did not seem content to speak with her in the open courtyard. He grasped her arm and pulled her toward the nearest receiving room.

She followed, mute.

The room was furnished to impress, with couches, sculptures, and painted panels that reached the lofty ceiling. The high windows opened to the west, and the room was still dim in the morning hours. Cato did not release her until they were well into the room, away from the door, and then he turned on her and took a deep breath, as though preparing for an attack.

Ariella waited, letting her resentment build again, preparing the sharp words she would use, the only weapons she still retained.

"Ariella."

She had expected arrogance. Flippancy, even. But her name was soft on his lips. Apologetic. She fought to hold on to the rage.

He dropped his eyes, as though the shame were his own. "When I saw you under his foot in the sand . . ." He breathed heavily. "I—I could not watch it happen again. I had to do something. To remove you from the arena."

She found her voice, icy and hard. "To keep me as your pet, then. Since I would not be your campaign prop."

His eyes returned to her face now and roamed over it as though to search out any injury. "To keep you safe."

Ariella licked her lips and swallowed, fighting that curious mixture of fear and anger—and something very different his presence always caused.

He stepped closer. "I did not know what else to do." His eyes went to her bandaged arm, and then his hand touched the knot that held the dressing. "May I?"

She said nothing. He stood so close, she did not trust herself to speak, or even to move.

With gentle hands he untied the knot, unwound the strips of rag, and touched the reddened skin around the crossed cuts with his fingertips.

Ariella bit her lower lip to hold it still.

"It should heal well. But you should try to keep it at rest awhile." He rewrapped the rags, still standing a breath away.

"That will not be easy." He stood so close, she spoke over his shoulder, focused on the wall behind him. "The life of a slave is not one of leisure."

He finished with her bandages but did not step back. His eyes were on her face again, and he leaned closer, his voice so low she nearly missed the words, only a breath against her ear.

"Forgive me, Ariella. I did not know what else to do."

31

With the dawn of each new day, Cato's priorities returned to him as sure as the sun reached through the high windows of his bedchamber.

Free his sister.

Defeat Nigidius Maius.

Avoid Ariella.

And not necessarily in that order. Indeed, the latter was becoming a challenge.

This morning he dressed quickly, anxious to begin the series of meetings awaiting him throughout the day—meetings with prominent citizens who had each been subjugated in some way by Maius, and whom Cato was attempting to sway to his side of the election. If time allowed, he planned to find his way once again to the old Jewish slave who had become both teacher and friend through days of furtive meeting.

He met Octavia and Isabella in the morning room, already dining on cereals and oranges being served by Ariella.

Her appearance in the days she had been part of his household had ceased to be a shock to him, as it was the first morning after he bought her from Drusus. Isabella and Octavia had taken Ariella under their collective wing at once, refusing to allow the disguise to continue. They dressed her in the finest robes a slave could be given, then decorated her in the way of women, with baubles and glittering things Cato could not name. And she no longer smelled of leather and metal, of the sweaty training barracks. Instead, the scent of the gardens sometimes lingered when she bent over him to serve his wine or passed him in the courtyard or back halls of the house. Her hair, too, had begun to grow out since he had first met her, wavy and thick, and he found it rather complementary to her petite features. Only the metal collar made her position clear.

All of it was quite disturbing, and almost he suspected his mother and sister of confounding him purposely. He nodded a morning greeting to the two of them, and each smiled sweetly. Surely they had placed Ariella here this morning in anticipation of his arrival.

For Ariella's part, she continued to ignore him. He could not understand her attitude any more than her appearance. She seemed to always be about, almost as though she followed him in his movements through the house, and yet she did not speak to him nor even look at him unless necessary.

And she was sad, this he could see.

"Mother, Isabella." He lowered himself to a cushion and ladled his own wine into a bowl before Ariella had a chance to attend him. "What plans do you two have on this lovely summer day?"

Isabella shrugged. "I thought I would hang about the doorways of your receiving rooms and listen to your meetings."

Cato narrowed his eyes. She was only half jesting. Isabella's curiosity about the workings of politics had become insatiable. "And if one of those men should take offense at your listening ear and draw a dagger against it?"

She gave him a sly smile and shrugged. "Perhaps Ariella has been teaching me the way of the warrior."

Cato glanced sharply at Ariella, but the slave's eyes were on Isabella, and her tiny smile and shake of the head were for the girl alone.

"I'll not have any sister of mine—"

"Oh, hush, brother." Isabella laughed. "I am only teasing. My, but you are so sensitive of late!"

Cato grabbed at a hard crust of bread and bit down on it, then cursed at the pain.

Ariella's glance flicked to him for a moment, but her amusement had fled and he saw only resentment, which pained him more than the crusty bread.

Later in the day—after an exhausting round of noblemen, civic leaders, and wealthy businessmen had paraded in and out of the house, in turn rejecting or supporting him—Cato found Ariella in the kitchen, kneading dough.

Octavia held sway in all things domestic in Cato's house, and he had not specified how Ariella was to be put to use. Besides a position requiring learning, such as a tutor or overseer, a kitchen slave had the most chance to move about the house and the city at will, and Octavia had placed Ariella here for the relative freedom, no doubt sensing that the girl was special to her son.

He watched from the doorway as her arms, well muscled from the months of training with a sword, pounded and flipped the tanned lump until it was silky smooth.

"You attack the dough as though it were your enemy."

She startled, and her reflexes clearly remembered their training. Her floured fists jerked to chin-height, she took a step backward with one leg, bracing her weight, and she was once again Ari of the arena.

But the reaction lasted only a moment. She returned to her bread the moment she saw who had startled her, the gladiator dissolving once more into a woman.

Cato leaned against the doorway and folded his arms. "I must remember not to come upon you in the dark."

She did not look up, but he could see her face flush red. She did not appreciate the reminder.

Already he had forgotten his morning objective, to avoid her. "You have been nearly silent since coming here. I have never found you with so little to say."

She did not pause in her kneading. The ball of dough fell from her hands to the floured board, sending a puff into the air around her hands. "Perhaps the company has grown dull."

He could not help smiling again, but was glad she did not see it. This provocation was closer to their former interactions than anything since he brought her to his house. "Hmm. Yes. My mother and sister can be quite tedious."

"Your mother and sister are the best things about the Catonii."

Ah, a little flare of anger, perhaps. It pleased him, not only to see her spirit still alive, but to hear her praise his family, even at his expense. "I would agree."

She did glance at him then, as if to judge if he were mocking.

He drank in those eyes for the brief moment he had them, before they returned to rest upon the dough.

"Yet still you are always angry, Ari. Would you truly have preferred to remain with those clods, to remain in danger? At least you are safe here."

She kept at her kneading. "Safe, yes. Forever safe. But never free."

In the days since purchasing her, it had of course occurred to Cato that he could give her freedom. Such a thing was done occasionally, when a slave had served faithfully for many years, perhaps. Or saved enough to purchase his own freedom. But to buy a slave and then set her free immediately? It was not done. What effect could it have on his campaign? He had already drawn attention to his interest in the young gladiator, Scorpion Fish. It would come out that he had bought the fighter. And then to set him free? And if it were revealed that Scorpion Fish were a woman? It showed a certain softness of heart that would not recommend him as a worthy rival of Nigidius Maius.

At least, this was the reason he chose to give himself for not letting her go.

"Better safe and alive." He crossed the room and stood before her, on the other side of the table. "You can make a home for yourself here. We will treat you well." He indicated her clothes and jewelry. "You have seen this already."

She blinked a few times, still looking down. Was it possible that she shed tears?

"This will never be my home. My home is in Jerusalem. The city you destroyed."

Cato inhaled, feeling the bite of her anger, wishing he could deny its truth. He circled the table and fumbled in a pouch at his belt.

Ariella kept her eyes on his hands. "What are you doing?"

He reached for her neck, for the metal collar fastened there by Drusus. "Something I should have done long ago."

The key was tiny, and the click of release soft, but as the collar fell away in his hands, Ariella's relief was palpable. She studied his eyes, too close to be safe. "Thank you."

He backed away. "Perhaps Pompeii cannot feel like home, but what about the old man? Jeremiah, was it? He is one of your own. Like family?"

The name elicited a small smile. "I should like to see him again, to see if he is well."

Cato poked a finger into the dough, which had begun to toughen with the excessive kneading. "And I should like to see those people again, to inquire about my sister. So we shall go together."

The closest thing to happiness he had yet seen crossed her face. "I would like that."

"You do know what those people are, do you not?" She had not seemed to understand the symbol of the fish when they had seen it together that night.

She lifted the board that held the dough and slid the loaf into the domed oven in the corner of the kitchen. "They are Christians. Gentiles who claim that Jesus was the Jewish Messiah, but that he came for all people."

Cato inclined his head, surprised at the concise explanation. "Is this something you also believe?"

She turned back from the oven and dusted the flour from her hands. "I do not believe in anything."

Cato chose not to argue, but there was something there. Some flicker of doubt, of curiosity. He recognized it because it had started that way in his heart. But he would not yet speak of his own nearness to accepting this radical faith.

He waited until it grew dark that evening, several hours after the evening meal had been served and cleared, before he sought out Ariella. He found her bent over a pot of thyme in the atrium, clipping its fragrant leaves.

"Ready, Ari?"

She straightened and placed the snipped herbs and the knife in a small basket, then set it on the paving stone in front of the plant.

Cato accepted this as her silent way of agreeing without having to speak. He extended an arm to allow her to walk ahead of him, and did not miss the look of surprise as she passed.

They were both silent in the dark street. He had been so determined to avoid this girl. How did he keep finding himself alone with her?

The night air was warm and the city was quiet, save the activity that spilled its noise from the occasional tavern or brothel. Moonlight poured down on the stones and lit up the white cat's eyes like silvery pearls. Occasional footfalls sounded behind them, as though their own passage through the city echoed from the stone homes that lined the streets.

They crossed half the city toward Seneca's house before he spoke. "It is the first time I have left the house today."

She did not answer at once. "No need to leave when the city comes to you."

"Not so willingly as I would like."

They turned into the street where Seneca and his wife, Europa, had their home and reached their door. Again Cato heard the echo of footsteps behind them. He turned, curious if they had been followed.

Two dark figures shot from a doorway.

Cato raised an arm and stepped between Ariella and the two men.

They lumbered toward him, snarling like rabid dogs. They were two ugly beasts, both with more fat than muscle and matching rotted teeth.

Robberies in the street were uncommon, but perhaps this attack was not about money. He squared his body against them, unsure how he could take them both. "Stay back, Ariella."

But she was beside him a moment later, then in front of him, flying like a barbarian warrior at the thug closest to her. Cato started forward to intervene. The other attacker blocked him and Cato turned on him.

It seemed only an instant later that Ariella was behind her man with a choke hold around his neck. She dropped him, unconscious, to the ground. Cato had taken more punches than he had landed.

Ariella leaped onto the back of the second man and pulled him backward. Cato aimed a kick at his exposed belly.

Somewhere behind them, Cato heard a door open and the shouts of women.

Ariella swung off the attacker's back and landed flat-footed on the pavement, crouched and ready. But others tumbled from the house now. The man's massive head swung to Ariella, then to Cato and the growing crowd behind him. He glanced at his partner, still on the street, then turned and disappeared into the night.

"Portius Cato!" Europa's velvety voice was unmistakable. "Were you robbed?"

Cato straightened and went to Ariella, grasping her arm and studying her eyes. But she shook him off and stepped away.

"No, mistress. Thank you. That was not a robbery, I fear."

Seneca strode into the street. "They were Nigidius Maius's men, I've no doubt." He spoke to the assembled group, fifteen or twenty of the followers who met in his home. "He's resorted to this now, to intimidation of not only the common people but his rival as well."

Ariella joined Cato. "They came to kill, not to intimidate."

Europa clucked her tongue. "Well, we thank the Lord that you two are like a matched pair of fighters!"

Ariella cleared her throat and shifted her feet, and Cato tried to mask his amusement.

But Seneca was not finished. "Do not fear, Portius Cato. Word of this attack will make its way through the city. Maius cannot assassinate his rival, the very attempt of which he has accused your sister, and remain untouched by it! The people will know."

Cato crossed the space between them and gripped Seneca's arm. "Thank you. I appreciate your support."

And yet as the crowd returned indoors, and he and Ariella were pulled once again into the home of these strange and secretive people, Cato could not help but wonder if their support was more of a danger than an advantage.

32

~~~~~

Cato's battle was coming to an end. Not the war he waged against Nigidius Maius, but the conflict in his own heart between the truth so evident in Jeremiah's words and the lies he had believed all his life.

To yield was dangerous beyond anything he had yet done in Rome or even in Pompeii. And yielding did not come easily for Cato. Yet the repeated visits in the generous home of Seneca and Europa, the teaching of Jeremiah and the other Christians, and more than anything the revolutionary community that bound them all together, became too much to dismiss.

This day, this ordinary moment in the garden atrium of the wealthy home, would change the future.

He knelt at Jeremiah's feet and prepared to die to himself.

The fledgling church that spread its message of love throughout the Roman Empire and its provinces was not without fault. From the letters of Paul he had learned of years of divisions, of heresies that threatened, of cowardice and corrupt behavior. And yet what he had witnessed here in Pompeii was radical. The breakdown of all barriers between slave and free, man and woman, even Jew and Roman. The great preacher Paul said that the sacrificial blood of the Messiah, the Christ, had destroyed the dividing walls of hostility, bringing near those who were once far and without hope.

And while Rome grew more threatened by and more dangerous to the new sect that undermined its rituals and pulled people from the temples and the gods, the Christians themselves became a shelter within chaos for the poor and broken, a community of belonging that had opened its arms to Portius Cato.

It was this community, this unnatural and wonderful belonging, that became the final proof that their message—and their Messiah— had the power to change lives, to heal brokenness. To save him from himself.

Jeremiah laid a hand on his bowed head. An anointing. He spoke softly. "All your life you have followed the customs of Rome in your worship, Quintus. You have made offerings to the gods and in return expected their favor. At best, a transactional religion. More often, empty ritual."

This was truth. It had been empty, all of it. All based on a presumption that he could obligate the gods into blessing him, based on his own actions.

"There *is* a transaction that the One God offers, however. You give Him your sin, your brokenness, your weakness. And in return He gives you righteousness, healing, strength. Freedom."

"You ask me to give what is broken? That which has no worth? Why would a god honor such a gift?"

"Ah, but you are wrong. All that you offer is wrapped up in the greatest thing that the Holy One desires. You."

He longed to believe it. No . . . he *did* believe it.

"The sacrifice He desires most is a broken and contrite heart. The gift He desires most is a relationship with His children." Jeremiah lifted Cato's head and smiled down on him. "Quintus, He is waiting to fill you with power as you have never known. To work through you, against evil, with a mighty and glorious strength. But you must first make that exchange. His righteousness for your transgression. Only through the Messiah, only through His sacrificial blood."

Cato let the truth flood through him. There was only One God, who offered salvation to Jew and Roman alike, slave and free, and with it, His love and His strength.

He sagged against the flagstones, felt the release of all the effort to be a good man, to be worthy. He was accepted by the only true God. Loved and accepted because of what that God had done for him, not because of what he had done for God.

The beginnings of a prayer came to his lips, awkward and unfamiliar, yet true. Jeremiah gripped his shoulder as he poured out his gratitude to the One who had been waiting for him and received the new life he had been promised.

When the words were spent, he lifted blurred eyes to Jeremiah. "What now?"

The old man's lips twitched. "Oh, this is only the beginning, young man." He patted Cato's cheek. "Only the beginning."

33

Ariella came back to life in the home of Quintus Portius Cato. Though she would not have admitted it to the man for anything.

In truth, it was primarily the two lovely women of the house whose presence and affection began to heal her shattered heart. The young Isabella mirrored her mother in compassion and humor, if not yet in sophistication. As the days passed, the façade of gladiator shed like a false skin, and Ariella's truer self emerged. Even her hair had taken on a more feminine appearance, short as it still was. The sadness, though, had burrowed deep, and this did not abate no matter how her body thrived.

She ignored Cato as much as possible, though their paths often crossed in the house. He always called her "Ari," as though he preferred to think of her as a boy. As though she were not woman enough. For this she did not fault him. She saw how his eyes followed the pretty girls who served and cleaned in his household. How he watched them move about, then dropped his eyes as though ashamed when he saw her. Her early fears of being used in the way all Roman men used their female slaves turned out to be unfounded.

He had others to pursue, it would appear.

And so she turned her attention to whatever tasks Octavia had for her and became a favorite of the matron of the estate. This morning Octavia tended one of the brothel women in a small room off the atrium. The girl had been beaten in the night by one of her patrons and had run to Octavia, whose reputation was well known through the city.

Ariella knelt at the girl's side where she lay on a low couch and blotted the dried blood from her swollen lip. The girl stared at the ceiling above her, as though oblivious to all.

Octavia paced behind her, directing Ariella's ministration, but clearly angry. "Every week one of them comes to me like this." She paused to huff out her frustration, hands on her hips. "I clean them up, give them a few *denarii*, names of friends with whom they could seek honorable work." She began her pacing again. "And yet where do they go?"

Ariella brushed the girl's hair away from her bruised eyes. Did she comprehend Octavia's words?

"Back to the brothel, that is where." Octavia knelt beside Ariella and gripped the girl's hand. "Why?"

Ariella glanced sideways at Octavia, awed by her compassion.

"Why can I not make a difference for them?"

She seemed to wait for an answer. Ariella inhaled and shook her head. "It is very hard to make a change. Sometimes the familiar, no matter how terrible, feels safer than the unknown."

Octavia's eyes were on Ariella then, peering into her secrets. But Ariella dropped her gaze.

"Mother?" Isabella's voice at the door brought Octavia to her feet immediately. She hurried to the door, blocking the girl's entrance.

"This is no place for you, daughter."

"I was looking for Ariella. I was hoping she would brush my hair. It always shines after she is finished."

Octavia turned to her and nodded once. "You may go." She took the rag from Ariella's hand. "I will see to the girl."

Ariella followed Isabella through the atrium.

Octavia's work with the brothel women often brought the girls to the house, and the lady had explained to Ariella that she was always careful about their interaction with the family. She did not desire their influence to taint Isabella. And Quintus—well, her Quintus needed to find himself a suitable wife, and did not need the distraction of the wrong type of woman.

Octavia's words stung, but Ariella could not deny their truth.

In Isabella's small bedchamber she took the bone comb from the girl's bedside table and sat her down at the large bronze mirror. Isabella loosened her hair from its gold ribbons and let it fall.

Like a waterfall of black silk. The image took Ariella back to the hills that surrounded Jerusalem, to the Mount of Olives, where once, during the rainy season, she had seen water cascading in a sheet from rocks above. The memory brought other images with it—smoke rising from the Temple beside the Mount of Olives. She pulled the comb through Isabella's hair and forced away the memory.

Isabella's eyes were focused on Ariella's reflection in the bronze. "Your hair will be wavy when it grows, will it not?"

She smiled. "Yes. I could never train it to behave the way yours does." Isabella shook her head, and Ariella laughed. "Hold still."

"Your hair will be beautiful, Ariella, I know it. I wish that mine were not so boring." She sighed and Ariella hid another smile.

"Was it very terrible when you had to cut it?" She started to turn her head, but Ariella directed her toward the mirror. "I would not want to join the gladiators if it meant cutting my hair. Tell me, Ariella, *why* did you become a gladiator?"

Ariella ran the comb through the length of her mistress's hair several times before answering, and when she did, it was with only half the truth. "My last master in Rome was not as kind as your—as your mother. Valerius was very rich and had a great many important visitors. Even your Nigidius Maius here in Pompeii had been in his house several times. But he treated me badly, and when I fought back, he decided he could fetch a good price for me as a fighter, so he sold me to the troupe." *End your questions there.*

But Isabella was too bright. She turned on Ariella and grasped her arm with all the curiosity of a younger sister. "But he knew you were a woman, of course. How did you end up disguised as a boy?"

And so the lies must multiply. "I—I did not stay long with that troupe. It did not work out. But to appear stronger I cut my hair and dressed as a man. When the lanista sold a group of us together, he did not mention my gender, and neither did I. Eventually, I was sold to another troupe where no one knew. It was easier to be a man among all those men."

Isabella giggled. "But living among all those men. The things you must have seen . . ." The girl blushed scarlet.

Ariella tried to smile, but the truth was not amusing, even now. "It was a dark time, Isabella. Do not think anything else."

The girl nodded, serious again.

But Ariella could see the notion still intrigued her. In this room of soft colors and even softer fabrics, Isabella could have no idea of the barracks life.

Later, when Ariella worked alone in the kitchen, chopping parsnips, the conversation came back to her, this time with the truth of those days with Valerius. Now that she found herself once again a household slave, could she not run again?

But even the thought of it wearied her. To whom would she run? Would it not be better to remain here, in a house of kindness, where she would be safe and healthy, even if she were not free? There were worse things, as Octavia's work with the women of the brothels had made clear.

And here, in this house, at least she would be near *him*.

She evened out the sections of parsnips with her fingertips, sliced through them quickly, and indulged in a few moments of rare honesty with herself.

Yes, she would rather grow old as a slave in this house, watch him take a wife and build a family, stand by as the house filled with the laughter of children who were not her own, than escape into a world that had only been cruel. He was pompous and arrogant and juvenile, and *Roman*—and still she did not want to be anywhere but in his house.

Ariella scooped the parsnips and tossed them into a bowl with a force that bounced some onto the table. She swiped at a foolish tear with the back of her hand and cleaned up the parsnips, and when she looked up from the bowl, he was in the doorway, watching her.

Her knife clattered to the table. "Do not do that!"

He smiled, that amused half smile he so often wore. "Walk about my own house?"

"Watch me in silence. It unnerves me."

Again the smile.

She wiped her hands on her tunic. "Was there something you wanted?"

He was silent for too long, his amusement fading a bit as he studied her. What serious thoughts ran through him at her question? "I am going back to the Christians again tonight. Do you want to join me?"

"Do you need my protection?" She couldn't resist.

He rewarded her with a full grin. "Perhaps."

She straightened the utensils on the table. "I will come."

Along the way to Europa's house, Cato was at first silent, then cleared his throat as though nervous to begin. "Isabella told me of your time before the gladiators. Was it Clovius Valerius who . . . owned you?"

Ariella cursed her transparency with the girl. "He is a wretched man."

"It is strange to me, to think that we were both in Rome at the same time and yet I did not know you. I wish—I wish I could have saved you from that unpleasantness."

Ariella's heart tripped a few beats, but she kept her eyes on her feet as they walked.

"Isabella says that Maius visited in Rome while you were there?"

The stones blurred under her feet. *Do not ask me to remember.* "Yes. They have debauchery in common, those two."

Cato slowed. "Greed I have seen in our duovir, and a certain ruthlessness. But never have I heard him accused of debauchery."

Ariella heard the eagerness in Cato's voice. Stemming, no doubt, from the possibility of finding something to ruin his opponent. Could she help him without betraying her own past? "Nigidius Maius joined Valerius for a celebration"—*Careful, Ariella*—"of the Dionysian mystery rites." She kept her eyes averted.

Cato halted beside her in the street, but Ariella kept walking, hoping he would resume.

"Maius is a Bacchanalian?"

The words were uttered quietly, but Ariella heard the astonishment. She stopped but did not turn. "Yes. Valerius is high priest of the cult. Maius is an initiate."

Cato caught up with her and clutched her arm. "I know very little about them. Tell me what you know."

But Ariella was done with speaking of it. She pulled from his grasp. "What would I know? I am a Jewish girl, not one of you Romans."

He walked alongside her. "Maius has kept his secret well here in Pompeii. Is Valerius also so secretive?"

"Rome is perhaps more tolerant of such things. Valerius believes that although the rites themselves are kept a mystery, the initiates should publicly revel in their own involvement. He often leads the processions himself."

"He must disapprove of his friend Maius's timidity?"

Ariella remembered that last night and shuddered. "I do not believe they are friends any longer. Maius incensed Valerius by killing his favorite slave."

Cato whistled through his teeth. "What vengeance did Valerius take?"

"I—I do not know. I was . . . sold shortly after."

Cato was quiet at last. No doubt he pondered how to best use her revelations.

They met no one intent on their harm along the way, and when Cyrus, the Persian slave, met them at the door, he seemed delighted to see Cato. Had her new master been here without her since their last visit? The slave left them in the atrium.

She listened for any sound of the group. "Will they all be here again this night?"

Cato nodded. "It is the first day of the week. This is their customary meeting day."

Ariella bit her lip and looked away. Cato had become so familiar with these people who worshipped HaShem, when she . . .

She was still so far from the Creator.

But when Jeremiah hobbled out of the triclinium, assisted by Flora, Ariella's heart once again softened.

"Quintus, Ariella." The old man extended his free hand. "It is good to have you here."

Cato greeted her old friend with a kiss, which astonished Ariella even more than the familiar praenomen with which Jeremiah had hailed him.

"We missed you yesterday, Quintus."

Cato glanced at her, then gripped Jeremiah's arm and led him toward the triclinium. "I am sorry, friend, that I could not make our usual time. Business to attend."

Ariella followed, marveling. Cato had become a student of Jeremiah's?

The group filled the dining room as usual, and Ariella smiled at those on couches and the floor.

Europa's daughter, Flora, hobbled over to another wealthy girl and joined her with an embrace of close friendship. Ariella had seen the girl here before, remembered her striking blue eyes.

Cato sat alongside her, and the teaching began, this time by Jeremiah.

They listened to a slave—and a Jew—teach them. Women were welcome. Though it felt like a synagogue, it was something very different. Indeed, from what she had seen, the way their women were treated was nothing short of revolutionary. From birth onward, females had a greater chance at life and happiness in this society. They forbid the practice of exposing unwanted infant girls to die outdoors, they condemned the termination of inconvenient pregnancies that often resulted in a woman's death. They frowned on infidelity and divorce, thereby keeping women safe from disgrace and poverty. They took care of new mothers, attended the needs of widows. After all the mistreatment of her life, this esteem for the female sex was nearly enough in itself to cave in Ariella's hard heart.

Jeremiah spoke again of the sinfulness of people's hearts, incapable of good, just as the prophets taught. He expounded on the sacrifice, the blood that makes atonement for sin.

But then his voice deepened as though he were a prophet himself, and he opened the Scriptures to her in a new way—prophecy after prophecy of the Messiah that had found fulfillment in the life of Yeshua. The words of Isaiah, of King David, of the prophet Jeremiah and so many others. Hundreds of prophecies, Jeremiah said.

He finished by reciting a long passage from Isaiah—one that predicted the Messiah, and so clearly described the suffering of the one Jeremiah claimed came from God to destroy sin, to break down the barriers between man and his Creator . . .

"'He was wounded because of our transgressions, He was crushed because of our iniquities. The chastisement of our welfare was upon Him, and we were healed by His stripes. Like sheep, we went astray, we turned to our own ways, and HaShem laid all our iniquities on Him . . . He bore our sins, and made intercession for the transgressors.'"

Ariella listened as though spellbound, but could not accept. Though Jeremiah had nearly convinced her that this Yeshua was the Messiah, still the knowledge of it collided with her anger at the suffering HaShem allowed. And she felt nothing but fury.

Before the meeting had ended, Jeremiah lifted prayers to the Creator and gave a special blessing over her and over Cato. "Champion of the weak," Jeremiah called him.

Her hands trembled when he spoke the words.

Later they walked home slowly, both lost in their own thoughts.

Cato broke the silence. "These people, Ari. They have found a way to live."

She said nothing and kept her eyes on the stones under her feet.

"I must introduce Europa to my mother. Don't you think? The

way that they love, and the teachings of this Jesus—it's like nothing I've ever seen. 'Love your enemies,' Jeremiah says. And it's all possible because the sacrifice has been paid for all. Jeremiah says that when Jesus had suffered and been raised, He sat down at the right hand of the One God. What priest has ever sat down, Ari? Finished with his work?"

She held up a hand. "Enough. They are dangerous. I want to hear nothing more."

They walked in silence again for some minutes.

"You said that Valerius wants his initiates to be more vocal about their involvement in the Dionysian rites?"

She grimaced. Had his thoughts turned so easily from one sect to another? "He believes that it is the way to become filled with the gods. True followers should not be ashamed."

"And he was angry with Maius over the death of a slave."

Ariella did not answer. She could not read his thoughts. When he spoke, the words left her chilled.

"I believe it is time to invite Valerius to our holiday town. Surely he would like to see the way in which Nigidius Maius shows his loyalty to their sect."

Ariella's blood seemed to rush to her feet, and she swayed for a moment.

Cato took no notice and continued down the darkened street.

She swallowed with effort. Her mouth and throat had gone dry. "Please do not do that."

He turned at the anguish in her voice, and his eyes were sympathetic. "Isabella told me that Valerius was a harsh master. I promise, Ari, you will not need to see him. You can remain in the back of the house during his visit, and I will make no mention of you. But I must do this. The people of Pompeii need to know of Maius's secret activities, and I need more than the word of a slave to present it to them.

If Valerius still holds a grudge over the murder, a firsthand look at Maius's hypocrisy might cause him to back me publicly and expose Maius."

She shook her head, unable to speak through the dread.

Cato stepped close and gripped her fingers at her side. "I am sorry, Ari. But Portia grows weaker by the day, and I must do all I can to get her out of his clutches."

Ariella had never met Portia. But Octavia and Isabella had already tunneled deep into her heart, as though they were her own family. She could not ask Cato to give up a chance to save his sister. She shuffled forward, nodding.

For he was right. She was only a slave. She should be grateful for his offer to stay hidden from Valerius. And if that failed . . .

She had run from Valerius once, but that was before she had learned what it meant to fight.

The next time, she would kill him.

Vesuvius would not unleash its fury without a warning.

There were stirrings within, rumblings without.

Tremors. Felt at first by no one but the deer on the slopes. Bits of steam and rock, spit out upon the craggy summit. Poisonous gases escaped from vents, killing unsuspecting birds and rabbits.

It was coming.

The plates that had merely jostled now rammed their bony shoulders, each one driving against the other, neither giving way, both determined to be the victor.

The fantastic pressure under the plates built to unequaled heights as they battled upward in their conflict.

It could not last, this tremendous, magnificent pressure.

The mountain owed them no warning. But one would come, nonetheless.

34

Cato measured the length of the *parados*, the offstage corridor of the theater, with heavy steps, then turned and strode to the other end.

"Stop pacing, Cato. You are making *me* nervous." Taurus leaned one shoulder against the stone wall near the stage entrance, watching the crowd fill the seats. With his patrician nose and condescending brow, he was the picture of easy calm. Cato's most vocal backer felt none of his own anxiety.

"How many?" He should not be seen peering out at the citizens, but could see only the orchestra circle and the scaenae frons, the false front behind it.

"A good number. The controversy is bringing them out, as we hoped."

Cato resumed his walking through the musty stone corridor. In the days since Ariella had revealed Maius's hidden proclivities, Cato had kept the knowledge to himself, determined to disclose the information to the town only when Valerius had arrived to confirm the truth and accuse him of murder. The Roman senator was already on his way, invited to a short holiday in the home of former quaestor Portius Cato, to discuss a matter of mutual interest.

But today . . . today was about rhetoric and passion. The opportunity to address the citizens of Pompeii, followed by an address from his opponent, was the chance to confront Maius with other truths, equally damning.

"But will they listen? Will they hear me?"

Taurus pushed away from the wall and caught Cato's arm. His small eyes bored into Cato. "Everyone in this town knows what Maius is, Cato. They know he owns them, either because their pay flows from his coffers or because their money flows into his for protection or blackmail. You do not need to convince them of this. But change depends on your ability to stir them up to action. They must be willing to rise up, to band together, to put an end to the man."

"I am making speeches in the Forum almost daily, Taurus. My supporters are spreading the word that Maius fears my integrity and has made my family his target. I have made the rounds to guild leaders and entertained town leaders in my home. What will one more speech accomplish?"

Taurus looked out again at the growing crowd. "Never underestimate the power of the collective, Cato. Lesser men than you have been propelled into the very realm of the *divine* on a wave of public support. One that began with nothing more than a throng such as this, whipped into a frenzy over what could be."

The growing buzz of the crowd erupted in a cheer. Some entertainment had been brought to loosen them up, to bring them to their seats. Cato braced a hand against the wall. Somewhere out there, Maius waited for his chance to speak, but as the incumbent he would be given the last word.

Cato's newfound faith, his time under the teaching of the

rabbi-slave Jeremiah, had begun to open his eyes to the spiritual war taking place unseen in Pompeii. Jeremiah had spoken over him like a prophet, charging him with fighting evil, showing him where true power resided. His faith in the Messiah did not save him from the fight—it gave him the strength to win the war. And in this war of evil, Nigidius Maius was a chief participant.

It was time.

Taurus gave him a nudge, and he strode onto the stage with a forced confidence. A smattering of applause filtered down from the seats. The eyes of thousands were on him. That protective surge he had experienced when he first took the platform in the Forum swept him again, an emotion that thickened his throat and blurred the sea of white togas into the white marble of the theater. How could all of that gleaming white hide so much corruption? He bent his head to the orchestra floor, cleared his thoughts, then raised both his head and his voice.

"Citizens of Pompeii! It is time for change!"

In preparing for this speech, one truth had hounded Cato. There was only one way to defeat a tyrant, a man who ruled by intimidation. Someone had to stand up. Someone had to show him as weak. If this could be accomplished, then it remained only to rally the people together and convince them that together they were strong enough to rid themselves of their oppressor. Once he would have run when faced with a stronger opponent. No longer. The Spirit of the Living God was his ally.

And so he spoke to them, from his heart and from his passion, and as his voice warmed to the truth, it rose above the people and seemed to carry above the theater wall to the very sky. He spoke of justice and of integrity with a raised fist, and was rewarded with courageous applause and cheers from the people.

He turned on Maius, where he sat in his customary raised box, and unleashed his righteous fury. "Pompeii has long suffered under the greed and malice of one man, and I tell you the truth, citizens, that man is a coward! Gnaeus Nigidius Maius, you have burned my vineyard, you have falsely imprisoned my sister, you have even tried to have me killed." He spread an arm to the people. "I ask you, citizens, are these not the actions of a man who works in fear? A man who knows that if someone takes his position, he will be forced to answer for his many crimes?

"I say it is time to make him answer for them. It is time for a change." He paused, drawing out the moment, and the theater was held suspended in the hush. "It is time, my friends, to shake the very foundations of Pompeii!"

At these words, as though God Himself concurred, there came a thunderous crack from earth and sky at once, like the snap of a giant whip over the back of a monstrous, unruly horse.

In the beat of silence that followed, the face of every spectator seemed anchored to his own.

And then a heaving began, a bucking of the massive horse—only it was the earth itself that sought to throw them each from their place.

An earthquake!

Cato held his ground, his stance wide on the stage floor. The people were not so fearless. The mass of them rose as one, shrieking and turning on each other in their panic to leave the theater.

Cato scanned the crowd, frantic to find his mother and sister, who were to sit with Lucius. Why had he not sought them out before he began?

It was impossible now. He turned to where Taurus had been waiting in the parados. The man was gone. In the seats, the people tripped and shoved and streamed up to the outer staircases and down to the lower exits.

The swaying of the ground ceased a few moments later, but the townspeople knew better than to remain inside the theater's stone ring. Cato looked over his shoulder, eyeing the unstable scaenae frons that soared two stories at his back.

With the quake over, he needed to find his family.

What about Portia?

The theater was nearly empty already, and no doubt Isabella and his mother were safe. But Portia, in her underground prison? A wave of nausea overtook him, and he leaped from the orchestra to the pit of seats and shoved through the remaining stragglers to the exit.

The city was still in turmoil, like a pot boiling over. People dashed through the streets, some fleeing to their own houses to assess the damage, and others, fearful of a second quake, sought open spaces. Cato hesitated outside the theater, thinking of his mother and younger sister—as well as others he cared about—still in his home.

After Portia.

He pushed through the crowds that flowed against him. Few headed for the Forum and the magisterial buildings, as all the homes and fields outside the city lay opposite and only the sea awaited on the other side of the Forum. People ran with hands outstretched, as though the earth still rocked and they sought balance. Arms and hands poked at him and knocked him to and fro as he crossed the city. He cared little for the damage, but was aware enough to see that this quake had not toppled much of the city, as the one seventeen years ago had.

The guard placed inside Portia's prison stood at its entrance, no doubt unwilling to be trapped underground, but leaving the prisoners to their own fate.

Cato pushed past him, ignoring his shout. The steps held, and there appeared to be no cave-in.

"Portia?" He called her name before he had even reached the cell floor. "Portia, answer me!"

He skidded to her cell, its tiny square opening the only window. A tiny whimper responded. He pressed his face to the hole. "Sister, are you hurt?"

It was too dark to see within. He heard a scraping, as if she dragged herself across the floor, and then her hand was at the opening, the fingers white and thin as a specter. He wrapped his own warm fingers around her icy ones and kissed them.

"What has happened?" Her voice was raspy, as though her lungs had taken on the thick prison air.

"An earthquake. You are unhurt?"

"I am fine."

Cato cringed at the word, knowing it to be far from truth.

"Lucius? Mother and Isabella?"

"We were all in the theater when it happened. I lost track of them, but the walls held and everyone got out. I am certain they escaped. I came to check on you."

She put her forehead to his hand, as she had the last time he visited.

"You are still . . . healthy, Portia?" He lacked the words to speak of womanly things, but his mother and sister would press him for details.

She nodded. "The baby moves within me now, Quintus." Her voice took on awe. "It is the only thing that keeps me from going mad down here."

The guard must have regained his courage in the lack of aftershocks, for Cato heard him lumbering down the steps.

"You there, you're not supposed to be here!" He brandished a short sword, though he looked slow enough for Cato to take it from him.

Cato held up a hand and nodded. "I am leaving." He squeezed his sister's fingers and whispered to her, "It will not be long, I promise you."

And then he pushed past the guard, up the steps, and back into the vacant Forum area, still sun-drenched and warm as though nothing had shaken it.

Portia was safe, but what of those at home? He broke into a run once more, taking narrow alleys and side streets to avoid the crowds.

His house still stood in the center of the block, though a few terra-cotta tiles from the roof had slid to the street and shattered. He stepped over the shards and through the doorway, calling out to his family before he crossed the threshold.

His mother's face appeared at the far end of the courtyard. "Quintus! Where have you been?"

At her shout, Isabella rushed out of the back corridor.

The three met in the midst of the courtyard shrubbery. "I have been to check on Portia."

His mother gripped his hands, wordless.

"She is well." He closed his eyes. "As well as she could be."

"The baby?"

Cato smiled on his mother and Isabella. "She tells me that the baby's kicking keeps her company in that foul place."

Octavia put delicate fingers to her mouth and turned away as though ashamed of her emotion.

"She asked for Lucius, of course."

Isabella nodded. "I sent him to his home to check on his belongings and servants. He is unhurt."

Cato surveyed the interior of the house. "And the Catonii? Did we fare so well?"

Octavia was once again the brisk household manager. "A few broken pots. A crack in the south wall of the triclinium. Nothing more."

Cato's eyes strayed to the servants' corridor that led to the kitchen. "No one hurt?"

Octavia didn't answer. He brought his attention back to her, and was surprised to see annoyance there.

Her brow furrowed. "Perhaps there are slaves you'd like to check on personally?"

He inhaled and looked away. Despite her disapproval, he intended to do just that.

He found Ariella bent over a large basin, washing pottery. At his entrance, she jumped to her feet, circled the basin, and rushed to him, her eyes wide. "Were you hurt?"

Her swift approach and obvious concern left him a bit breathless. He shook his head, wrapped his hands around her arms, and pulled her close. "You?"

"I was outdoors, at the fountain. I am well."

They remained there for a moment, and he allowed himself the indulgence, but soon released her and stepped away. She was a Jewess. And she was a slave.

"There is no Jew nor Greek. No slave nor free. We are one in Christ Jesus." Paul's words, spoken by Jeremiah, but still too hard to accept. Still . . .

How much longer could he keep Ariella physically close but distanced from his heart?

His mother was right to be concerned.

35

Maius returned from the theater, still fuming. The towns-people had reacted as though the world were coming to an end, when in truth the earthquake had been minor. Maius would not care, except for the stolen opportunity for a rebuttal to Cato's speech, and the way in which the earthquake had seemed to fortify the would-be duovir's message.

He strolled through his house, inspecting walls and sculptures for damage, and found only a few minor pieces broken in the front halls and no structural harm. The city had withstood far worse years ago.

When he reached the sunlit gardens, Nigidia looked to him from her place on a bench. He had expected frightened tears, but she only smiled, a sad smile he could not understand, that did not reach to her lovely blue eyes. She seemed to be pulling away from him of late.

"I am glad you are unhurt," she said simply.

He left her there in the gardens, unwilling to draw her out this afternoon. His thoughts were all for Portius Cato.

The man refused to quit, refused to die, refused to be silenced. This was unacceptable. But he could not kill him now, with the city watching.

He crossed to the cages that held his birds, needing to be greeted by those who never questioned his authority. But the birds were strangely silent. The red warbler, always vocal when Maius approached, hopped in circles behind its wooden bars, but did not sing. The silent garden, though bright and green, had an eerie feeling about it, as though even the flowers and birds feared the shaking of the earth.

"What is wrong, my pretty?" Maius reached a finger through the slats. The warbler responded with a sharp peck to his finger.

"Aahh!" He yanked his hand backward. The stupid bird had drawn blood. He put the finger to his mouth and turned from the birds, his unease building.

Perhaps some time in the baths would relax his tense muscles. Maius was not forced to attend the public baths, as his home on the outskirts of town had been built to receive public water and supply its own luxurious and private accommodations.

He summoned a female slave and ordered the baths prepared.

"Master." She bowed at the waist, her unbound hair hanging about her head. "There is no water."

He growled and pushed past her. "What foolishness is this?"

She hurried along behind him. "The water comes only in a trickle since the quake."

Indeed, when he reached the baths, the basin that normally bubbled with fresh water was stagnant. Some piping must have been damaged. Maius cursed the earth, but then thought better of his anger. It was a time for appeasing, not for cursing, and he should have gone to the gods first.

His spirit disturbed, he sought comfort and reassurance in his special room, the triclinium used only for the feasts that honored Bacchus. Bordered by a narrow colonnaded porch on its western end, the room received only the late-day sun, and still lay in dim shadow this afternoon. Maius reclined on one of the long couches, waited for the slave to attend with food and wine, and surveyed the delightful frescoes he had commissioned for the room.

The series of paintings told a story, one that had been enacted thousands of times by celebrants of the cult, and would be again here in this very house, at the time of the next initiation. Maius's eyes wandered over the face of the young initiate in the paintings, her expression moving from compliant to terrified, and then finally to wiser, experienced, even resigned. Nigidia should not feel the terror that the frescoed girl displayed. But if so, it would be over soon enough, and she would understand at the end.

Hours later, after he had sought the will of the gods and appeased them with incense, Maius took reports from Primus on the terrace that overlooked the mountain. He reclined in ease with a cup of warmed wine on the iron table beside him, but his mood had grown darker as the sun descended, and the mountain view that afforded such pleasure left him cold. This must be the lowest point of his political career. Never before had someone challenged his position with any chance of success.

A new visitor appeared out of the shadow, interrupting Primus's tedious accounting.

"Sulla." Maius extended a hand from his position on his chaise, but did not rise. "This is an honor." In truth, he hadn't seen the man in months and didn't care much for him.

Sulla curled a lip. Maius's posture must have contradicted his words. "What are you going to do about all of this, Maius?"

Maius folded his hands over his ample belly. "All of this?"

"Portius Cato! He turned you into a fool today."

At this, Maius did stand and stepped to Sulla until the man could feel his hot breath. "Be careful, Sulla. I have not been beaten yet."

But the man displayed the same lack of intimidation that Otho, the fuller, had days earlier. He barely blinked. "And you should remember which way the winds are blowing."

"So what do the winds tell you today?"

"People are saying that he is bringing someone from Rome. To endorse his candidacy, perhaps?"

Maius waved a hand and again reclined. "He is too young to have powerful allies. It is no one of concern, I am sure."

"Clovius Valerius."

Maius felt himself blanch at the name and inwardly cursed the reaction. "Is that so?"

"You know him?"

"Certainly, we are acquainted. I have been in his company when in Rome."

Sulla folded his arms. "And he would set himself up against you here? Support Cato?"

Maius sipped at his wine, forcing his hand to hold steady. "Quite the opposite. I've no idea what Cato hopes to accomplish through Valerius. He and I are on quite friendly terms."

Sulla watched him through narrowed eyes.

"I thank you for your report, Sulla. Now if you will excuse me, I have business to attend to." He motioned to Primus, who came forward to sit cross-legged at Maius's feet once more, books and reed in hand like an Egyptian scribe.

Sulla bowed and backed away. "As you wish." Unconvinced, Maius could see.

Only the election would convince them now.

And yet it was just this thought that worried him most. Cato's support increased daily, and his speech in the theater today had been too persuasive, too full of the rhetoric that swayed common people and convinced them to vote for the candidate whose personality pleased them most.

And now . . . Valerius.

The name brought with it visions of smoky rooms and poppy-laced wine and long hours of revelry that lifted the participant to a higher plane, infused him with the life of the gods themselves, and left him unable to remember most of the acts he had committed while in the thrall of wine and drug.

Valerius, high priest of the Roman Dionysian cult, who was outspoken in his desire to see all his initiates proclaim their appetites publicly. He believed such assertions would lift the official sanctions and alleviate society's disapproval of their practices. All this Maius could suppress, if it weren't for that cursed slave boy's blood on his hands.

What possible reason could Portius Cato have in bringing Valerius to Pompeii? Whatever it was, it did not bode well for Maius. The town was much more conservative than the mother city, much less tolerant of behavior considered aberrant in their prudish opinions.

The feast was only a few days away. He had promised the gods that the reenactment would take place at the first new moon after the Feast of Vulcan, though Nigidia still knew nothing of it. Valerius would no doubt want to join the celebration. Did he dare invite him?

His mind had wandered far from Primus's reports, but the slave's monotonous voice called him back to the terrace when he heard his enemy's name. "What about Cato?"

Primus sighed, seeming perturbed at his master's lack of attention. "I was saying that it is strange Cato would seek association with a man such as Valerius when he also has become so involved with the Christian sect."

Maius straightened at once and swung his legs over the side of the chaise. "Cato has become one of the Christians?"

Primus shrugged. "He has been taking some kind of training in their rites. This is all I know."

Maius grinned and clapped Primus on the shoulder. "Why did you not tell me this sooner?"

The Greek slave sighed again and said nothing.

Maius rubbed at his chin, stubbly with late-day growth. And what a day it had been. Cato's damaging speech, the earthquake, then news of Valerius's visit. And now this latest bit of gossip about Cato associating with the Christians.

The entire day had bucked and heaved like the earth itself. But in the end, when the dust settled . . .

It was Maius who was left standing.

36

The days evaporated like morning dew on the stones of the Pompeii streets. *Vulcanalia*, the festival dedicated to Vulcan, god of fire, crept closer and then at last arrived.

The day began early for most of the city, with work starting by the light of the candle. The traditional propitiation of the god by the beneficial use of fire was only the start of the festivities that would last throughout the late-summer day. With any good fortune, Vulcan would be appeased, and the summer heat that dried out crops and granaries would not result in devastating fires this year. Vulcan also gave his name to the mountains that occasionally rained down fire, though no one in Pompeii had ever seen such a thing.

It was on this feast day that Cato expected Valerius's ship to arrive from Rome with his retinue. Cato had several slaves positioned at the city gates to run a message to him when the senator was sighted, and the rest of the household busied themselves with preparing for the feast later in the day.

For Cato, the day was one of conflicted emotion. His newfound and unquenchable thirst for the teachings of Jeremiah left him cold over the thought of honoring Vulcan in his home. And Valerius's impending visit had driven Ariella deep into the house—and into herself—where he was unable to draw her out.

He spent the morning in the wine shop, hoping for distraction and finding it in the surly comments of Remus, who was still convinced that both the vines and the business would fail. Cato remembered his early dedication to both as though it were distant past now, so focused was he on the coming election and Portia's fate.

The wine shop had taken on a cheerier appearance since those early days, due to Remus's efforts to clean up and whitewash the walls. The amphorae that lined the shelves were empty, awaiting the start of the harvest in a few short days. Cato counted the amphorae, reciting the sizes and number to Remus, who scratched out marks on a wax tablet.

"Master, he comes!" The slave, Italicus, stood outlined in the doorway, his breath labored.

Cato rubbed at his forehead. "Valerius? So soon?"

"He is at the Marina Gate."

Cato grabbed his toga, thrown over the counter, and glanced at Remus. "I will leave you to it, then, man."

Remus shrugged as though Cato were a madman bent on destruction and he could do nothing to stop it. "Blessings of Vulcan on you, then, I suppose."

Back at the house, Octavia had received the news and emerged to meet him in the atrium, wearing her finest white robes and with her hair piled elaborately atop her head. Cato raised his eyebrows at the effort, but she narrowed her eyes and he would not comment.

She eyed the door. "We have had replies from all the invited guests. Everyone has accepted. We shall have a full house."

"And all is ready?"

"Quintus, do you think it will work? Will he reveal Maius to the town? Make them see what kind of man has jailed your sister?"

Cato scratched the back of his neck, damp already. "I do not know."

And what kind of man would Valerius be? Was the reputation of the Bacchanalians perhaps exaggerated?

A cart rolled to a stop in the street, and the time for answers had come. Cato squared off to receive the man he had convinced to make the two-day voyage from Rome, and Octavia stepped to his side and stood tall and erect.

Three slaves lumbered in first, burdened with trunks. And then Valerius appeared in the doorway, slightly built and surprisingly short. He was young enough to stand alone, yet leaned on the arm of a younger man, dressed as a slave. He seemed at first to be infirm, but as the senator moved into the atrium, it became clear that his grasp on the slave was one of affection, not need. The slave did not appear to share the sentiment.

Valerius's eyes swept the atrium. He smiled at the dancing faun at the edge of the impluvium, passed over Octavia without much attention, and stopped instead at Cato, whom he looked up and down. He pursed his lips, then smirked. "I had heard you were fine-looking, but you are even better than that."

Cato heard his mother exhale and he put a hand to her back. "We hope to surpass *all* your expectations, Clovius Valerius. Welcome to Pompeii, and to my home." He turned to Octavia. "My mother, Octavia of the Catonii."

Valerius sauntered forward, unaided, and grasped Cato's arm in a weak greeting. He had girlish features and unnaturally red lips, and Cato forced himself to return the grip rather than shrink back.

"Such a long trip we have had." Valerius used the corner of his toga to dab at his throat. "Where can I rest?"

Cato motioned to a nearby slave who hurried forward. "Italicus will take you to a room."

Valerius sighed and surveyed the interior of the house. "It is a crime to be away from my villa on a feast day and caged out here in the country. You *are* planning a celebration this evening, I assume?"

Cato bowed. "Pompeii's leading citizens will be here to greet and celebrate with you."

Valerius waved a delicate hand. "I care nothing about the company of rich men." He stepped closer to Cato and lowered his voice, as if it would keep Octavia from overhearing. She looked away and Valerius wrapped his fingers around Cato's forearm. "There are better ways to celebrate than the pompous discourse of fools. You will have women? Boys, perhaps?" His grin became lecherous. "A little opium mixed with the wine, to honor the god?"

Cato fought to hold his ground. He could feel the man's breath on his cheek. "I hope to make it an enjoyable evening for you."

His noncommittal reply did not seem to please the senator. Valerius stepped back and a furrow formed between his eyebrows. "You have brought me here to seek something from me, Portius Cato. Understand that I reward those who favor me." His expression cleared and he clapped his hands together twice. "I know how you can please me. I hear you have a gladiator here!"

Cato's stomach turned over. "How—"

Valerius waved a hand again. "I have ears everywhere. Tell me, is it true? Have you bought a boy from the gladiator school?"

Octavia joined the conversation again. "Why should that interest you?"

"Ah, dear lady, it interests me very much." He turned on Cato. "I want to see a fight."

"There are no games scheduled—"

"Not in the arena, silly man. Here. In your home. Tonight."

Cato felt his mouth drop open.

"Don't look at me as though I am mad. Bring one of your slaves in and pit the two against each other for me. Come, don't tell me it's too much trouble after I've come all this way?"

Valerius turned to the slave to lead him to his chamber, as though the matter were decided. Cato watched him cross the courtyard and flounce down the colonnade.

"Vile man." Octavia's voice was low. She used the same words to describe Nigidius Maius on their first meeting, and, indeed, the two men were much alike in attitude, if not appearance. "What will you do, Quintus?"

Cato turned away in silence. There was another to whom he needed to speak.

"Never. You cannot ask me to do this."

At Ariella's vehement response, Cato rubbed at his throbbing temples. "I would not, if I did not believe it necessary."

Her eyes were wide, accusing. "Necessary to humiliate me?"

He held out his palms. "Ari, the man demands entertainment, and I fear he will not help me expose Maius if I don't please him. He would have me bring in the worst sort of debauchery, but you could wear your helmet and he would never recognize you."

He stepped toward her, but she moved away until her back was against the wall, her hands flat against the stone at her sides. "Nothing has changed, then. You still force me to fight, for the sake of your own popularity!" Her voice pitched higher. "Why did you not leave me in the barracks where you found me?"

"It is not the same! It is *one* fight, not even a real fight—only an exhibition. You will be masked and there will be no danger." He crossed the room to stand before her. "And I do not ask you for my own sake, but for my sister's."

"Yes, your *sister*." She nearly spat the mocking words in his face. "Everything is for your sister. You bring my enemy to the door, then force me to perform for him. All for Portia."

"Yes, for Portia!"

"For yourself, Portius Cato! You would win this election at any cost because if you fail you cannot still consider yourself a man."

Cato unconsciously formed a fist and pounded the wall beside her head. Ariella winced and turned from him.

"What? Do you think I would strike you?"

She leveled dark eyes at him. "You have already proven you will do anything to get your way."

Cato whirled from her. She was unreasonable. She would wear a mask, and with the fight staged to make her the winner . . . there was no reason for her to refuse. And she clearly had forgotten that she was a slave to be commanded, not entreated. "Be ready after the first course is served. I will have Italicus fetch equipment from the barracks for both you and Ruso, and you can work out the staging with him."

She said nothing, and he left her to think through her irrational obstinacy.

Hours later the triclinium had been laid with enough delicacies of food and comforts of appointment to render it the slave quarters' antithesis. As Cato surveyed the work of his slaves, he felt the first twinge of uncertainty over his request of Ariella.

But the sun had set, and guests were arriving. Cato greeted each at the doorway of the triclinium and seated them around the U-shaped table arrangement according to their status, as was customary. They wasted no time in setting to the wine and breads and speaking in low tones of money and property and politics.

Valerius appeared some time later with several of his slaves, including the young man for whom he appeared to have a special fondness. The senator took the middle couch.

Cato welcomed them all and summoned the slaves to bring the first course of oysters and wild poultry. Hired musicians began to play stringed lyres in the corner, and the wine was kept flowing. His younger sister's face appeared at the room's entrance and he shooed her away, to Isabella's great annoyance.

Cato had planned this dinner party for days, but now found himself unable to concentrate. He reclined next to Valerius, but the man's grating, high-pitched laugh and vulgar conversation forced his thoughts elsewhere. Ariella would appear soon. She feared interaction with Valerius. Why? Should he have asked?

He tried to taste the oysters with their spicy *garum* sauce. Had it gone rancid? No one else seemed bothered. But even the smell sickened him.

He was beginning to think he had made a mistake when a figure darkened the doorway. Ruso, the slave Cato had assigned as Ariella's opponent. He wore the simple armor of a Gaul and stood silent, his eyes on Cato.

"Ah, here we are!" Valerius sat up at once. "Something to save us from the tedium of this party." He patted his fingertips together. "Is this the fighter you have purchased for yourself, Cato? He looks a bit weak in the chest, if you ask me."

"This is Ruso." Cato half rose on his couch, his stomach churning. "He will fight my gladiator, Scorpion Fish."

At that, Ariella stepped to Ruso's side, and the room applauded.

Cato's choice of entertainment had won them over, but the victory felt hollow and his mouth had gone dry.

Ariella wore her helmet with the fish insignia. He could see only her eyes, and they were trained on him and him alone, as though even to look at Valerius would invite recognition.

Do not look at me thus, Ariella.

"Come." Valerius pushed himself to standing. "It will not do to see a battle here. To the atrium!"

The rest of the guests followed suit, as though Valerius were their host. It was just as well, for Cato had lost the use of his tongue.

He was the last out of the triclinium and reached the atrium with his heart pounding and his palms slick with regret. It was a mistake. Her eyes told him that and more. He crossed the paving stones to where she stood opposite Ruso.

"You do not have to do this." He kept his voice low, for her alone. "I was wrong—"

She jerked her trident up between them, and Cato had to pull backward to avoid injury.

The dinner guests hooted in amusement. One of them shouted, "Careful, Cato. You'll be the first casualty!"

"No, he is a seasoned fighter," another called. "Remember the arena?"

More laughter, but Cato's eyes were still on hers. Pleading.

But Ariella had made up her mind. Her eyes were like two dark bits of stone shining through the slatted helmet, cold and hard as Bellona, goddess of war. Ari lowered the trident until its three prongs rested at the base of his throat.

Again he heard the catcalls of his guests. Cato took two steps backward and was pulled to their circle, leaving the open space for the two fighters.

Ariella faced her opponent, legs slightly bent in that familiar stance he had first seen in the training yard so many weeks ago.

And then she rushed him, trident upraised. With the first clash of iron on iron, Cato's hand went to his forehead, eyes covered.

He had brought this shame on her—and now he could not bear to watch.

37

Balance the weight. Slightly forward. Back and forth.

The training flowed back into Ariella's arms and legs as though she had left the barracks only moments ago.

Eyes on Ruso. Always watch the eyes.

She and Ruso had not had much time to drill together. Had her rushed lesson on exhibition been enough to keep the slave from stupidity?

Cato stood apart. His hand shielded his gray eyes, as though he could not watch.

She forced her attention to the fight. Only the fight. To think of her audience was to invite danger. She would not even look on her enemy's face.

Ariella thrust forward to her opponent's pullback and noted his pale face.

Follow me, Ruso. Focus.

She flutter-stepped back and forth, circled the young man, swung her sword arm. Her weapon clanged onto his and the sound echoed off the stone walls and pillars. The green of the courtyard's shrubbery blurred with the white togas of her audience, their purple- and red-edged robes like strange flowers among the garden.

At the first strike, the party guests sent up a raucous cheer, like young boys watching a street brawl.

She would not look at Valerius. The thought of him there in the circle, his pretty face and vicious temper focused on her, made her sick. Snatches of memory fought for her attention, images and horrors from their time together.

She drove forward, propelled by angry memories, backing Ruso toward the guests. Then parried and circled, her feet sliding and scraping the stone pavement in a familiar rhythm.

The trident and net brought back some sense of invincibility. She welcomed the feeling. Behind her helmet, she was unknown and unknowable.

He had promised.

In the blur of garden and guest, somehow Cato's face alone remained distinct. She saw his agonized look. An illogical pity flamed in her chest. *Do not fear for me. I am invincible.*

They had only to give a good show, a believable display, with no harm on either side. But such a feat was more difficult than it looked.

Ruso's steps faltered. He tripped and fell toward Ariella's trident. She yanked the weapon away, but not before it had pierced the leather across his chest.

The men around her once again let out a yelp, and Ruso's eyes widened.

Ariella saw the panic there and backed away to give him space. But it was too late. He had lost the confidence of the display, and she could read the fear. He believed the fight had become real.

Ruso came at her in a rush, their choreographed movements forgotten and the fire of self-preservation in his eyes.

Even in the fury of battle, Ariella's sense of Cato's every expression did not waver. He stood now with hands on his hips, as though angry at the entire proceeding, and a deep channel furrowed between his brows. She could smooth out that furrow if she could end this farce.

A flash of yellow behind a thick column revealed Isabella watching. Ariella swished her net toward Ruso's feet, ashamed that the girl should see her once again degraded.

The guests had gone silent with anticipation, and only the scrape of sandal sounded in the atrium.

And then she heard the laugh. That shrill, discordant laugh that she reviled.

Though she knew it to be a mistake, she looked toward the sound, as one who looks at a dead animal on the roadside or at a public execution. She could not help herself.

Her eyes swept Valerius's fine-boned features, saw that he had not changed at all, then pushed past him. To the young man at his side. A slave.

At the slave's features, a heat like lightning blazed through her body and seemed to spark from her fingertips. Her feet stilled, then her arms. Silence swallowed the atrium, and her mind, and her heart.

Micah.

Her brother.

Ruso's panic swept him across the stones toward her.

A moment later she hit the pavement on her back. Her helmet smacked the stones and air whooshed from her chest. The stars shone down through the roof opening above, cold and harsh.

Ruso's sword point was at her throat. She heard the cheers and waited for death.

Another yell. Cato's voice. Then Cato's feet and legs were at her head. He shoved Ruso backward.

Valerius crowed. "An ignoble end for your gladiator, Portius Cato! Beaten by an untrained slave!"

She felt the odious man patter toward her where she lay.

"At least we must see his humiliation!"

Before she knew what he was about, Valerius reached down and yanked the helmet from her head.

Cato was there, stepping between them, full toga shielding her. But it was not to be. He could not protect her from the circle that closed upon them, from the toes that prodded her to stand.

And in truth, she wanted to stand. Wanted to stand and turn and look upon the face that she had longed to see for nine torturous years, never knowing if he were dead or alive, fearing the worst and not daring to pray for hope.

It was Micah alone that she saw when she stood and lifted her eyes. His lips parted in sudden recognition. She felt the tears spring to her eyes, and then they were in each other's arms, the embrace of two who had believed they were forever parted.

"How?" Micah's voice was a whisper in her ear.

"I did not know where to find you—" Oh, for a hundred years to sit and talk with him.

But the voice she hated trilled from behind them.

"Well, this is most surprising." Valerius circled the two of them like a beast admiring its prey. "The gladiator is not only a woman, but she is a woman who belongs to me!"

Cato stepped between them, facing Valerius. "Not any longer. She is my slave now, purchased from the gladiators you sold her to."

The guests had gone silent, like an audience before an impromptu theater performance.

Valerius laughed, the sound high and juvenile. "Is that what she told you?" He patted Ariella's cheek.

She jerked away from his touch. Her brother circled her waist with an arm.

But Valerius was not put off. He leaned in close. "Lovely as always, despite the hair." He turned to Cato, whose face had gone as dark as a summer storm.

"I did not sell her, Portius Cato. Why would I part with such a beauty? No, I fear you were duped into purchasing a runaway slave. And as such, she must be returned to her rightful owner." He clapped his hands together like a delighted child. "And that is me!"

The heat that had coursed through Ariella at the recognition of her brother drained away, leaving her icy.

Cato's eyes were on her, inquiring. Pleading, even. She had to look away.

"What will you take for her, then?" Cato's voice was edged with something like fear, and it hurt Ariella to hear it.

Again the sick laughter. "I would not take all the wealth in the world for her, my friend." He lifted Ariella's chin with his fingertip. She kept her eyes trained downward. "The little Jewess and I have unfinished business, do we not?"

He turned from her, giving Cato his attention. "I knew when I found her brother it was a good omen. She could not be far behind. But I must admit, I did not expect to find her in Pompeii."

"Her brother!"

Ariella met Cato's eyes, and a moment of exultation flowed between them. It meant everything to her to find Micah, he knew that. Without taking his eyes from her, Cato spoke to Valerius. "I will purchase them both from you. At whatever price you name."

Valerius clucked his tongue and elbowed Ariella. "It would seem your illegitimate master is as taken with you as your rightful one, my girl."

She was going to be sick and grasped Micah's hand for strength.

Valerius shook his head, then spoke to the group at large. "You are all my witnesses. Portius Cato is in possession of my property and I am reclaiming it." He clapped his hands. "We shall not be guests in this house. I fear that Cato's affection for my slave would overcome his good judgment and I should find her missing in the morning. Micah, fetch the other slaves and my things."

Cato grabbed his arm. "I must speak with you of other matters, Valerius." He eyed the other dinner guests, as if weighing his options. "The reason I brought you here."

Valerius waved away Cato's words.

Ariella watched the drama play out, too stunned to think. Her brother disappeared, obedient to his master.

"I know, I know. You are opposing Nigidius Maius and you want information that will damage him." He chuckled. "Really, Cato, you must think me an idiot. Would I come all this way without knowing why?"

Cato's voice was low. "Will you help me?"

"Will you let me take my slave girl and leave?"

Ariella's breath shallowed. The election, his sister, these were objectives Cato would not surrender. Not for a gladiator-turned-slave. She watched his face drain of color.

Valerius smiled. "Ah, but I will save you from making a choice, Portius Cato. For you have no choice. She is my slave. And Nigidius Maius, for all his cowardice, is my ally."

His slaves rushed into the courtyard carrying his baggage. Valerius took Ariella's arm and yanked her toward the door.

Behind them, Cato called out, "Stay the night, Valerius. You cannot leave for Rome at this hour!"

The desperation in his voice shredded Ariella's heart.

"Oh, but we do not go to Rome, Cato." Valerius's words dripped with sweetness. "We go to the home of Nigidius Maius."

With that, he pulled Ariella into the night street where slaves and chariot waited. She glanced over her shoulder, back into the torch-lit atrium, for a last look at Cato framed by the doorway.

It seemed to her that he had aged ten years since the evening began.

38

Ariella gripped Micah's hand as they ran behind Valerius's chariot through the dark streets of Pompeii. One of his other slaves held the horses' reins, but the other two ran behind the brother and sister, keeping them penned.

She ran on wooden legs, numb to both feeling and thought. Only one truth sustained her. She had found her brother and he was alive. Everything else had crashed like the basilica's columns after the quake.

The road to Maius's house on the outskirts of the town led upward, through the eerie Street of Tombs, toward the mountain barely visible in the night sky. They arrived at the huge estate breathless and weary and were prodded through the doorway on the heels of Valerius.

Ariella had not faced Nigidius Maius since the last time in Rome, when he had visited Valerius. She had seen him only from a distance since coming to Pompeii. But she would have known him anywhere, and when his florid face appeared in the atrium, she swayed on her feet in the rush of unwelcome memory.

Micah released her hand and wrapped an arm around her shoulders.

It was like a nightmare, all of it.

"Clovius Valerius." Maius held his arms wide in welcome. He was clearly intoxicated, and his lascivious lifestyle had aged him. "I had heard you planned a visit to our little town. Welcome, welcome."

The two men gripped arms. Joined by a common depravity.

"It has been a fortuitous arrival already, Gnaeus." He turned on Ariella and she shrank back. "I have found a runaway slave girl whom I have been longing to recover."

Maius turned drunken eyes on her, and she could see his confusion at her gladiator's costume. He looked at Micah. "Hmm. A matched pair, it would seem."

Valerius cocked his head. "Yes, they are much alike, are they not? Let us hope she continues to give as much pleasure as her brother has."

At this, there was a first stir of awakening, and the hair at the nape of her neck prickled with dread.

Micah's grip on her tightened.

She felt the tension of his body.

HaShem, what had happened to him?

"Come, come." Maius beckoned the group to follow. "You have arrived perfectly. We are just beginning the Feast."

Valerius grinned. "And I expect a better celebration than I received in the home of Portius Cato."

Maius's face darkened. "Cato." It was not a question, but a statement of betrayal.

"Fret not, Gnaeus. Cato's desperation marks him as your inferior, even if there were nothing else to disparage him."

A smoldering anger sparked to life in Ariella's chest.

Maius bowed. "Then let us enjoy the evening as it should be enjoyed."

Valerius followed the larger man, then glanced backward at his other three slaves. "Bring the two."

They were herded through Maius's fantastic estate, past the courtyard garden, down a long hall, and through another smaller atrium. The home seemed to continue forever, as another hall bent and led toward the west. The sounds of celebration wafted on an odor of cooked flesh, and Ariella slowed, only to be prodded from behind by one of the slaves.

A small portico opened at this edge of the house, and they rounded the corner onto it, catching a breath of the night air. To her left, a large triclinium adjoined the portico, and the room was crowded with celebrants and lit by an abundance of flaming torches.

But it was not the many guests, nor the lavish spread of rich foods, that stopped Ariella and held her captive where she stood. It was the paintings.

The three walls of the room were painted from floor to ceiling with panels of plaster frescoes, each one its own scene, divulging a horrific story that was both the stuff of legend and the truth of her past.

Ariella's mouth went dry, then flooded as though she would be sick. Confronted so visually with the events of her life, she felt her legs tremble and her stomach rebel.

It was all there. The panicked female initiate, the god Bacchus sprawled naked, the priestess ushering the terrified girl toward her descent to the underworld. Satyrs, nymphs, the winged god Eros, the man-horse Silenus—all looked down on the proceedings with approval. Even the final scene of the now-wiser girl being whipped by the priestess. All of it wrapped around the room in color and details so real, for a moment she felt again the trance-inducing effects of the *Kykeon*, the wine that brought on frenzied hallucinations.

Ariella became aware once again of her surroundings. The humiliation of her memories came to life before Micah. She looked to him, hoping he would not understand. But when he turned his face to her, she saw more than understanding. She saw the pain of a shared humiliation.

He knew. He knew too well.

Her anger flamed, building as though fanned by a hot wind. The stupor that had numbed her since leaving Cato's house began to lift, washed away with a wave of hatred.

They were pushed into the triclinium behind Valerius and pulled to a couch on his left and right, his private pets chained to his side. The eyes of the guests barely registered the newcomers, so far gone were they with their drugged wine. The room smelled of body odor and a sickening sweetness—a smell Ariella could not identify that soured in her stomach.

Valerius was commenting on the paintings.

Maius laughed from his place across the room. "You were my inspiration, of course, Clovius. My time in Rome with you was most . . . enlightening."

Valerius reached across to the table in front of them and lifted a lump of sausage. He brought it to his mouth and bit off a chunk, then pushed it against Ariella's lips.

She turned her face and leaned away, but he would smash it against her lips and so she at last opened her mouth and considered biting off his fingers.

Not yet. Her time would come. The sausage was vile in her mouth. She chewed and swallowed.

The Feast of Vulcan had given each of the guests reason enough to indulge in excess, if indeed any reason were necessary, and the night wore on with lively music played by flutes in the corner and half-dressed women brought in to dance in the center of the three tables. Knowing her brother watched, Ariella felt her face flush at their explicit display. But the night had only just begun. The partygoers had barely begun to indulge their flesh, and her vision blurred at what was still to come.

Some of the guests still retained enough sobriety to speak of politics, and it was not long before Cato's name was mentioned. Valerius raised a cup to Maius. "He is young and eager, Maius. Are you assured of victory?"

Maius grinned and reached out to yank at the arm of one of the dancing girls and pull her down onto his couch. "I am making certain of it even as we enjoy the evening, Clovius." He pressed his full lips against the girl's mouth, then pushed her away and stuffed a date between his teeth. "I have spent the day writing letters and sending messages." He spoke around the date, chewing it with an open mouth. "It would seem that our Portius Cato has made some unfortunate allies. Christians."

Valerius's hold on her tightened. Could he feel her racing heart?

"Christians! Why would he do such a thing?"

Maius shrugged. "His foolishness is my gain. By the morning, everyone who matters in this town will know of it." He swallowed his mouthful. "If I can manage it, I will bring some charges against him and toss him into a cell next to his sister. With the blessing of the gods, we will see him executed before the election even arrives."

Sweat dampened Ariella's tunic under her leather and her shoulders tightened.

Valerius indicated the paintings once more. "You are planning initiation rites soon, I expect?"

"Indeed." Maius waved the dancing girls away, clearing the space between himself and Valerius. "At the next new moon." He swept a hand around the room. "Everyone is in great anticipation."

"You will be Bacchus?"

Maius shrugged with false humility. "Of course."

"And your initiate?" Valerius leaned against her. "Who shall play the part of Ariadne?"

Maius smiled and rubbed his lips. The room quieted, as though his guests also wished to hear who would be the female initiate in the ritual marriage. "My daughter, Nigidia."

Ariella's body jerked. To use a slave in such a way was contemptible, but one's *daughter*? Incest was frowned upon, even in Rome's depraved society. The guests around the tables held their silence, and the moment seemed suspended on bated breath.

Valerius dipped his head toward Maius. "A bold decision. I applaud your courage."

Guests relaxed visibly.

But for Ariella, the declaration sickened her beyond tolerating. She pushed away from Valerius.

He seemed to anticipate her and snaked out a thin hand to clutch her arm in a vicious grip. He smiled at Maius. "Sadly, since I lost my favorite here, I have had to use a substitute." He pressed his lips against her arm. "But as you said, the two are a matched pair. So I have not suffered too greatly."

The truth of what Valerius had declared rained down on Ariella like a torrent of hot coals. She could not look at her brother. Could not breathe.

Oh, God. How could you allow such a thing?

But it was a question with no answer, a question she had asked too many times in the past nine years. She expected nothing in return. Nothing but the hollow burning where her soul had been.

Maius was laughing. "And I applaud your creativity."

Valerius rubbed her arm with his fingers, as if to erase the welts he had caused. "I must confess that I've grown quite fond of her replacement. Ah, well, perhaps when we celebrate again, they can *both* participate." He lifted his eyebrows and winked in Maius's direction.

It was too much. Fearing she would vomit and suffocating with rage, Ariella yanked herself away from Valerius and stood, unsteady and breathing hard.

Valerius sighed. "She is not as submissive as she once was, I fear. And I grow tired of her tonight, Gnaeus. Can you find somewhere to keep her for the night?"

"Of course." Maius signaled a slave at the doorway. "Place the girl in the cells and put a guard on her."

Ariella sought out her brother's eyes once more, even as the slave yanked both her arms behind her back. Micah turned to her, but there was a dullness there, a slackness about the mouth. She had not noted this before, and she trembled with fury to see it.

Valerius reached out to stroke her leg.

She kicked his hand.

He yelped with pain and anger, and she laughed.

It seemed only moments later that she sprawled on the mud floor of a tiny chamber under Maius's terrace. Little surprise that the man kept private cells in his house. At least Portia had not been chained here.

The thought of Portia brought memories of Cato on its heels, of Maius's threat to have him executed, of Cato's eyes on her as Valerius led her away.

She paced the cell, her wrath building to the breaking point.

It was all absurd, everything Jeremiah had taught her. There was no freedom of spirit without freedom of body. She belonged to Valerius once again, all of her. The Creator had forsaken her, as she had always believed.

Her heart pulsed with the desire to lash out, to hurt someone as she had been hurt, to destroy and to tear apart, and in the destruction to dull her own pain.

The searing hatred for Valerius, for the Romans who had razed her city and destroyed her family and annihilated her faith rose up inside her with a boiling heat, overwhelmed her, and set her screaming. Screaming out her rage and pain at the God who had allowed all of it, her fist raised to the low ceiling as though she could reach through it into the night sky, all the way to the heavens above.

No one came. No guard chastised. No God either.

She was alone.

Spent, she dropped to the floor and lowered her head to her bent knees.

She would forget everything that Jeremiah had nearly made her believe. There was no contentment to be found in injustice and despair. There was no community here to help her. And most of all, there was no God who cared.

She would not give up fighting. Never. But she would fight alone. For herself and for her brother, she would do what must be done. In the darkness, she made a vow. And through the long, sleepless night, she repeated this vow until it hardened into solid rock within her soul.

Even if it brought about her own death, Clovius Valerius would not live to abuse them again.

39

Late into the night Cato paced the city streets, reliving the day and berating himself for his foolish pride. He never should have brought Valerius to Pompeii. What a stupid, arrogant thing to do. To think that he could control the situation, manipulate Maius's ally for his own ends.

He reached the southern edge of the city, his feet having taken him toward the arena of their own accord. The circular stone wall loomed gray and black against the night sky, its series of arches like hooded eyes, scowling down on him.

He would lose the election. Of this he was certain. He had made inroads into Maius's corruption, but it was not enough. The failure of it nagged at his pride, but it was pain over the fate of his sister that crushed him.

And Ariella.

Ariella.

Her face was before him in an instant. The way her eyes had rested on him as Valerius hauled her into the street with her newly found brother. Her lips parted, as though she would say farewell. But she did not.

He crossed the grassy field that led to the arena, ignoring his vineyard on the left. The amphitheater was silent, like a massive tomb awaiting its occupants. He walked down the darkened ramp that led to the arena floor and stepped into the soft sand.

The memory of ten thousand cheers seemed to echo from the hollow seats, as though a spectral audience wavered, ghostly and unreal, in the empty marble tiers. Cato moved on soundless feet to the center of the arena.

He turned a slow circle, remembering the day he had sworn that Ariella would not face another opponent. Self-reproach washed over him. What good had he done her? Taken her from one form of slavery to another, then brought an adversary more dangerous than any her net and trident had seen.

He saw her again, pleading with him not to summon Valerius. Why had he not understood?

Suddenly weary, Cato lowered himself to the sand, spreading out with his face to the cold sky and his back to the cold sand. It still smelled of blood and death here. Of the thousands of men and animals that had died to entertain.

What would happen to Portia? To Ariella?

He faced the truth that he had brought harm to both of these women whom he loved, and he was helpless to change anything.

Helpless.

A failure.

All the pain of Rome. He had been so cocky, so sure of his fight against the corrupt praetor, Maximus. Outspoken and arrogant and immature. In the end, he had failed to convince the consuls and had been trounced, even ridiculed for his position.

He had come to Pompeii to forget and had only caused more harm.

He tried to pray. Reached out to the God who had saved him from his sin, but not from himself. But there was only the black sky above, and the stars seemed to accuse with their brightness. Cato threw his arm over his eyes and lay there in the sand, defeat as sharp as if he had fallen by a gladiator's sword.

The despair swelled in his chest and overflowed, spilling tears from his eyes, down over his temples. The sand that had soaked up so much blood over the years drank in his tears as though they were nothing, and the sobs that wracked his chest bounced back at him from the stone surrounding him.

Hours later he lay on a bench in his courtyard, half-frozen but uncaring. The family and household had all gone to their beds, but sleep came only in fragments of uneasy dreams for Cato.

His mother found him nearly senseless in the morning, unwashed and cold. She roused him enough to swallow some cold porridge. Lucius arrived soon after, his face as white as marble.

"Have you heard?"

Cato pushed the porridge away. What else could there be?

"It is all over town this morning." Lucius's voice cracked with emotion.

Octavia gripped her son-in-law's arm with both hands. "Portia?"

Lucius eyed her as though he did not comprehend the question, then turned back to Cato. "Maius has sent letters throughout the town. Telling everyone that you have taken up with the sect of Christians and are practicing their unnatural rites with them, defying the emperor. There are rumors of your arrest."

Octavia gasped and took an unsteady step backward. Lucius had the sense to catch her.

Cato did not move.

Lucius spoke through pale lips. "What are we to do, Quintus? How can you free Portia—"

"I cannot!" He jumped to his feet. "I cannot free Portia, or Ariella, or anyone in this town! I told you. All of you. I told you not to force me to take a stand against this man. I failed in Rome and I have failed here. And I never should have expected anything but failure."

Octavia and Lucius said nothing, but their stricken faces accused and Cato could bear it no longer. "I am going to work in my vineyard. When they come for me, they can find me there."

He left them both, open-mouthed and staring, in the atrium. Left behind the house and the election and his empty promises to find justice for anyone, and returned to his vineyard where he should have stayed months ago.

The vines had matured in the months since he had come to Pompeii, and they hung heavy now with ripened fruit. Cato spread a cluster across his palm and felt the weight of it, pleased.

Remus came up behind him, startling him. "The harvest is ready."

Cato nodded and surveyed the rows that remained healthy and strong even after Maius's fire. The vineyard seemed unnaturally silent today, perhaps feeling the emptiness of his own heart. Somewhere across the city, a dog howled, and then another. A chill shuddered through Cato, like a portent of evil to come. He lifted his eyes to the protective mountain, purple and green against the blue sky, like a reflection of the grapes and vines. A wisp of cloud hovered above Vesuvius's dome, almost as though it wafted from the mountain itself.

More dogs howled. Somehow, something was not right. But it was likely the disturbance lay within him. He shook off the feeling and turned to Remus, trying to smile. "Have you been taking a holiday, Remus? This soil looks as dry as an Arabian desert."

Remus straightened and scowled. "Not much I can do with no water, master."

Cato clapped his shoulder. "Easy, Remus. I was only joking with you. Who has stolen our water?"

His forced humor fell short with Remus. "Ask the gods, master. It's them that have dried out the city."

Cato frowned. "What nonsense are you talking?"

"Where have you been since yesterday? The water has slowed to a trickle through the aqueducts. The city is growing panicked."

As if in response, a small flock of black birds erupted from the vineyard, wings beating in unison.

The birds. That was the unnatural silence he had noticed. No birds sang this morning.

"What are you doing here, master?" Remus's question cut through his puzzlement.

"Did you forget I own this vineyard, Remus? I came to get my hands dirty."

The laborer scratched at his neck. "You do not belong here. Not any longer. You have more important work to do."

Cato looked away, focused again on that wisp of smoky cloud that hung over the mountain. "Not anymore."

Remus stepped in front of him, demanding his attention. "I do not know what has happened, but I will tell you this, Portius Cato. You are not this man anymore. No longer the carefree winemaker who arrived in Pompeii." He drew himself up, strangely assertive. "Go back and fight your fight, Cato."

His words were punctuated with another howl of a dog.

Cato ran his hand through his hair. "The whole city has gone mad, and you with it, Remus."

But the man was right. He did not belong here. No more than he belonged in the arena or in the magistrates' offices. He was neither winemaker nor politician. He belonged nowhere. So who was Portius Cato, in truth?

"You are a champion of the weak."

Jeremiah's words, spoken over him that night, in a holy hush that felt like a calling.

Somehow, in all of the sprawling decay of Rome and the countryside beauty of Pompeii, there seemed to be only one man who could see into his heart.

Cato turned from Remus and left him to the vineyard.

If it was truth he sought, there was only one place it would be found.

40

The Empire had more festival days than it had gods, or so it seemed. On the heels of Maius's feast to honor Vulcan and appease the fiery underworld god, he prepared for another holiday the next day, the Festival of Luna. There would be no feast today, only the opening of the *mundus* pit outside the city. Three times each year the stone covering of the pit was pulled away to allow the departed spirits trapped in the underworld to escape and, for a brief time, roam the world of the living.

As duovir, Maius was expected to be present at the lifting of the stone, but he made his way outside the city walls, anxious to be about his more pressing desire this morning—to begin the raids.

The morning was bathed in that unnatural stillness he had noted yesterday, as though the earth held its breath, listening for what would come next, like the gray serenity of the sea in the moments before a mighty storm. The silence unnerved Maius, and he quickened his steps along the shadowed eastern wall of the city and through the arched stone of the Marina Gate. He sought reassurance above in the bright yellow orb of the sun, already scorching a pale blue sky, and the mountain behind him with only a trace of wispy whiteness above it. There would be no storm today.

Only the storm of his wrath.

He smiled. Yes, he would sweep through the city in a tempest of retribution.

But first, the mundus pit.

The pious had already begun to assemble around the large pit with its stone covering when Maius arrived. From a distance he could identify the blinding chalk-white toga of the priest, surrounded by the lesser white of the townspeople. An air of agitation prevailed. Did they also feel the strangeness of the morning air? The crowd was smaller than it had been even last year. The people grew less religious with each passing season. They preferred the arena to the temple, the public baths to public worship. Ah, well. They could be controlled either way, it made little difference to him.

The priest chanted over the pit as Maius approached and lifted his head in a subtle acknowledgment of the duovir, as though the magistrate were inconsequential in these religious matters.

Maius curled a lip and scowled at the presumptuous little man, who began the official opening ceremony.

"Mundo nomen impositum est ab eo mundo qui supra nos est." The mundus gets its name from that world which is above us.

He would participate when the stone was pushed aside. That would communicate to the priest where he stood.

In the beats of eerie silence after the priest's declaration, there was a whispering, like the touch of a breeze through a leafy tree, and it raised the hair on his neck. He surveyed the people. Did he alone hear the murmurs of the dead?

But it was not the dead that whispered. Beyond the circle of peasants who waited to toss their firstfruit offerings into the pit stood a tight circle with clasped hands, facing inward, and it was their hushed prayers that had sounded so sinister. The very Christians he had been dreaming of raiding now prayed against him, prayed against the good fortune of the city bound up in the mundus pit opening. Maius shuddered, part disgust and part mystical fear. Would that he could push each of them into the pit when it opened.

"Mundus cum patet, deorum tristium atque inferum quasi ianua patet." When the mundus is open, it is as if a door stands open for the sorrowful gods of the underworld.

Four lesser priests bent to the stone, and Maius pushed his way through the sparse crowd to bend over the lip of the stone beside one of them. The high priest frowned, but Maius ignored him. They lifted the large piece away from the pit, revealing the black earth beneath, deep enough that one could not be certain where the bottom lay. A musty, rotten smell escaped the pit. Was it the odor of decaying spirits rushing out of Hades?

The Christians' prayers increased in volume, as though they also sensed evil escaping. He clenched a fist, ready to leave the ceremony and begin the day's arrests.

The high priest said a few words over the pit, and the rites ended. The people dispersed, but the high priest grabbed at Maius's toga before he could leave the grassy hillside.

"A word, duovir." The small man's eyes bored into him.

"I have pressing business—"

"Yes, so I have heard."

Maius turned on him. "You question my actions?" He pointed to the disbanding Christians. "Even after this?"

"It is the Festival of Luna. In honor of the blessed dead there are to be no military or public matters undertaken this day."

Maius waved him off. The priests alone cared for such trifles.

"I am certain the blessed dead will understand the urgency of the situation."

The priest's face darkened. No matter. Maius stalked away, reentered the city with haste, and found the *contubernium* of eight legionaries he had requested awaiting him in the Forum, arranged in two silent rows of four.

Somewhere in the city the wretched howl of a dog punctuated the odd atmosphere. Maius crossed the paving stones to the *Decanus*, their leader. "All is ready? They have instructions?"

The Decanus gave a sharp nod.

Maius clapped him on the back. "Then be about your business!"

The quiet morning was in need of shaking up. The chaos they would cause throughout the city pleased him. He followed the contingent of soldiers as they began their march.

Street after street, house after house. Had the mystery sect believed they had gone unnoticed? Oh, but their names had been catalogued and recorded long ago, and now it took only the stomp of military boot, the splintering shove of a wooden door frame, the sharp end of a soldier's *pilum* to bring them to heel.

Maius stuck close to one bulky soldier who seemed to delight in his work. The excitement of it built in his own stomach, as though he himself bore the weapons, as though his hands grabbed and yanked the Christians from their hearths and gardens.

Rich and poor alike were snatched from their homes, but it was the rich who gave the most delight. In one large city house, a family of six gathered in the leafy atrium at the sound of the soldiers, mother clutching young children to her side and father standing before the huddled group as though he could protect them. The home smelled of freshly baked bread. Beside them, a table had been set with midday breads and cheeses, and a bowl of glossy black olives watered Maius's mouth.

A soldier jabbed at the father. The man smacked the pilum away, bringing the wrath of the soldier. Two grabbed at him, and the children cried out.

Maius pushed past the soldiers to the woman. "Take them both. Leave the children." No one could say he was not merciful. He snatched a handful of the olives, filled his mouth, and bit down on the moist flesh.

They were all crying now, the children and the mother. They should have considered the consequences before they aligned themselves with impious traitors to the Empire.

The troops stomped out, the man and his wife gripped between two of the lead soldiers. Maius followed, ignoring the cries of the children.

It was good, this purging. Good for Pompeii and good for him.

Even better would be the moment when they came upon Portius Cato. Perhaps he would fight the soldiers. Resist and force them to run him through with a sword.

Maius shut the door of the house as he left, and he couldn't help but smile.

41

By the time Cato reached the home of Seneca and Europa, he questioned himself a hundred times. Why did he keep crossing the city to hear the opinion of an aging Jewish slave? Did his future rest in the old man's leathery hands, as though his life were nothing more than an evening meal prepared for gladiators?

And yet the brokenness and desperation that had left him cold in the sand of the arena drove him forward, until he stumbled out of the stink and noise of the street and over the threshold of the warm house, as though he had reached the comfort and safety of a fortress, with an invading army snapping at his heels.

The Persian slave, Cyrus, met him near the door and led him in silence to a receiving room off the main atrium garden, where he collapsed into a chair. Seneca appeared moments later. Cato lifted his head from his hands.

Seneca started forward. "What has happened?" His brow furrowed deeply. "They have not come for your family?"

Cato scanned the room, feeling as though invaders had arrived. "Who?"

"Maius. His soldiers. They are sweeping the town for the Christ followers."

Cato breathed deeply, trying to free his chest from the pressure of this latest news. "No. I knew nothing about it. Except that he has identified me along with you."

Seneca said nothing. No doubt he weighed whether such an honor were justified.

"Seneca, I—I need to speak with Jeremiah."

The man's lips twitched into a sad smile. "Remain here."

Seneca disappeared, and Cato waited in the chair until he was drawn to the doorway by a lilting voice in the atrium.

Flora worked in the garden, plucking blood-red blooms, clipping stray green stems, and singing of her Savior. Curious girl. Her uneven gait from shrub to shrub was unfortunate, for otherwise she was lovely. He rode a wave of guilt once more, as he did when he had seen her last. Was there not something wrong with a world that would have disposed of this infant, simply because she would never walk correctly? And was there not something extraordinarily fine about Seneca and Europa, who had saved her?

Jeremiah limped across the atrium, carrying a tray. He drew a smile from Flora, who must have seen in him a strange reflection of herself, as their disability was much the same. Cato crossed the open space to take the tray of bread and wine from Jeremiah.

"Haven't spilled any yet." The old man's usual quick smile welcomed.

Cato tried to return the smile. "Nor shall you."

They retreated to the receiving room once more. The food and drink were hospitable, though they only brought more guilt at his imposition. He did not come to have Jeremiah serve him.

Or perhaps he did, but not his physical needs.

"You are troubled." Jeremiah sat beside him, his eyes sparkling with that inner light.

Where did one find such a light? "I have lost everything, Jeremiah."

The slave nodded. "That is good."

Only Jeremiah would speak cryptic and wise nonsense.

The man gripped Cato's hand with his own strong one, skin like soft leather.

The touch made Cato want to weep.

"Emptiness always precedes filling, son."

Cato could do nothing but look at those hands.

"Eat something." Jeremiah released him and offered a cup of diluted wine.

The tray had been filled with small loaves of a grainy bread, a bowl of oranges, and a small pile of walnuts, their wrinkled brown shells again reminding him of Jeremiah's hands. He took the wine and sipped at it, from courtesy rather than thirst. "Maius is spreading word about my involvement with your sect, which will cost me the election. And with it, my sister's freedom."

"What else?"

Those eyes, they could read his very soul. "Ariella."

The name ruffled the old man's peace. "She is in danger?"

Cato nodded, swallowing at the tightness of his throat. "Her former owner—Clovius Valerius of Rome—has claimed she ran away and has taken her back."

Jeremiah sighed deeply.

Cato shuddered in response. Had he hoped the old man would offer some reassurance?

The slave shifted in his chair, perhaps to relieve the pressure on his hip. "The election. Your sister. Ariella. These are those whom you have lost?"

"What else is there?"

"There is hope."

"Then I have lost that as well. Evil has triumphed once more, and I have done nothing."

Jeremiah smiled, a sad and wise smile. Would that he could read every thought in the man's heart.

"Tell me what to do, Jeremiah." Ludicrous statement, given their positions. And the only words that made sense.

"What do you want to do?"

He stood and paced, too restless to remain in one place. "Destroy Maius! Free my sister. And Ariella."

"Champion of the weak."

Those words again, yet they were untrue. "It is I who am weak, Jeremiah!"

"His strength is made perfect in weakness."

More paradox. "How can I be both weak and victorious?"

"How indeed? Do you ask in earnest, or do you only wish simple answers?"

He came to Jeremiah then, kneeled before him as he had before, and opened his heart, bruised and bloody. "I seek the truth, Jeremiah. Tell me only the truth."

"There is so much more for you, Quintus. Abundant life, a life of His calling and your responding to do the work He has prepared for you."

"I don't know how, or what, He wills."

"You have been set free from your sin, my boy. Freed for a battle yet to come, if you will join it. But first, before there can ever be victory, there must be complete surrender. *His* battle, *His* fight, not your own."

Again, talk of surrender. Cato struggled against this paradox. Called to fight, asked to yield. Like any true warrior, under his general's orders.

The room fell silent, as all of Pompeii had been silent today, waiting. Waiting for his decision, for his will to flow in one direction or another.

He dropped his head again and felt Jeremiah's holy hands on him. There was a power there, and it seemed to pulse through him, to set his body trembling. But no, there was more than Jeremiah's power at work here. The very ground beneath him shook, as it had in the theater when he had given his speech.

He lifted his eyes to Jeremiah, saw the confirmation. The earth again convulsed. He stood and gripped Jeremiah's shoulder. "Stay here."

In the atrium, Flora had suspended her gardening, her hand still raised above a flowering rosebush, as though she had turned to stone. Her eyes followed Cato as he ran through the courtyard to the doorway.

In the street, a roar began. Like a rumbling thunder that did not lessen, like the hoofbeats of a thousand bulls pounding through the cobbled streets, the sound rolled onward, shot upward through the soles of his feet to shake his very core.

This was no minor quake.

The incident on the day of his speech had been swift, over before he had realized what occurred. But this tremor was different. It reverberated through the street and buildings like an evil warning from the underworld, on and on. Did the spirits released from the mundus pit this morning bring destruction with them?

Cato's gaze traveled the length of the street, saw the panic of townspeople as they turned on each other, unsure where to flee. Stone walls cracked. A column splintered and crashed to the pavement, knocking a woman to the stones. At the end of the street, he could see the mountain.

Vesuvius.

Something ominous hung above its peak. Gray and thick, like a storm cloud that had collapsed inward, condensed and threatening.

A cloud of death.

The time had come at last.

Under the rocky depths, one shifting plate at last gave way to the other, and as the victor hurtled over the vanquished, escaping gases shot upward with unrivaled force.

In the rivers below, turtles jumped out of the water. Animals were often quicker than humans at sensing doom.

Vesuvius garnered strength as the poison flowed upward within it, gathering debris, rock, ash, all it could consume on its way. The pulsing flow bulged the sloping sides impossibly, as though it would give birth to a hideous monster of death.

Above the peak, a roiling cloud of ash and rock signaled that the birth pangs had begun.

42

The dawn did not reach into the cells deep under the countryside estate of Nigidius Maius. Ariella stirred with the vague awareness that the night had passed and stretched her limbs, grown stiff with the chill of the brown muck in which she spent the hours.

She stood and walked off the numbness, willing her body and her spirit to be ready for what should come next.

But it was hours before she saw or heard another. Had Valerius forgotten her, underground and out of sight? More likely he was sleeping off the excesses of last night. Best not to think about her brother, and what Valerius's celebrations may have included.

Micah. The momentary joy of finding him washed over her once again. Damaged, yes. But alive. And once they were away from the stench that was Clovius Valerius, she would love Micah back to health. They would be a family. She swiped at the unbidden tears with her palm. Later. She could give way to emotion when they were safe.

For today, for this moment, she would be Scorpion Fish once again.

They came at last, two of Valerius's slaves, with the news that her master prepared already to leave Pompeii, to return to Rome via the ship that had brought him. The two brutes seemed to enjoy dragging her upward to the daylight, though she would have come willingly, her singular focus driving her to face the vile man.

When to kill him? And how? She indulged a moment of imagination, of her trident in her hand once more, of Valerius on the ground, three prongs driven through his empty chest.

The wagon sat ready outside Maius's villa, and a muscular horse had been harnessed to a two-wheeled gilded cart. Slaves loaded Valerius's belongings into the wagon, his prime slave shouting directions and insults. The two who had brought her from the cell yanked her forward and lashed her wrists with a lead-rope that trailed from the wagon. The late-summer sun beat without pity on her face, and the day was still, silently watching her shame.

Micah appeared moments later to be tied to the rope beside her.

She drank in the sight of his tanned face, even his wide, white eyes, and lifted her roped hands to touch his cheek. She sent him encouragement with her eyes, but dared not speak.

He nodded, the only indication that hope also lived in him.

Perhaps Valerius meant to humiliate them with the forced march through the town, but they were together, and that was a blessing.

Blessing. Had the Creator brought them together? Or was it chance, and the evil hand of Valerius? Could she accept their reunion as His gift? Would He also bless her hand as she raised it against the evil? Unknowable.

The voices of Maius and Valerius emerged from the villa behind them. She did not turn, but fixed her eyes on the winding gravel path that led downward from the estate, into the town. Their route to the sea would not pass through much of Pompeii, and she was unlikely to see many she knew.

Unlikely to see Cato.

She inhaled against the tightness of her chest and blinked away the sting of the sun.

She let them have their laughter and their fond good-byes.

Yes, say good-bye, Maius.

Her limbs trembled with fury and tension and she coached herself to remember her training. She had only to secure a weapon somehow and find opportunity. There would be no difficulty in the task itself.

But she must also be wise. She desired more than vengeance, more than his death. She fought for freedom, as she always had. But now it would be freedom for them both. She could not risk capture or death in the pursuit of freedom, for that would be to once more abandon Micah.

A cool shadow fell against her face. She lifted her chin, eyes still trained forward.

"Rather worse for your night in the mud, I see." Valerius's voice mocked, but in a low and familiar whisper at her ear. "No matter. We shall make you pretty once we are at sea."

She turned her face to his, focused on his grinning mouth, yellowed teeth, those blood-red lips. "You shall find me dead before your vile hands touch me again."

He slapped her. His delicate fingers stung her cheek.

She tasted blood inside her mouth, swung her face back to his, and let her hatred pour from her eyes.

His nostrils flared and he shoved her backward into Micah, who kept her upright with his roped hands.

"You have grown uglier during your holiday."

He mounted the gilded cart with a wave to Maius, and the entourage jolted forward. Ariella and Micah struggled to keep pace with the wagon. Its wheels churned dust into her lungs and her eyes burned.

Away from one despicable man, on the heels of another, they trotted downward, through the Street of Tombs and past the towering north wall of the city that separated Maius and his estate from the common man. Valerius kept to the inner east wall of the city, choosing the most direct route to the harbor. The noonday town seemed peaceful, and she remembered the strange pagan holiday.

They passed through the Marina Gate, leaving the town once again.

Good-bye, Pompeii.

One foot caught against the other, and she nearly went down. The rope bit against her wrists, bringing tears.

Boats clogged the harbor, more than Ariella would have expected. They bobbed in the sapphire-blue water, their white masts a reflection of the white sand. She inhaled the sharp tang of salt and fish, letting it purge the road dust from her chest.

Valerius's cart was met at the beach by more slaves, perhaps his ship's captain and oarsmen. She heard the words *ill wind* pass between them.

So that was the reason for the excess of ships. The current did not favor setting sail. How would this affect her plan? Would they return to Maius's villa? When would her opportunity arrive?

They would wait, Valerius announced peevishly, though not long. He desired to reach Ostia Antica, the port of Rome, before nightfall.

Ariella and Micah were left where they stood, though the other slaves ranged themselves in the sand, shadowed by the wagon. Valerius paced the waterfront, as though his petulance would drive away the winds.

She surveyed the beach. Was this her chance? It seemed unlikely that she could free them both, find a weapon, deliver the blow, and escape unhindered. Did she need a weapon? She had been trained to kill without one.

Into her musings came a throaty growl, like a mighty beast trapped beneath the sand. Micah's eyes met her own. "The wind?"

But it was not the wind.

On the beach, slave and sailor alike stood in silence, every head inclined to the sound.

And then came the tremors.

The sand shifted beneath their feet, but this was a deeper shifting, she could sense. She had felt it weeks ago, when Cato had been giving his speech in the theater.

One of Valerius's slaves stood beside her. She turned on him. "Untie us. You must free us."

He glanced at her face, her bound wrists.

"Have mercy, man. Where would we go?"

He threw a furtive look toward Valerius's back. Their master stood at the shoreline, his stance wide and his arms extended, as though he balanced on a racing chariot. With a burst of decision, the slave released the loop of rope from the wagon's back and freed Ariella. She did not wait for him to free Micah. She could do it herself.

The underground snarl became a roar and the tremor turned to heaving. The sea swelled and those at its edge fled backward.

Were they not safe here on the beach? No columns or statues to crush them, no roofs to collapse on their heads. They needed only to ride it out. Micah wrapped his arm around her shoulder and she pressed into his strength.

Ariella lifted her eyes to the mountain. How did it fare under the earth's treachery?

With the question and its answer above, her courage failed.

Micah followed her gaze, and they watched as a gray-black cloud, darker than any storm cloud, churned and swirled above the mountain's summit.

And then, then—impossible yet undeniable—with the force of a cork blown off the top of the world . . . the peak of the mountain exploded.

The noise was a thousand dragons breathing fire, a million bonfires roaring, the screaming shriek of the end of the world.

Every person on the beach fell away from its force, knocked to their backs to watch the inky gray column shoot upward from the mountain like a massive tree trunk sprouted before their eyes. The malevolent tree spread outward in branches of fury.

Lying in the sand, Ariella could not tear her eyes away. Her muscles had turned to water and her mouth hung slack. Shock numbed her mind. She was a rag doll thrown at the feet of a goddess and she lay nearly senseless as the wicked storm raged in the sky above the mountain.

Vesuvius's spewing went on and on. The tree grew, like a mighty umbrella pine, impossibly high, until the spreading branches must have scraped against the floor of heaven itself.

On the beach, astonishment had turned to terror. Slaves, sailors, and townspeople scrambled to their feet, dashed left and right, bawled instructions and questions and fear.

Micah and Ariella linked arms and stood against the side of the wagon. Was this their chance? In the chaos, they could run. Was she willing to forfeit her vengeance and simply have freedom?

But where did one run while the world came to its end?

Valerius was yelling, directing his slaves on the docked ship to send the dinghy to the shore so that he could board and sail away from the disaster. Even Ariella could see the angry waves chasing each other to the sand, each one outpacing the one before.

Valerius was a fool.

But it would seem the town was full of fools, for a screaming horde of them poured from the town's gate, seeking refuge by escaping into the Bay of Napoli.

She and Micah were caught between the sea and the masses, and chaos erupted on the beach as those without boats begged and bribed to be rescued.

She held tight to Micah in the press of people. "We must run." Her voice was lost in the roar of the earth and the continued belching of the mountain. She pulled Micah's head to her own. "We must run!"

He turned wide eyes on her, but she could see that he was ready.

At the water's edge, Valerius still shouted to be put out. They would leave him to his folly.

She waited a few moments, with measured glances at the other slaves, none of whom seemed interested in anything but their own safety, then grabbed Micah's hand and nodded.

But impossibly, Valerius was beside them, his long fingers wrapped around her upper arm, dragging her backward toward the sea. "We must sail now!" His voice was pitched toward hysteria.

She tried to shake off his death grip.

"The sea is raging just as the mountain, Valerius. You will not reach two *stadia*!"

He seemed not to hear her, still pulling her toward the water.

This was her moment, then. At last, there was to be both vengeance and freedom. In the crush of the mob, many of whom were now fixed on Valerius's ship as their salvation, no one would care when he went down.

She planted her feet as best she could, dug her heels into the grainy sand, and halted their progress. He turned to her, his eyes pleading as though she were his daughter and not his slave. "There is still time!"

It took only a quick twist of her arm to release his grasp, a puncturing kick to his midsection to double him over, and a fore-arm blow to his neck to send him to her feet where he belonged. She moved, swift and sinuous, and the action warmed her limbs and flushed her with confidence.

Her sandal dug into his neck, poised for the death stroke. She had trained well. She could kill a man in a dozen different ways, even without weapons. Which would cause the most pain? Which method would kill him surely, yet let him linger in agony?

This is not My will, child.

The words were audible, even over the screams and shouts of those on the beach and the bellowing roar of the mountain. She looked for Micah, found his eyes, but could not tell if his fear came from the voice or the imminent murder of Valerius.

I gave My life to redeem yours. And vengeance belongs to Me.

She inhaled sharply, then coughed, the air noxious in her lungs. *Yeshua?*

Valerius's face had paled beneath her foot. His pinched, unnatural lips hung open. She was his Scorpion Fish, leaping out of the fishpond to stand over its master, full of venom.

But the poison drained from her. It ran down into the sand and left her with nothing but impossible compassion for the vacant shell of a man beneath her. He would meet his death today, she felt certain.

But it would not be at her hand.

She shoved against him with her foot, signaled Micah, and ran. They pushed against the flow of people, two small fish travel-ing upstream against a powerful current of fear, and were lost in the mob. Above them, the spreading gray cloud blocked out the sun like a heavy curtain, turning noon to dusk in an instant.

It proved nearly hopeless to shove through the bottleneck of the

Marina Gate, and Ariella squeezed Micah's hand until her fingers were numb. She would not lose him again.

But then at last they were through, bursting into the open air, fighting through the panic that flowed toward the city gate.

And from high above them, like a toxic, dirty snow, ash began to fall.

43

Cato watched from the street, mesmerized, as the gray cloud above the mountain bubbled and foamed. But nothing prepared him for the explosion.

The top of the mountain blew off with such force it knocked people to the street. Cato kept his footing but raised stunned eyes to Vesuvius, seeing it bellow out gas and rock, its peak shattered into fragments that shot to the heavens.

Merciful God, protect us.

Townspeople got to their feet, the earthquake forgotten, and faced the mountain, like children cowering before a wrathful parent. The roar of the rock raining upward drowned out their cries.

He ran back into Seneca's home and found the entire household assembled in the atrium, slave and family alike. They turned panicked eyes to him, as if he held an answer to the blast that had rocked the city.

"The mountain—" He labored to speak, as though he had run a distance to give the news. "The mountain has blown."

A slave cried out, her voice tearful. "Vulcan is displeased!"

He had left such beliefs behind. It was a sudden realization. Still, it was impossible not to think of the god of fire's feast day yesterday and the townspeople's efforts to earn favor. They had sought safety from crop fires, never dreaming that their beloved mountain seethed with flames.

Seneca pushed forward to Cato. "Should we flee?"

Cato inhaled and surveyed the group. "Not yet. We would not know where to flee to escape. Or if there is a need. For now, the rocks fly straight upward."

"And at some time, they will come down."

True. "But the mountain is miles away. We are safe for now. Besides, the street is already filled with panicked peasants. The quake will have set fires through the *insulae* and the poor will run for safety. You are better off in your home."

Seneca nodded and turned to his household, opening his arms to include them all. "We will stay here."

Cato clapped Seneca on the back. "Bar the door behind me. There will be looters about."

"You are leaving?"

"I must get to my own family." He eyed the group. How many would he see again? Flora clung to Europa. Jeremiah stood near the two, leaning on his staff. He caught Cato's glance and nodded slowly.

A swell of emotion caught Cato off guard. He placed a hand over his own chest, bowed to the old man, and received the blessing of his smile in return.

In the street, he heard the bar slide into place behind him and breathed a prayer to Jeremiah's God to keep them safe.

It had grown darker since he entered the house. The gray ash cloud had spread, dimming the sky. In the streets, rich and poor alike streamed toward the edges of the city. Carts rumbled past, piled with furnishings and valuables, and their owners yelled at slaves to hasten.

And yet as crowded as the streets were, it was clear that with the quake over and the threat now coming from the sky, the majority of the town had taken refuge in their homes.

He shoved his way through the panicked citizens, past taverns and brothels, bakeries and thermopolia, all gone silent, their inhabitants either hiding or fleeing. People knocked him against the stone walls and once down into the gutter. He pushed on, heart pounding.

He found his own door barred when he reached it. Octavia's doing, certainly. Good woman. He smacked his palm against it and heard the call of a slave in return. "It is Portius Cato! Open the door!"

The bar slid upward, the door cracked open, and he shoved through the opening, turned, and barred the door himself.

Isabella and Octavia rushed from the atrium. His sister called to him in her dramatic way. "Is it the end of the world?"

He opened his embrace and caught them both, breathed a prayer of thanks over their heads. "Only the end of the mountain, my good women."

And perhaps the town.

Octavia's eyes were red-rimmed and she held a letter in her hands. "Everything is coming to an end." She waved the letter. "I have just had word that my brother Servius is dead."

Cato exhaled, unable to take in this news with all else that had transpired.

"Where should we go?" Octavia was all practicality, though he could see the fright in her eyes.

"Nowhere at present. The buildings are unsafe because of the quake, and fires are raging. There are enough panicked people in the streets. You are safer here."

Isabella was quick to note the *you*. "Quintus, you are *not* going back out there!"

He faced his mother. "I must see to Portia. It is madness to leave prisoners underground during a quake. She must be freed."

Octavia's face blanched. Clearly, she had not thought of the danger to her elder daughter.

"Courage, Mother. I will be back soon and return Portia to your arms. Keep Isabella secure." He spoke of courage, even as fear dampened his neck and forehead.

Octavia seemed torn between duty to each of her children, as though she wished both to stay with Isabella and to go with her son to see Portia freed.

He kissed her cheeks, kissed Isabella also, and turned to go, calling over his shoulder, "Stay away from the walls and the columns. Keep to the garden."

He had no doubt his mother would secure the door behind him. He launched back into the street, joining the human current flowing toward the prison, the Forum, and the Marina Gate.

He would free Portia if at all possible, but in truth it was not his only errand. There was another woman whose safety concerned him, and he would see her protected before he returned home.

The mountain still poured forth its foul contents, a column so high he had to crane his neck backward to see the spreading summit. The edges of the black cloud reached the sun in its midday position and crept across it, eclipsing the day and turning it to dusk in moments.

The darkness seemed to cast unreasonable fear into the people in the streets, and the chaos spiked. Horses and wagons plunged down the narrow roads. People fell beneath cart wheels to be trampled underfoot. Cato kept to the walls, turning his body sideways at times to avoid the press of madness. His breath came in gasps, as though the air had thickened.

Halfway to the prison the ongoing rush grew sluggish. It took only a moment to discern the cause. The people stood in the street, faces and palms raised to the sky.

Snow? In the heat of Augustus?

But it was not snow. It was ash.

Seneca's prediction. It had begun. The mountain was beginning to rain down on them.

In the lull caused by wonderment, Cato pushed forward and gained ground. By the time he reached the prison, the ash was falling heavily. The white marble paving stones of the Forum grew gray with a layer of it, and footprints could be seen where people trod.

He hurried across the Forum toward the magistrates' buildings and the prison beneath. The crowd thinned here, freed from the confines of the narrow streets.

He did not see it coming. One moment he was pushing across the Forum, and the next a burning boulder larger than his head dropped from the sky as though hurled in spite. The black-and-orange projectile smashed the paving stone only a cubit in front of him. He jumped backward, safe by only a fraction from the superheated rock. The bitter taste of fear rose in his chest.

The scare gave new meaning to the danger. Falling ash could be brushed away. Burning rocks could not. He risked a glance upward, expecting an avalanche from the sky. He could see no other blackened rocks, but it began to rain light pebbles that stung the skin. He bent his face to the ground, held out his hand to catch a few in his palm.

The stone hail was dirty-white, light and porous—like bits of bleached sea sponge from Greece—but solid. The sound of it hitting the Forum stones brought memories of echoing theater applause.

Again, this new revelation from the sky gave the townspeople pause, and the spacious court ceased its churning for a moment, then resumed in earnest.

Cato, too, pushed forward toward the prison, his mind keeping pace with his feet. First the thick ash, and now rocks, some light and some fatal. It was growing more dangerous aboveground than below it. The quakes had stopped. Would Portia be safer in the prison than they were aboveground?

He was not the first to consider it. The prison entrance thronged with people shouting to be allowed underground. Several guards fought them off, striking down men and women alike with their heavy rods. Cato kept his distance, measuring his chances, measuring the danger.

In the end, he followed his instinct. For now at least, Portia was safer underground. How ironic . . . when this nightmare ended, perhaps the prisoners would be the only survivors.

And what of those toward the north? Of Nigidius Maius and his estate outside the north wall of the city, and the one who was held there against her will? To run there was to run toward the mountain. Which meant she was even nearer the danger.

Cato raced through the Forum to the north end, where the Temple of Jupiter still stood unrepaired from the last quake that had wrought destruction. Would Pompeii survive this disaster?

The stones assaulted his face and arms, raising welts. He ran through the Street of Tombs, empty and silent save the continued rush of the fire-breathing mountain and the clatter of pebbles hitting the street.

The street wound upward slightly, to a rise outside of town where Maius's estate farmed the rich, black soil and the grapes grew in abundance.

He reached the villa breathless and beaten by the falling pebbles. The gravel accumulated underfoot now, crunching beneath his sandals. No more flaming boulders had accosted him, but he ran half-expecting to be struck down. Above him, the black cloud had reached to every horizon. Daylight had been overtaken by a foul mid-day night, a darkness that traveled on an evil wind and wormed its way through mind and heart.

Cato ran the length of the empty peristyle along the southern end of the villa, under a doorway, and into Maius's first atrium. The pleasant *plink* of rocks falling into the impluvium basin's water deceived. The reds and yellows of the garden's flowers glowed with the strange light of a coming storm.

He'd formed no plan as he ran. Foolish. Where would Valerius keep Ariella? Where would Maius have housed his guests? The household had fled the safety that open space provided during an earthquake to hide from the falling sky.

Should he yell for someone? Would they hand over Ariella? He must at least be certain she was safe, that she had survived the quake.

He ran through the house, coming upon a girl in a shadowy colonnade, about Isabella's age. She paced the hallway alone. She turned on him as though he might save her. Maius's blue-eyed daughter, Nigidia. With a flash of recognition, he realized that he had seen her several times—among the Christians. Flora's friend.

"Have you seen my father?" In the murky light her face seemed luminescent.

He shook his head. "I am looking for the slave girl Ariella. She belongs to Valerius."

Nigidia blinked several times, her lips parted.

He shook her. "Have you seen Ariella?"

"They have gone."

"Gone? Where?"

"Valerius. All of them. He left for Rome."

Cato released his grip on her. It had only been last night that Valerius arrived. "Because of the mountain? Is he a fool?"

Nigidia shook her head slowly. "No. They left before the quake. He wanted to sail today."

Cato turned from her, left her in the hall, guilt nipping at him. But she was not his responsibility. He already had four women to look after.

"Will you tell my father I am waiting for him?" Her voice was plaintive, childlike.

"Keep out of the open," he yelled in response, already across the atrium and heading back through the house. His tunic was damp with sweat now.

The ash seemed to have thickened while he had been indoors. He stopped under the peristyle roof to rip a swath of fabric from the bottom of his tunic and tie it around his face, to cover his nose and mouth. Chest heaving, he ran back toward the town, through the dirty ashfall that lay ankle-deep, mixed with the pebbles and rising fast. When would it stop?

More important, could Valerius have put out to sea before the disaster? And if he had . . .

What had become of his ship—and the slaves it carried?

44

Ariella and Micah pushed against the foot traffic on the inside of the gate and threaded through the crowd in the street. Ahead, though she could not see it past the people, lay the Forum. But between the gate and the Forum, people flooded into the entrances of the basilica on the right and the Temple of Apollo on the left, seeking refuge together. Stones began to fall on them, stinging bare skin. How could such a thing be? She understood the ash—it settled out of the sky from unseen fires. But stones from the heavens? It was beyond understanding.

Where should they go? There was something illogical about fighting against the flow of people. Did it not mean she and Micah were headed the wrong direction? And yet any direction away from Valerius seemed right.

She longed for reassurance that Isabella and Octavia were safe. And Europa and her household. Jeremiah. The faces flitted across her mind. She fought the desire to weep and kept pressing onward.

They reached the basilica and joined the flow into its central courtyard. The structure built for handling legal matters of the town had not yet been repaired since the quake that damaged the city years ago, as broken columns and a partial roof attested. Citizens clogged the nave, huddled in tight family groups. Children wailed and mothers tried in vain to comfort them, all the while looking at the treacherous black cloud spreading across the sky and the ash and pebbles it rained down on their heads.

Ariella slowed to watch the sky. It was unreal, like something from one of Maius's dark frescoes, with its billowing darkness blocking out the sun. How could they find safety from such a widespread, fearsome thing? She had been trained to defeat any foe. But this was an enemy far beyond her reach, and the helplessness both angered and terrified her.

Micah pulled her to the front of the building, to the raised apse that had retained its stone roof. They pressed against the wall, watching the turmoil as though they were ruling magistrates, looking down from positions of authority. Throughout the crowd, prayers to the various gods, chief among them Vulcan, were shouted from frightened lips.

Beside her, Micah spoke over the people. "This is what the Holy One says: 'Soon I will shake the heavens and the earth, the sea and the dry land again.'"

Ariella looked up at him, into the man's face of the boy she had known. Yes, a man now, of twenty years. A man who quoted the prophets as though their words were part of him. Since their meeting yesterday, they'd had so little time to speak. Who had he become in the nine years since their separation? Had he carried anger as she had, refusing to bow his knees to a God who would rip him from his family and give away his inheritance?

He met her eyes, looked deep into her heart.

Regardless of what would become of them, for this moment they were together and they were free. She gave way to her emotions at last and reached up to wrap her arms around his neck. Tears flowed unchecked, so unlike her and yet a welcome release.

Micah held her head against his chest and patted her back as she sobbed out her fear and her joy. She had been a fool to think him still a boy, and the relief of being in his protective arms brought more tears.

"I have missed you, sister." He pulled her away and held her arms. "I never gave up hoping that I would find you."

She dried her face with the back of her hand. "Nor I, you."

Memories of that last day in Jerusalem, of the terrifying chaos, the raging fires, the screams of people fleeing the streets, burned through her mind. Memories so like this very day that it was as though they had reunited only moments after they had been lost to each other, as though the years did not exist.

"Have you been in slavery these nine years?"

He shrugged. "Among other things." It would be a story for another time. "But when I eventually learned that you served under Valerius, I arranged to be sold there myself, hoping to find you." He touched her cheek and smiled.

She grasped his hand and held it there. "I am beginning to believe HaShem *does* watch over His children, even in the midst of suffering."

"You must believe it, sister." Micah's eyes grew serious. "I have much to tell you, things I have learned. The Messiah has come, Ariella, and we missed it. He walked Jerusalem with our grandparents . . ." He frowned. "What is it, Ariella? Why do you look at me that way?"

But she could not speak. Micah too? Did everyone she loved believe in this new Messiah?

The ground trembled under their feet, and Micah pulled her farther into their shelter, but Ariella's heart was too raw to notice. The words spoken to her on the beach resonated: *I gave My life to redeem yours.*

Could it be true? Though her body remained in slavery, had her soul been purchased with holy blood? Could she be set free?

She had been fighting for so many years, fighting the God of her fathers for all the evil He had allowed. And yet, if it were also true that He had provided a way for her to be accepted, this way of shattering grace that defied all understanding, then was He not good? And what was there to do but surrender? To continue to fight was to throw herself in the path of death.

Her heart hovered there, on the edge of a precipice, looking into the unfathomable. She still did not understand His ways, how He could allow such horror and still love. Yet if the Messiah had come and died to save her, then what more proof did she require of the love of HaShem? She hovered . . .

And then she leaped.

It took only a moment. While death rained down around their heads, Ariella passed over to life. She felt it in her body, knew it in her mind, embraced it in her heart.

Micah waited, his eyes locked on hers.

"I know," she breathed. "He is also my Messiah."

Micah once more pulled her to his chest, and the ground heaved again.

He turned to the open nave, to the ash and pebbles that littered the floor. "I do not know that we are safe here."

As though in response, a huge chunk of blackness flared into the courtyard, angling out of the sky as though thrown down from heaven. A moment later a woman's scream cut across the wide space, silencing the crowd. A circle widened from where she screamed, hugging two small children to her side. At her feet, under the flaming rock, lay the crushed body of a man. She screamed again and then again, the sound bouncing from the stone walls of the basilica, enveloping them all in a wave of panic.

And then there were more. A shower of flaming rocks like falling stars. With them came a strange smell, rotten like the smell of death. The people scrambled over each other in their race to escape the basilica, as though there were safety to be found in the streets.

Ariella's mouth went dry and she, too, pulled toward the crowd. Micah held her back.

"Where else would we go, sister?" He pointed upward, to the roof. "We are protected here."

Ariella panted, watching the people pour from the basilica to the street. "Micah, I—there are people I care about . . ."

"You want to go to them?"

She reached up to touch his cheek. "It should be enough to be with you. But if we are to die, I want to see the world end with my friends."

His mouth was tight. "Portius Cato."

"No!" Her denial was too quick, too sharp. She saw it in his eyes. "His mother, his sister. And there are others. Others who have loved me."

He nodded. "Then I should also like to meet HaShem in the presence of those who have loved you."

They joined the crowd pushing from the damaged building into the street, then turned right, toward the Forum. The Temple of Apollo's narrow entrance across from them also disgorged citizens. Inside the temple, someone had lit torches on the platform to combat the strange dusk, and Ariella caught a glimpse of the gold-trimmed altar, glinting in the torchlight.

The crowd flowed both directions now, as though half were

convinced that their escape lay across the sea, and the others had determined to return to safety under their own roofs.

They reached the Forum, and Ariella took a deep breath of relief at the thinning of the crowd. But her breath caught, ash-filled and chalky. Had it grown worse? The layer of ash in the Forum, deeper than her ankles now, muffled the sound of the falling pebbles. They paused inside the Forum's wide rectangle, empty as most of the people crowded under the colonnaded roofs at its side. Black chunks of burning rock, some the size of a man's head and others as big as chariots, littered the Forum's expanse.

The central gathering place for the city had been oriented toward Vesuvius, as though all important business should occur at the foot of the mountain. There was irony here now, as the mountain beyond the end of the Forum continued to spew upward, as though the underworld were emptying itself into the sky.

Micah grabbed her hand. "Are you ready?" They would have to dash across the Forum, taking their chances in the open.

She turned to look across the space, tracing the path they would take. To her left a single man ran toward them. She tried to draw courage from his bravery. He had tied a strip of fabric across his face to filter the ash. They should do the same.

Something about him drew her gaze again. That familiar build, shoulders and chest. Her heart surged with something she could not name.

Micah was pulling her forward. "Ariella, come!"

But in that moment the masked runner slowed as well, drawing up as though in surprise. In recognition.

She could not move. A chill ran over her flesh.

And then he was running again, pulling the mask from his face, shouting her name.

She struggled from Micah's grasp and left him behind, her feet carrying her toward the other.

Cato reached her with his arms already open, and she fell into them. He held her tight, buried his face in her neck. "She told me you had sailed. I was so afraid for you."

Ariella could not speak. How could she say what was in her heart?

He was kissing her cheeks now, holding her face in his hands, kissing her forehead, her hair, like a husband who had thought his wife lost and had her restored.

His kisses left her more breathless than the ash.

Perhaps there would be time for truth between them later. Perhaps not.

He circled her shoulder with his arm and pulled her toward Micah. "Come. The city is going to fall."

They reached her brother and she read his disapproval. No doubt he believed Cato had used his slave girl for more than kitchen chores. Again, the truth must wait.

Cato led them all to the covered colonnade and they circled together beside a pillar, holding their ground against the tide of people.

Ariella found her voice at last. "What do you mean? How will the city fall?"

He pointed upward. "Look at what the sky still holds for us." He kicked at the calf-deep ash and pebbles. "If the city is not buried, at the very least the roofs will not hold. It is not safe indoors, nor outdoors." He lifted his head toward the magistrates' buildings at the end of the Forum and the prison. "And those underground will be trapped beneath it."

Micah straightened and spoke to Cato. "What is there to do, then?" He spoke as an equal, and a glow of pride flickered in Ariella's heart.

"We must leave Pompeii. Escape to the south, across the plains and away from the mountain." He eyed Vesuvius. "I am not certain she is finished yet. I have heard that rivers of fire can pour from Vulcan's mountains. We may not have seen the worst."

Ariella kept her eyes from the monster. "But what of the others—your sisters and your mother?"

Cato turned again to the prison and his face grew as dark as the sky. "We leave no one behind."

45

Cato feared for them all. Isabella and Octavia. Portia and even her husband, Lucius, wherever he might be. And what of his new friends, so recently dear to him? Had Europa and Seneca and the others survived the quakes? Did they also take to the streets, where burning boulders were as lethal as falling columns?

Whatever came of each of them, of the city itself, Cato had found Ariella. He would not be separated from her again. He ripped another strip from his tunic, wrapped it around her face, and leaned forward to tie it behind her head. The fine powder of ash coated her short hair, whitening it, and the desire to see her hair grow white with years flashed over him. Her dark eyes never left his own.

He did not take the time to ask himself the obvious questions. She was a slave and he a patrician. She was a Jew and he a Roman. But disaster made all people equal, and as they ran together toward the prison, Cato counted on the city magistrates' agreement. They could keep no one in chains while the city burned.

They dodged people and fallen rocks, crunched through the ash and stone with progress far too slow. The detritus from the sky was knee-deep now, and though the solid particles made it possible to walk on its surface in most places, in others they floundered in soft ash, alternately sinking and climbing.

The townspeople were like animals trapped in an arena, running to and fro with no plan, and it grieved Cato to see it. They reached the suggestum, where he had once stood above the Forum crowds to announce his candidacy. He climbed again, yelling to the people who rushed past.

"The sea is not safe, nor are your homes! We must flee the city. Gather your households. Move south!"

Some stopped to listen. Most hurried on, as though he were a crazed prophet, foretelling doom while the sun still warmed them. He smacked a fist against his palm and paced the platform. The message he shouted today outweighed any political speech. The vicious enemy above them overshadowed even Nigidius Maius.

Ariella grabbed at his ankle from beneath the dais. "It is not your responsibility to save them all. You have done what you can."

She was right, but the useless flight of the people toward the sea frustrated him. Still, he must see to his own.

He expected the entrance to the prison to be untended, but when they reached the narrow set of steps that led underground, they found that the guard had been tripled. As though the escape of criminals threatened the city more than the evil in the sky. Two burly soldiers stood at the steps, their pilum crossed at the opening, and another stood within the recess, shoveling out the ash and rocks that clogged the opening.

Cato scrambled through the remaining distance, Ariella's hand in his own and Micah somewhere behind them. "You must let them out."

The guards wore a mixed expression of fear and duty.

"They will be trapped under there!"

One of the soldiers inclined his head to the third. "He'll keep it clear."

"And you will be buried beside him. Think, men! Who will hold you accountable for fleeing your own death?"

But they had been trained too well and looked over his head, silent.

Cato cursed under his breath. Could the three of them, unarmed, overpower the soldiers? "Who has given the order to keep them here?"

"Nigidius Maius. He was here only a short time ago, ensuring that the prison remains full."

Maius. So this was where he had been when Cato had searched for him in his villa. Had he now returned to his daughter? Would they run to safety, leaving some to die in cells?

Ariella squeezed his hand and turned her face to speak to him. With the fabric covering her mouth, the guards would not hear. "We must find weapons and come back. They will not give up their duty without a fight."

Cato looked down on her sweet face, so earnest in her willingness to take up arms for him, for Portia. His beautiful and fearsome warrior. He kissed the top of her head once more, then led her and Micah from the prison.

"There are those with more influence here than we have. Seneca and Europa will know how to get into the prison." And it would give him a chance to see how that family fared.

Ariella's eyes brightened above her mask. "I have been worried for them."

"It should not take long to reach their home." He turned to Micah. "You should cover your face. The night is not over yet."

The grand house of Europa and Seneca lay in the eastern district, perhaps a league from the Forum. Could they reach it without being pummeled by falling cinders? They would have to stay close to the walls and stay together. What time was it? The early dusk was disorienting. Did it near the time of the evening meal?

But the townspeople were unconcerned with food. Many of them had strapped small cushions to their heads to soften the blow of the falling fist-sized rocks. Strange sight. Man, woman, and child hurrying through the half-buried streets with terrified faces under their comical head coverings. Many clutched ornate wooden lock boxes. All they could carry, fearing the worst—that they would not return.

Cato had not released Ariella's hand since the Forum. They twisted through the crowd. A sudden and white-hot flash of light drew him up, and she rammed his back.

The crowd paused, as they had when the stones began to fall. As if an unseen god controlled the movement of each one, halting and setting them in motion according to his whim. They looked to the sky, to the menacing gray cloud.

Another flash. A collective scream. Summer lightning, but arcing horizontally through the darkness. No daggers thrown to earth, these ragged red sparks branched from one side of the sky to the other. Lit up the underside of the cloud with an angry orange glow.

They pushed on. Every new flare brought sharp screams. Ash coated his tongue, burned his eyes, rattled in his lungs. How long could they survive?

Fires cropped up throughout the city. He glimpsed them through the open upper portion of abandoned doorways—both the insulae and wealthy homes. The city burned above and below.

At last they reached the house. The door was unbarred, though rock and ash buried a third of it. Had they left? He entered without a call of greeting, pulling Ariella across the hidden threshold. Micah brought up the rear. The three pulled their masks below their chins.

Silence reigned. Ash drifted through the open atrium roof and settled on the bright flowers. Bizarre paradox of vibrant life coated with the cremated remains of the mountain.

"Europa? Seneca?"

Ariella ran to the triclinium. "Jeremiah?"

No answer.

A shadow caught his eye in a doorway near the back of the courtyard, familiar in its massive build. "Cyrus?"

The bald Persian slave edged forward.

"Are they hidden?"

The slave crossed his bulky arms. "Taken."

Cato's heart lurched. "Killed?"

Cyrus's eyes narrowed to angry slits. "Arrested. Because of the faith. They were accused of treasonous acts and imprisoned."

Ariella gasped and extended her hand to the ruined garden. "Now?"

"The soldiers came this morning, after the first earthquake. Rounded them up and marched them off."

Cato raked a hand through his hair, finding it full of ashes. "And now he keeps them there, in certain death. He has gone mad." A flicker of madness threatened Cato's own mind. Could he do nothing to help anyone?

Ariella grasped his hands, brought his eyes to her own. "We must free them, Quintus. The believers and Portia. We can do this together." Her steady voice sharpened his focus. Portia and the church. But there were others he could not forget.

"Micah." He turned to Ariella's young brother, always so quiet. "I need your help. My mother and sister, in my home . . . will you go to them?"

The young man straightened and nodded.

"They will be frantic at my absence, and they need to leave the city. Help them gather what valuables they can carry, and bring them both to the Stabian Gate. We will meet you there. Will you remember the way to the house?"

His eyes were somber. "I will find it."

Cato looked into his eyes and gripped his arm. "Watch the sky, Micah. And the mountain. If we do not come—"

Micah returned his grip, the clasp of friends. "I will keep your loved ones safe." His eyes flicked to Ariella.

Cato nodded, offering Micah his own vow. "And I will do the same for you."

Ariella threw her arms around her brother. "We will come to you soon, I promise. Do not fear."

Should he send Ariella with her brother? Was it wrong to force them to part? And yet he had sworn he would not let her go again. And he needed her help. He let them say their good-byes and went to Cyrus. "We need weapons."

The loyal slave drew in a breath that expanded his mighty chest. "You shall have them." He pounded a fist across his chest. "And another to fight by your side."

46

Ariella watched Micah climb through the half-buried doorway, back into the open street. Tears welled, but it was right. He should go to Octavia and Isabella. And she must help free Portia and the others. Her heart ached at the separation, but she would see him again.

Cyrus brought bread and wine. Not hungry, she ate and drank for strength. The bread tasted of ashes and the wine soured in her chest.

The home had some weapons, but not many. Two swords and a small assortment of time-dulled daggers.

They covered their faces once more, gripped their weapons, and trudged through the gravelly atrium to the door, ducked through the opening, and regained the street.

They moved in a single line now, holding their weapons instead of each other. He had not spoken to her of his heart. How could he? But his eyes and his lips had said much. She would refuse to be his mistress, but he knew that. She followed him through the streets, which had grown quieter since they came this way. Cyrus walked behind.

The lightning continued. Would it ever stop? Night had fallen, and with the walls of houses blocking the view of the mountain and the darkness obscuring the sky, one could almost forget the horror that overshadowed them. But those flashes of terror—each one screamed the truth.

Deliver us, HaShem.

"The name of the Lord is a strong tower, the righteous run into it and are safe."

Words from childhood. Were they still so much a part of her? What kind of Jew called on the Creator only in times of distress?

Most of them.

This was truth, and the history of her people. And yet, did He not deliver, again and again?

She struggled to keep up, her breath coming in short gasps, but her mind was fixed elsewhere.

Yes, HaShem was sovereign over the affairs of men, whether her rebellious spirit chose to acknowledge it or not. Refusing to bow her knee, raising her fist, these actions did nothing to put her in control, did they? She could accept His sovereignty, or she could deny it. Either way, HaShem still ruled. Extending blessing and allowing evil, and who could fathom the mind of the Creator?

True, her life had been mostly evil of late. But still, there was good. Micah had been returned to her. She had found Quintus.

Quintus. She had called him by his praenomen earlier, and he had not reacted. It had come naturally, for in her heart, she had called him such since the first time she learned his name.

Another flash illuminated the ash-clogged street. With the crowds dispersed, the light revealed a scattering of dead bodies, lying where they had been struck down. Some lay abandoned, others cradled in the arms of their loved ones. They passed a young girl clutching an older man to her chest. She rocked and wailed, insensible to danger. Ariella's heart wrenched. But they must move on.

The sight of such tragedy might have crushed the spirit of another, but Ariella found that the will to fight, the flaming heart of a warrior she had claimed in the arena, rose up within her with a strength she had never known. She clutched her dagger securely, her heart pounding and palms slick with the familiar anticipation of battle.

Invincible, no. But a warrior for HaShem. Would He accept her, after all she had done to refuse Him? There was only one way to be accepted, she saw that now. The once-for-all atonement of Yeshua's sacrifice, applied to her.

They passed an open doorway, and her right leg dislodged gravel, slipping down into the entrance. Cyrus grabbed her from behind and lifted her back to the loose upper level of stones. They marched on.

The strange smell that had drifted through the city strengthened. Sulfur. The smell of fire . . . of the underworld.

Halfway to the prison, a wrenching crash sounded to their left. They paused, listening. Another quake?

Cato turned, his eyes dark. "The roofs are collapsing. They cannot hold the weight."

Ariella closed her eyes. The sound was horrific. The sound of a city dying. The streets had emptied. Where were the people? Had they escaped out of the town, or did they huddle in their homes, believing they were safe, while the gray world crashed down on their heads?

Cyrus prodded her from behind. "We can do nothing for them."

They reached the Forum at last. Ariella called on the fight within, readied her mind for the battle. In the darkness it was impossible to see how many guards remained at the entrance to the underground prison.

They fought their way across, still a single line, a feeble front with no rear guard. The mountain drew her irresistibly, and she paused to stare at the orange flames at its peak, a grotesque and colossal torch, lighting up the trunk of ash and rock. In the ash-covered world, the flaming mountain seemed the only thing that lived. How was it possible that after all these hours, it still disgorged itself into the sky?

But she must forget the mountain. Think only of the battle.

When they reached the prison steps, they found only a slight depression in the gravel where the entrance had been. No guards blocked them. Only stone.

She wiped sweat from her forehead with the back of her sword-hand. "They heeded your advice." The guards had fled and left the prisoners buried alive.

Beside her, Cyrus yanked a handle sticking up from the ash. A shovel. He set to work immediately.

Ariella tossed her weapon aside and used her feet to kick the gravel away from the opening as he dug. Cato did the same.

The mountain blazed, rocks landed around them, and an urgency fell upon them all. They worked in silence, clearing the entrance bit by frustrating bit. When they had opened a narrow channel, enough to squeeze through, she and Cato took up their weapons once more and pushed through. Cyrus remained above, in case of a cave-in.

Singing.

They heard singing as they descended. Ariella's heart swelled with the melody.

"Portia?" Quintus called into the gloom. "Seneca?" He grabbed a torch from a wall socket, still burning even in the sealed-off tomb.

The singing ceased, a beat of silence followed, then the sound of a crowd scrambling to its feet, hurrying to cell doors.

"Cato?" Seneca's voice was strong, confident.

They moved toward the voice. A hand stretched through the small opening in the door.

"We will get you out."

They had prepared themselves for a battle with the guards. The cell doors fell before them easily. Ariella hacked at the wooden bars with her swords and Cato kicked at others. The prisoners, innocent and guilty alike, tumbled from cells, chattering and embracing each other and their rescuers.

Ariella fell into Europa's embrace, patted Jeremiah's aging cheek. But above their heads, she watched Cato as he searched for his sister.

"Portia?" He clutched at various prisoners in turn. "Portia of the Catonii? Where is she?"

It was Europa who gave the answer, her hand gentle on his arm. "He came hours ago, when we first arrived. He took her with him."

Cato stared down at her, uncomprehending.

"Nigidius Maius. We were placed here on his orders. After the disaster began, he visited the prison. He seemed fearful that you would come for her, so he told the guards he was removing her to his private cells, in his villa."

Ariella's arms trembled with fear and fury. It had taken so long to reach the prison. Could they ever hope to rescue Portia from the estate outside the town? A house that lay in the direct path of the spewing mountain? She met Cato's eyes, tried to convey her sorrow.

His own eyes had gone cold. He gripped Seneca. "Take your family and get out of the city. The roofs are collapsing and I believe the mountain has more death to rain upon us. There is nowhere safe."

Seneca wrapped an arm around Flora and said nothing.

Ariella could read his heart. How could Flora make such a journey? She clutched Europa's hand. "You must find a way. Please. We will meet you south, beyond the city gate."

Europa looked to her husband.

Would they leave? She could not be sure.

Cato was pushing the freed prisoners up through the opening they had cleared. He yelled encouragement to move forward. Many of them must have found the prison a safe refuge compared to the falling sky. But it would not remain so. He called to Cyrus to lead them to the city gates.

Aboveground, she fought her way to his side. "Can we make it?"

"To the Stabian Gate?"

She touched his face. "To Portia."

He shook his head. "I cannot allow you to come. Go with them, help them flee, meet your brother, and my mother and sister."

Her mouth went dry and she gripped her sword tighter. "You promised Micah you would keep me safe."

His eyes flashed. "And this is how I will do it! Do you think you will be safer heading toward that?" He jabbed his sword toward Vesuvius.

She ignored him and said her good-byes to the believers. When they had ventured off, following Cyrus, she turned back to him. "You do not even know where Maius keeps his private cells."

He rammed his sword down into the rubble. "I will find them." He took her in his arms, pulled his mask away so she could read his face. "Please, my love, be safe."

The words struck the breath from her chest, but she would not be dissuaded. She pushed away, took up his sword, and handed it to him.

"I stay with you."

47

They traveled across a foreign landscape barren of life, devoid of color.

Cato led the way, both grateful and fearful that Ariella followed. Their sandals sank in the ash and rock, sometimes to the ankle but often deeper. Progress was slow.

It must be well after sunset now, though the sun had been absent since midday. The column of fire ahead of them lit the gray streets and the fields beyond with an unnatural warmth, a glow that sickened rather than comforted.

They picked their way up the Street of Tombs, many of the repositories of the dead already buried. Not even the dead were safe, and the sight proved that there was nowhere to hide. There was no end to the falling ash, and Cato tried to calculate the rate at which it fell. How many hours until the city ceased to exist?

Behind him, Ariella yelped.

He spun to the sound. Had she been hit?

She held up her hand as if to signal that she was unhurt, but then rubbed at an angry red welt on her arm.

They were both scraped and burned, but he was grateful it was no worse. He nodded his sympathy and they moved forward. It seemed a miracle that they had not been struck down by anything larger. Perhaps it was a miracle.

If Jeremiah's God, his God, were indeed intervening, it had better be only the beginning. The approach to Maius's house was the final approach to evil. The villa lay in the shadow of the mountain, a fitting place for the culmination of the fight that had begun the moment Nigidius Maius had stepped into his wine shop.

It was about more than the election now. About more than even his sister's freedom. Perhaps it always had been.

The pull of God was strong on his heart tonight. All that Jeremiah had spoken over him seemed words from a prophet. It was for him to rise up against evil, to wield the sword of God against it. Trusting in God, not himself. Willing to fail, praying to succeed. Had he been chosen? Could he believe the old man's words?

It seemed hours until they reached the path that led to the front of the house. Perhaps it had been. A weariness he had never known washed over him. He paused before the buried front garden, unequal to the task.

Ariella drew up beside him, panting. "What is it?"

It was growing harder to breathe, the sulfuric odor thickening the air. "I do not know if I can do this."

She seemed to feel it too. It was not merely the exhaustion. The house seemed enveloped in a special darkness, a settled dread that wormed its way into his soul.

"Evil." Her voice was low, perhaps angry.

He looked at her eyes, tried to read her expression beneath the ash-coated mask.

She watched him. "Can you feel it?"

He turned back to the house. If he had needed confirmation that the battle about to be waged was more than man-against-man, this was it.

Holy One, go before me.

The prayer strengthened him. A piece of his soul lightened as though a candle had been lit. A tiny flicker at best, but enough to guide him onward. He lifted his sword toward the house. "Are you ready?"

She did not answer at once, perhaps finding her own strength. But then she was climbing upward, toward the peristyle. Always the warrior.

Inside the house, the atrium's garden and floor mosaics had been erased. Only a sea of rocky ash greeted them. It tapered down at the edges, to the roofed colonnade surrounding the atrium. They slid down the pile to the empty walkway. It was a relief to be on firm ground. His calf muscles twitched with the strange solidity.

Ariella hurried ahead of him. "The cells are this way."

They twisted through the silent house. How could she remember where to go through this labyrinth? It hurt his heart to think of her firsthand knowledge of Maius's special cells.

Ariella slowed as they neared a smaller peristyle porch on the west side of the house. Torchlight flickered against the columns and Cato could hear voices coming from the room that opened onto the porch.

She turned to him, held a finger to her lips beneath the mask. "The entrance is past the triclinium here. But there is someone present."

A laugh echoed to them.

Maius.

Ariella's eyes flickered her fear and confusion. Could the man truly laugh at such a time as this?

A slave turned the corner suddenly. He bore an empty tray and stopped short when he saw the two. Cato moved quickly. He grabbed the man, twisted behind him, and covered the slave's mouth with his hand. His back slammed the wall and he held the man fast. Ariella lifted her sword point to the slave's chin.

Cato hissed into the man's ear, "Do not make a sound." The slave nodded and Ariella signaled with her eyes that she was ready to hold him to it.

He eased his hand off the man's mouth.

The slave took a gulping breath but said nothing.

Ariella held him against the wall.

Cato pivoted to face him. "Is Maius alone?"

The slave shook his head.

"Who?"

"His daughter."

"Anyone else?"

Another shake of the head. "He is feasting."

The words were offered as an explanation, but they only explained that Nigidius Maius was either a fool or a madman. Perhaps both.

Cato pushed him toward the hall. "Go. Take anyone you wish and flee the city. He will not have need of you again."

The slave hesitated a moment. Cato was unsure whether it was loyalty to Maius or a desire to fight alongside Cato that held him, but then he was gone.

Speed and good health, my friend.

He drew Ariella close and spoke in whispers. "I will deal with Maius. You find Portia, bring her out."

She nodded her understanding.

"Ready?"

Another nod.

He touched her face above the mask, traced a line under her eye.

Then he strode ahead, to the opening of the room. He felt Ariella slip behind him, toward the entrance to the lower levels.

Maius did not look up at once. He reclined on a couch with Nigidia beside him and a table filled with excess before them. His distraction gave Cato a fleeting moment to absorb the scenes of horror painted on the triclinium walls. He took in the story at once, the terrible mystery rites of a young girl's initiation, the horror on her face before, and the resignation after. The sight filled him with something he could not at first name.

Righteous anger. His chest swelled with it, and it burst from his mouth in a shout of rage. "Gnaeus Nigidius Maius! The Holy One has looked down on your acts and has passed judgment!"

Maius's head jerked up from the table, his mouth still stuffed with grapes and his eyes wide.

Cato stood at the center of the room's opening, his stance wide and his sword raised. A tremor shook through him, deeper and more profound than any earthquake.

Surrender. He gave it all in that moment—all the responsibility he felt for his sisters, his mother, for Ariella. All the commitment to free Pompeii of Nigidius Maius, to free the world of all injustice. It was not his battle, it was the Lord's.

And he was full of something new, something with power and glory, a strength he had never known, a freedom from bondage. He was a sword wielded in the Name of the only Just One.

And in that Name, he had no doubt of victory.

Maius struggled to his feet, lifting his bulk above the cushion and stepping back against the triclinium wall, beneath the fresco of the lounging Bacchus. Nigidia did not move, and Cato sensed in her a fearsome dread, of the ending of both the world and her father. There had been guilt at leaving her earlier. It would not happen again.

Cato expected Maius to cower in fear, as he was unarmed. He had been naïve.

The man's face filled instead with amusement. And then laughter, such as they had heard in the hall, filled the room.

"I should have known you would come. You cannot leave a thing undone, can you, Portius Cato? Even on a day such as this." He gestured toward the darkness outside. "When everyone with sense is indoors. Still you come, always the rescuer."

"The mountain will kill us all, Maius. I am taking Portia with me."

"Are you?" He pulled Nigidia to her feet and wrapped an arm around her. Then turned his eyes to Cato and stared him down, his bushy brows drawn together.

Cato swallowed, trying to free a tightness in his chest. Around him, the frescoes blurred as though viewed through water, then seemed to come to life, to swirl around the room. Wispy satyrs playing their pan pipes, a nymph suckling a goat, the leering Bacchus. Evil personified.

Had he gone mad? Did Maius see the apparitions? Nigidia's face blanched and she ducked and swerved, still gripped by her father's right arm.

Maius opened his mouth but did not speak at first. When he did, the words seemed to stream from his mouth in a torrent, as the flames now poured from the mountain above them. "Come to me now, Jupiter! Heed my call and deliver me! Strike down my enemy. Accept my many sacrifices and grant me favor. Venus and Mercury, I call on your mighty power!"

Cato raised an arm, but his strength faltered. His limbs were weighted with the force of Maius's words.

Fight. He must fight.

No. You must surrender to Me.

341

The words were not his—they were spoken into his heart. He gave himself to the words, to the Word, who opened his mouth and spoke for him. "'If you say, "But we did not know," does not He who weighs the heart perceive the truth? Does not He who guards your life know it? Will He not repay each person according to their deeds?'"

Maius wavered on his feet, took a step backward.

"'The wicked are like chaff that the wind blows away. For the Lord watches over the way of the righteous, but the way of the wicked will perish.'"

The words were not his own. Never had he even heard them spoken. He was a mouthpiece only, a willing tool in the hands of a mighty God.

This is what it means to be a champion for God.

"Nigidia." He looked into the girl's frightened eyes, her gaze skittering around the room in terror. "Nigidia, look at me." She focused on him at last.

"We are leaving now. Come to me."

Maius's lips drew back from his teeth and a hiss like that of a snake rushed from him. The unnatural sound filled the room, but the man did not move.

"Nigidia, now." He spoke to the girl as a father to a daughter. Her own father did not release his grip on the girl.

"What are you doing, Portius Cato?"

"I am taking the only good thing you have, Maius. And I am leaving you to the demons you worship, to be judged along with them."

Nigidia did not take her eyes from him.

He nodded slowly, passing his strength to her, willing her to move. And then he saw something shift in her blue eyes, saw freedom unfold in her expression, and knew that she had passed through the unseen veil herself, into the arms of a Savior, mighty to deliver.

Her head lifted to the beams above her for a moment, and a smile broke across her face like the coming of dawn in this impossibly long night.

She stepped aside, Maius's hold on her broken.

Maius flailed out to grab her, but did not move toward her. She sidestepped his clutching hand, staring at it as though it were a foreign object.

Cato held his sword outstretched, pinning Maius to the ground. "'You lifted praise to the gods of silver and gold, of bronze, iron, wood, and stone, which do not see and cannot hear or understand. You have not honored the God who carries your life and all your ways in His hand.'"

Nigidia seemed to float across the room until she reached his side.

He nudged her to stand at his back.

Maius's chest heaved, and flecks of white dotted his mouth. He glanced back and forth between Cato and his daughter. "You think you have defeated me?"

The election. Cato smiled. Such matters seemed to belong to another world. There would be no election now. And yet it had never been about the election, had it? He had always been meant to defeat the evil that Maius represented, and this he had done, here in the man's own villa, through a power not his own.

"Not I, Maius. The One True God has defeated you. You and your gods." Again the words that were from elsewhere. "Your gods hold sway over the hearts of the Empire now. But it will not always be thus. A day is coming when even the names of those you worship will be forgotten. Even then, the One God will make His name great, and His people will remain!"

Beside him, Cato felt Nigidia draw herself up, his ally against the evil she had known. Maius saw it too, and the loss of her seemed to steal whatever arrogance remained. His knees buckled, and he lurched forward onto a couch.

Cato pulled Nigidia with him, away from the triclinium and toward the hall that led to freedom.

And behind them, Maius began to scream.

48

Ariella ducked through the opening to Maius's private cells, leaving Cato to contend with Maius in the triclinium above.

Would she face guards at the bottom? She adjusted her grip on her sword and moved downward on silent feet into the darkness.

The cells were nothing more than a mud hole beneath the house, but the fact that Maius kept such a place spoke much about his character.

Little light filtered down the steps, and no torch extended from the wall socket at the bottom. Ariella felt her way along the narrow channel, tracing the wall with her left hand, while her sword hand remained extended.

There appeared to be no guard. Small wonder, given the destruction that reigned above. If Maius had not dismissed them, they likely fled their posts.

"Portia?" She whispered the name, unsure why she felt the need for stealth, except that the place seemed unholy, as though she trod in the domain of Rome's underworld. She breathed a prayer to HaShem once more and felt His presence.

No answer returned to her. She called for the woman again, then paused to listen for any sign of life. A rattled breathing sounded from beyond.

Ariella edged forward. She had been insensible with rage when Maius had consigned her to his cells and barely remembered the arrangement of them. That there was no latrine she remembered well, and the smell disgusted and angered her.

She reached a small barred gate, its post anchored in nothing more than solid dirt. The latch would require a key, but she saw none about.

So Maius would leave Portia to die. Not surprising. His grudge against Portia's brother had become much more than personal or even political.

"Portia, are you there?" She drew up close to the gate and tried to discern something in the dim light. A whitish form on the ground. Ariella heard again the labored breath.

Whether it was the woman she sought she could not be certain, but whoever it was would perish if Ariella did not open the gate.

She searched the murk for a tool, found nothing, and set to work on the dirt around the latch with her sword. Pity about the dullness it would cause, but in the past hours she had needed a shovel more than a sword, and it was the best she had.

The dirt gave way with difficulty, and Ariella felt her neck dampen with the effort. In the end, it was thoughts of Maius, his feast with Valerius, and the beliefs the two men shared that gave her the furious energy to hack without mercy at the latch and the earth that held it. The latch became to her the bondage the two men forced upon others, and her sword the instrument of freedom. A frenzy of redemption swept her and she drove at the dirt again and again, until her hands blistered and her muscles ached.

At last, the latch gave way with a *thwack*. She kicked at the gate.

Inside the cell she heard the scuttle of rats and made out a prone body. She bent to the form, felt leg and arm and face, chilled with a fine sheen of sweat. "Portia, I am Ariella. A friend of your brother."

"Hmm." The woman stirred and shook her head.

"Can you stand?" She switched her sword to the other hand and slipped her free arm under Portia's body.

Portia struggled in her grasp and moaned. "Leave me be." The voice was cracked and hoarse, the flesh too warm. A fever, perhaps. Could she carry the half-conscious woman up the steps?

"Portia!" she whispered harshly into her ear, trying to rouse her. "It is time to leave. Quintus waits for you."

"Quintus?"

In the darkness, Ariella saw the woman's eyes flutter open. "Yes, he is aboveground. You must stand. It is time to leave this place. Time to go home."

"Home."

The word was uttered with heartbreaking simplicity. Ariella cradled her body. "Come, Portia. Let me take you home."

She succeeded in getting the woman to her feet, pulling her through the cell door and toward the steps. The light that drifted down from the torches above shadowed Portia's face, but still Ariella saw a reflection of Cato's features there and her heart swelled with a love for the woman, because she was his sister. She felt the pain of Portia's imprisonment in her own body.

The steps were steep and painstaking, with Portia propped on her. Above them, she could make out angry words, but not their meaning.

They reached the head of the steps where the light was stronger, and Ariella looked over Portia's chalky face and bloodless lips. Even if they should escape Maius, how would she make it from the northern outskirts of the city, all the way to the south wall?

She saw Cato at once, exactly where she had left him, feet planted at the entrance to the triclinium. Had he not moved?

Maius yelled to him, something about defeat, and Nigidia drifted across the feast room, away from her father. Portia bent her head to Ariella's shoulder as though she would sleep.

She watched as Cato drew himself up and delivered words that sounded to her ears more like prophecy than argument, a denouncing of Maius's gods, indeed of all the Roman idols, and the pledge that the Holy One would ultimately triumph.

He spoke as a Jew. And yet more than a countryman. She could see it in the set of his jaw, read it in the corded muscles of his outstretched arm, hear it in the force of his voice. He had become a follower of the Jewish Messiah, had given his heart and his allegiance.

What did this mean for them? *No slave or free. No Jew or Roman.*

There would be time enough to think on it later. For now, Cato was leaving.

And Maius was screaming.

49

Against logic, Cato left Maius in the triclinium and left Ariella underground. His newly heightened sense of God's word spoken over him said, *Go now. Trust now.* And so he did. With a hand at Nigidia's elbow, he sped through the inner halls, toward the devastated atrium, filled with a strength and confidence unknown since the mountain exploded over their heads.

Maius's screams followed them, echoing through corridor and mind with a demonic shriek. Had he rooted the man to the floor through the power of God?

However it had happened, the duovir was alone, bereft of that which he most prized.

They twisted through the halls when Cato heard footsteps behind. He turned, still holding Nigidia. Ariella gave him a half smile from the end of the hall. Supported by her arm, but alive and upright, was his sister Portia. His heart leaped with the sight of her. Of them both.

They met in the middle of the hall, and Cato took Portia from her, bore the weight of his sister's feeble body with his own.

"Maius saw us outside the triclinium." Ariella's voice held wonder. "We walked right past him. He shrieked at us but did not move."

Cato shifted forward and led them again, helping Portia. "It is an act of your God."

"And yours?"

He glanced at her. Of course she would somehow see the change in his heart.

Portia stumbled, and the group slowed.

"She is a bit feverish, I believe." Ariella touched Portia's face gently. "But I think most of all she needs food and water."

Cato dared not ask his sister about the child she carried. Not now.

Beside him, Nigidia stirred to life. "Follow me." She turned and left them swiftly.

Cato did not favor the idea of staying any longer than necessary in this evil place, but it was clear that Portia needed strength for the fearsome journey ahead. He pulled her along.

Ariella hastened to support her on the other side. They followed Nigidia's disappearing figure through the night-dark house.

The villa had suffered. Cato heard the shudders and creaks that signaled the stress of rock and ash on the roof. It might hold longer than the poorer houses in the city, but not forever. Nor for long. He had grown so accustomed to expecting rocks to fall from the sky that it seemed little had changed indoors, as he waited for the roof to collapse.

They trailed Nigidia to the back rooms of the house, undecorated and deserted. Maius's slaves and staff had fled.

Nigidia lit a torch from a smoldering cookfire, mounted it, then hastened around the kitchen, gathering small loaves of fine bread, cups, and jugs of wine.

She tossed her finds onto a table. "Eat. I have no need of anything. I will pack more food for our passage."

A sudden hunger swept Cato. He could not remember when he had last eaten. Cold porridge in the atrium, a lifetime ago?

Ariella tore a small piece from one of the loaves and held it to Portia's lips.

Cato inhaled sharply, touched by the tender act.

Portia was unwell, she was weak, and she seemed unable to focus on her present situation. The night was dark and dangerous. He chewed his lip. How could they bring her safely across the city?

But Ariella's ministrations seemed to help. Portia took a cup in her own hands and drained it, chewed some bread and asked for more. Some color already had returned to her face.

Nigidia handed pouches to each of them, filled with more bread, some cheeses, and dried fruit. To Cato she held out a wineskin. "It will not last us long, but we cannot carry much more."

"Thank you, Nigidia." The girl had grown much since he had first encountered her.

A glance at Ariella and Portia. "Are we ready?" It seemed impossible that Maius had not yet sought them out. They should be away from here.

Ariella strapped the pouch over her head, picked up her sword once more, and nodded. Cato turned from the sight. She had done nothing but fight since they had met, and even now the battle was not over.

They sped along the colonnaded walkway that bordered the atrium, through the side entrance, and out onto the covered peristyle.

It was a shock once again. The ash and rock alongside the empty porch now piled higher than the heads of the women, higher than his own head. It drifted down to the terrace level, a gravelly ramp. They scrambled upward, sinking knee-deep or worse and fighting to reach the upper level and move forward.

It had to be midnight. No moon, no stars brightened their way. Only the fantastic orange glow on the underside of the dense cloud. He looked backward at the mountain, still churning out fragments of itself with that great *whooshing* sound that had dogged them all through the day's living nightmare.

The women moved on ahead of him, and he pushed forward to lead. Portia was walking in her own strength now, thank God. They headed once more toward the town. From the hilly rise of Maius's estate, what should have been a lovely view of the town below, with torches carried through streets and candlelight streaming from windows, appeared a dead and frightening thing. In the hours since they had left, few roofs could have survived. Between the accumulation in the streets and the crushing load on houses, the city's residents would be underground, praying for deliverance. Or dead already.

The difficulty of crossing the landscape wearied his legs within minutes. The long hours of climbing through it had taken their toll. There were fewer orange streaks hurtling death from the sky now. They could be thankful for that. He looked backward at the mountain once more. Had something changed to save them from the fiery fallout?

And in that moment, something did change. He could not at first identify it.

The women also stopped, and Ariella was at his side in a moment. "What is that sound?"

But it was not a sound. It was the lack of sound that had arrested their attention. The familiar roar of ash and rock surging upward had suddenly ceased, as though the mountain had run out of breath, as though a mighty hand had shut off the gushing upward fountain.

They watched, open-mouthed, as the entire trunk-like gray column supporting the massive cloud-branches collapsed upon itself with a shuddering groan and the sky above the mountain rained down.

Where would it flow—all that poisonous, torrential weight? The decapitated summit of the mountain bubbled orange and black.

Cato turned from the mountain and set his eyes toward the south, toward the impossible trek before them. It would take all night to cross the city.

"Come." He struck out ahead. "There is not much time."

The unceasing upward surge could not last forever, and when at last Vesuvius had expelled all the madness within, the tower of death collapsed.

But there was still so much destruction to come.

The hours of spewed ash and rock now tumbled downward, a molten river, mixed with water, and became an avalanche of fiery mud, surging downward at speeds no human could outrun.

All day, as the lethal cloud spread across the sky, many of the people of Herculaneum had thought themselves safe. They had watched the winds blow the poisonous ash toward Pompeii and believed that they were spared. The mountain was a curiosity to them, nothing more.

And in less than four minutes, they were all dead.

They had seen it coming, the surging river of melted rock. Some had fled toward the beach, as if the water could save them.

Rich and poor, slave and freedman, they fell first in the death throes of the noxious air.

And then the burning river incinerated them where they fell.

When the glowing cloud of death subsided, all of Herculaneum lay in its grave, buried under forty cubits of burning mud.

But Vesuvius was not finished.

50

How long had he stood in this room, his feet weighted to the floor, as though an anchor were fixed to his ankles and dropped through the mosaic tiles?

He gave up struggling, gave up screaming, as the night wore on. There was no one to hear him, no one to help him.

He was alone.

When at last his legs were freed, he fell upon the triclinium floor, exhausted.

The torch had burned itself out. The food had grown stale. He could not see his beautiful frescoes any longer, could not drink in the truth of them. He dragged his bulk to the couch, climbed upon it, and collapsed.

Did he sleep?

The night was unnatural, the darkness odd and perplexing. Unreadable.

He felt strength had returned to his legs and pulled himself to standing. He stumbled from the triclinium, calling for Nigidia. It was useless to search for her but he did it anyway. Through the halls and rooms, the hidden recesses of the villa and the buried gardens.

He slowed at the back garden. How long had his birds lived as the ash piled around them in a smothering silence?

The steps to his veranda were partially covered by a roof. The first few lay bare, but the rest had become a steep incline, covered with rubble. He climbed, and the porous little rocks cut his hands and knees.

He reached the veranda, though it was now foreign to him. The level of the terrace had risen more than his own height, and the half wall where he had stood and gazed on the lovely mountain for so many evenings lay somewhere far beneath. He stood as on a cliff, overlooking the valley that had made him a wealthy man.

Not a vine remained. The stony landscape led all the way to the foot of the mountain, an unbroken plain of death.

Maius planted his feet in the stones, balanced himself on the edge of his blighted world, and once more raised his eyes to the mountain and to the gods that reigned above her.

Deep in his chest, the words rumbled.

I have given you everything.

He had called upon them in the triclinium, beseeched them to grant him favor as his enemy laughed in his face and blasphemed their names. But the gods had been silent.

Still silent.

He had taken her. Portius Cato had taken Nigidia, his one comfort, his most precious treasure. She had gone willingly, he had seen it in her eyes, though he wanted to believe that some enchantment of Cato's had drawn her away.

He sensed a lightening in the sky to the east. How could the sun still rise on such a day as this?

To the north, the mountain had not yet finished its boiling and churning.

The wind shifted. He smelled, rather than felt, the change. The sulfurous odor that had drifted over the city all night grew pungent. His lungs tightened and rebelled, doubling him over with a slashing cough that seared the throat.

Behind him, he heard the sound of another coughing.

Not alone. *Not alone!*

He turned, his feet still planted forward in the rocks.

Below, under the roof, Primus stood, clutching his chest. His most faithful slave, advisor.

Friend.

He reached out a hand of welcome. But the man's eyes were dark with hatred.

"Curse you, Nigidius Maius! You bring nothing but death."

And then he fell, facedown along the length of the bare steps, and was still.

Maius turned back to the mountain. He lifted his eyes to the orange fires at the summit. And barely blinked when an explosion rocked the house. Stones cracked. Somewhere columns split. The veranda held, and he watched the mountain.

A mighty, vicious flow streamed from Vesuvius, up, up over its lip, boiling over with melted rocks and earthy flames, then surging down the hillside, a flood of fire and poison.

Maius raised his chin, then raised his fist in its face.

He roared above the surge, "Come and get me, then!" He yelled at all the gods to whom he had ever sworn allegiance, all the gods he had offered sacrifices and even those he had not avowed.

Yes, even Cato's God, the Jewish God and his God-man Messiah. He roared at him as well, for sometime in the early watches of the morning, the fear that this One God was more powerful than any other had overtaken him. And so he spewed his fury, shook his fist at Israel's God.

The flow of boiling rock raced down the mountain, faster, faster, a wave crashing from a stormy sea. He watched it come, faced it, alone and defiant, angry and fearful.

And in the end, as the scorching flow swallowed his vineyard, his gardens, and his veranda, Nigidius Maius spit in the face of God.

51

The morning approached, impossibly.

The eastern horizon lightened from obsidian black to the color of filthy wash water. The travelers had slogged through the city's destruction all night, and Ariella would have sworn that the streets had doubled in length, so slow was their progress.

They took frequent breaks for the sake of Portia, but always Cato urged them forward before they were ready.

Sometime in the middle of the night, another earthquake rattled loose stones and broken walls. They waited it out in the center of a wide street, away from the danger of falling masonry. Apparently Ariella had not gone numb to fear, for the quake still left her palms slick and heart pounding.

The deserted streets wore an eerie, haunted look about them. More than once Ariella had caught a flash of someone, something moving about the streets as though on their way to the market or the arena. But each time she looked again, there was nothing. Did apparitions of the dead already roam the town?

Whenever they did encounter townspeople, peeking out from

near-buried doorways at those who voyaged across the stone sea, Cato begged them to join their group.

"There is no protection here." He pointed to the mountain. "She is not finished. Come with us to a high place, a wide place of safety."

Some refused to leave the valuable property they could not carry. Others scoffed at the danger. Most heartbreaking were the obedient slaves left behind, charged with guarding their masters' households.

They were not far from Cato's house now, but their loved ones would have fled south.

Cato took a side street, a slight detour. No explanation was necessary. Seneca and Europa's house lay this way.

Their door was open, but the entrance was submerged. Did it mean they were well away? She joined Cato in stabbing at the pile of rocky ash, forcing it down into the open vestibule until it slid away suddenly, allowing passage. He propelled his body through the chute and she followed. Nigidia and Portia dropped through after them.

The vestibule was a pocket of empty space between the street and the buried atrium, but a hall led left and right, a covered perimeter of the piles of rock.

"Seneca? Europa?" The rocks muffled Cato's voice as though underground. He led them through the halls, still calling.

"We are here." At the feeble answer, Ariella's heart fell. Cato stopped in the hall and closed his eyes. Her mouth went dry. The journey had grown so difficult, how could they make it?

Europa appeared at the end of the hall, outside the triclinium where Ariella had first encountered these special people, the night she brought the injured Jeremiah to their door. She hurried to meet them, arms outstretched. "I am so glad you are safe."

Ariella fell into her familiar embrace. "For now. But we cannot stay any longer. You must come."

Cato stalked ahead, through the entrance to the room. Europa led the three women behind him.

She stood in the doorway, taking in the group before her. The triclinium's beautiful frescoes were as bright and colorful as always, the brazier fires flickering against the reds and yellows, illuminating the spread of food on the tables. Like that first night.

And her friends. Europa and Seneca. Flora, reclined on a couch, with Jeremiah beside her. Only these four remained. Nigidia crossed behind her and knelt to Flora.

"You should have left the city!" Cato's voice sounded angry, but he was only worried.

Europa smiled sadly and patted his arm. "We have traveled as far as possible."

Ariella pushed forward, a fearsome dread weighting her limbs. "No. We are going to the south wall. We will help you."

Seneca came to his wife and circled her shoulders with his arm. He spoke softly. "Flora and Jeremiah nearly did not make the trek from the prison to our home. They are . . . unable—" His voice caught and his eyes filled with tears.

Ariella looked from Seneca to Europa, then down at the two on the couch. They were not reclining, were they? They had collapsed there in exhaustion.

She shook her head slowly. "No. You cannot stay."

Cato grabbed Seneca's arm. "We can get them out. Together."

Seneca pulled them into the hall, out of hearing range of the young girl and old man. His eyes held sadness, but also a strange peace.

"The Lord is with us. He will not forsake us."

Cato breathed heavily. "The mountain—"

"May take our lives, yes. But not our souls."

Ariella tightened her lips, stifling a cry. They could not be left behind. She would not allow it.

Europa embraced her, whispered into her ear, "We are not afraid, dear one. This day we shall see the face of our Messiah and enter into His glory. Do not fear for us."

She clutched at the woman, drowning in memories of her last sight of her mother. "I cannot lose you."

Europa drew away and put her hands to Ariella's cheeks. "We shall see each other again. When there will be no more war."

Her breath came in short gasps now, and tears dripped from her chin. Cato grasped her hand and led her into the triclinium, where Flora and Jeremiah rested.

The old slave opened his eyes to them, and Ariella bent to kneel at his side. "Jeremiah—"

He patted her hand. "This hip will lead me home after all, my girl." His smile was undimmed by pain or fear. "I only regret that these two remain." He pointed to Europa and Seneca.

Europa clucked her tongue. "We would not leave either of you."

Beside her, Flora sniffed, trying not to cry. Europa went to her and held her, rocking her as she must have done when the girl was a newborn, exposed by the river, left to die alone.

They would not die alone, any of them.

The words were true, yet they shattered her heart.

Cato was moving behind her. He gripped her shoulder. "Come, Ariella. It is time."

Jeremiah grasped her hand. "My girl, the Holy One—"

She leaned to kiss his cheek, to whisper in his ear. "I have made my peace with Him, Jeremiah. Through the Messiah, as you taught me."

Jeremiah's smile was like the sun shining through dark clouds and his eyes filled with tears. *"Baruch HaShem."* Blessed be the Name.

CITY ON FIRE: A NOVEL OF POMPEII

She smiled in return. "And Cato joins us too."

He squeezed her hand and took Cato's with the other. "My two warriors. He has great plans for you." A tear pooled in his eye and escaped. "And I can face the end with joy, knowing that the Creator calls you out to do His work after I am gone."

She could not release him. It took the gentle pressure of Cato, untangling her warm fingers from his twisted ones, pulling her backward, away from Jeremiah, from Flora and her parents. She staggered and he caught her weight.

They paused in the doorway. Europa embraced a sobbing Nigidia, wrapped an arm around Portia, kissed them each, then patted Ariella's cheek one final time. Her eyes were bright with unshed tears. "We are well here, my girl. Go in peace."

And then they were off, retracing their steps through the corridor as the husband and wife waved farewell. Already a hole had been ripped through her heart. She followed Cato, numb with grief.

They climbed back to the street, pulling Portia from the opening last. Her face had grown pale again.

Cato studied her. "How do you fare, sister?"

She nodded. "I will not hold you back." No doubt she thought of those inside the house.

They moved on, reaching his house within minutes and repeating the process of digging through to get inside. This time Portia and Nigidia waited in the street. Cato found a torch still burning and grabbed it to light the way.

As expected, they found no one at home, even after shouting through every room.

Cato turned to her in the kitchen, the first time they had been alone since they had stood here once before. She pulled her torn tunic around her, embarrassed.

She looked at his eyes. From this moment, nothing would be the same. There was nothing left to do but leave the city. What kind of life would meet them in the world beyond Pompeii?

Cato also seemed to feel the hinge of fate. He put a palm to her cheek, ran his thumb over her lips. "Are you ready?"

She nodded. "It is time."

Up on the raised street once again they trudged south, high enough now that they walked on the same level as any of the remaining slanted roofs. From this unnatural vantage point Ariella could survey the entire city, all the way to Maius's estate if she chose to look that way.

Another explosion rocked them from their feet.

They scrambled to stand, turned toward the mountain, and watched, amazed as it gushed, the outpouring aimed for Pompeii.

Closer, closer. The surge flowed downward with a speed no one could outrun. They stood transfixed, huddled together, and watched it come.

It swelled down the hillside, then poured toward them, a fiery deluge.

It swallowed the northern fields.

It submerged the northern estates.

Nigidia gave a sharp cry and her legs gave way. Cato kept her upright. Ariella pulled the girl's head into her shoulder, whispered empty words of comfort into her ear. But she kept an eye on the surging tide of death. For their grief would end in moments, when they joined Maius under the whelming fire.

52

The northern wall of Pompeii halted the surge.

Cato watched it swell to the city wall, the height of five men, then settle. Barred entrance to the city, a failed siege.

But the proximity of the flow was telling. The mountain could surge again, and with the northern valley already filled with molten rock, the next one would race over its predecessor and sweep the town.

He turned to the women he had pledged himself to protect. No need for words.

They stumbled after him, a ragged, grief-struck group with little hope, but still the will to survive.

They were not the only ones to have seen the end coming. Survivors pocked the streets, eyes wide, their hope to remain hidden in safety erased.

"Come with us. Follow us." Cato spoke to each one they passed, each bewildered and dazed face that turned their way.

He heard his name spoken by one man to his wife, heard the word *Christian*, and smiled to himself. Such a short time ago he would have feared the association.

And yet, as it happened, it was this very connection that proved most effective. The Christians of Pompeii had made themselves known, it turned out. In their quiet way they had loved well and spoken freedom, and it was this that convinced people to join Cato and the women on the march out of the city.

More and more emerged from rock piles and hidden recesses. Cato urged each one, not willing that any should perish in what was to come.

The lengthening line of survivors twisted through the streets, a river of life flowing through the city of death, with Cato at its head. He had desired to win the election, to lead the people. Was this not a greater victory?

The Stabian Gate lay half-buried, but still open enough for the train of people to pass under its arch, out of the city and toward the plains.

Where was the rest of his family? He looked everywhere at once, along the city wall in either direction, out over the field of stone. Beside him, Ariella scanned the pale horizon, her hand to her eyes.

There was nothing to do but keep walking, away from the mountain. Toward safety. The rock and ash still lay heavy here.

And so they climbed. Trailed by patricians and plebeians, slaves and freedmen, all who left the city empty-handed, with nothing but the breath of life.

They moved quickly, fearing another surge from the mountain, unsure how far they must travel to escape.

The sun rose above the lip of the east, burning through the ashy air with a filtered pinkish hue.

Ariella grabbed his arm and stopped. Pointed.

He followed her gesture to the rise ahead. To four figures moving toward them. Two men. Two women.

"Micah!" Ariella's scream punctured the early morning air. She scrambled forward, falling in the rocks, running in a crouch with her hands to catch her.

Cato's chest rose and fell with the sight of it. With the sight of the others.

He moved toward them, and they met at last, the two groups.

Octavia held her chin high as ever, though her clothes were as dirty and torn as any serving girl's.

Isabella fell on his neck, weeping.

He wrapped one arm around her and the other around his mother. Watched the reunion of Lucius and Portia, so long in coming, through tear-blurred eyes.

Micah picked up his sister and swung her as though she were a child.

Cato's breath caught to hear Ariella laugh. To hear her laugh and see her smile.

Their reunion was brief. They were not yet safe.

But within another hour of travel, the rock and ash began to shallow, until at last they gained a hill and could see grass poking up from the rubble. A mighty crowd had gathered on the hill. Thousands upon thousands who had streamed from the city all the day before and through the long night. They had reached this knoll and had no strength to go farther, it seemed.

Cato wondered about those citizens he had not seen since the disaster began. His vineyard caretaker, Remus. The healed madman. Cyrus and the others of the believers. Were they among this crowd?

They had outrun the cloud, but was it enough?

As if in answer, the mountain roared once more, a sound to rock the heavens, a sound like the end of the world.

Cato turned to face Vesuvius to see what remained, of her and of them.

A massive surge of fiery mud, far greater than any previous, flowed down her sides, across the devastated valley, up to the northern wall. This time, the wall did not hold. The flow breached the barrier, swelled over it, and swept the city of Pompeii.

The fire pulsed on, filling the Forum, swelling the city streets, burning across his vineyards. It reached the south wall, overflowed the banks of the city, and poured across the plain beneath them, until at last it exhausted itself and settled.

The city of Pompeii was no more.

Cato pulled Ariella to stand in front of him, her back pressed against his chest, and wrapped his arms around her. "We are saved."

She leaned her head against his chest and he felt the tension flow out of her, released into quiet tears for their friends left behind.

Around them, a cheer went up from the crowd, proof that the resilience of the human spirit knew no bounds.

Their city was submerged, but they had come out from destruction, into a wide place.

And they would live.

53

Moments earlier, near the southern edge of town, Tullius Taurus the jeweler had his family in tow—two adolescent boys, his wife, and their young daughter—when he realized that he had waited too long.

He had such hopes for Pompeii once. How had it come to this?

Years of suffering under the corruption of Nigidius Maius, and now, just when it seemed they might have found a savior in Portius Cato, all his hopes had tumbled down the slopes of Vesuvius, so much ash and debris.

He had not wanted to face it, this invalidation of his own belief in the future. Even his own mortality, if he were honest. And so they had waited. Hiding their valuables from potential thievery, huddling together in a back room of their estate, hoping the roofs would hold.

All through the long night they had waited. Until it became clear that the house would become their tomb if they did not flee. But now, near the south wall of Pompeii, so close to freedom, he knew it had not been soon enough.

A blast from the mountain rocked them off their feet, all five of them. Nearby, two farmers and their families also fell.

Taurus clung to hope, fragile and worthless as it was.

He was still pushing himself up, straining to rise in the gas-filled air, when the next surge took his final breath.

———⟨∞⟩———

In the entry hall of the house of Emeritus the fuller, the guard dog he kept chained there to protect his riches was dead.

Emeritus stepped over the twisted corpse, its jaw open in the agony of poisoned lungs.

Indeed, the air had grown impossible to breathe. Emeritus fought to take shallow breaths. How could one suffocate in the open?

In the dark street, he stumbled forward, senseless as to where he might go to escape the air itself.

Within minutes, he felt his lungs collapsing.

In a final effort to defeat the atmosphere, he lowered himself with his back to a wall, knees bent in front of him, and used his toga to cover his nose, pressing the fabric against his face.

Still in this position, he was unconscious before the fiery flow swept the city.

———⟨∞⟩———

Drusus paced the roofed passageway that surrounded the gladiator barracks, his thoughts vacillating with his footsteps. All that he had worked for, all that he had, was chained within these cells. Nearly a hundred highly trained men who brought him wealth, fame, and freedom. His prizefighters, Celadus, Paris, Floronius. To release them was to give up everything.

And yet, could they survive the rising ash and rock?

If he had seen the surge that had come to the north wall, perhaps he would not have taken the chance. But he had been busy securing his future.

Or so he thought.

For in the end, they all perished together.

———◦∞∞◦———

In their wealthy home in the eastern district, Seneca pulled his wife, Europa, into an embrace where they reclined on the triclinium's couches and whispered final words of love and reassurance. They would meet on the other side, he said.

Jeremiah sat nearby. He wore a contented look, his eyes focused far off, as if he saw the dawn of eternity breaking on the horizon.

Across from them, Flora smiled bravely at her parents.

They could have left her there on the riverbank, all those years ago. Perhaps things would be different today if they had. But there were no regrets. None. They had answered the call of God on their lives, and though He should slay them, yet they would trust Him. Always.

Let the fires come.

They would only purge away what was left of this fallen life, this fallen world that twisted feet and twisted hearts and left all men longing for their true home, whether they knew it or not.

As they would have wished, Jeremiah's whispered words were the last that they heard.

"Thanks be to God, who rescues us from this body of death."

The city was no more, and thousands within it were now asleep, tucked into graves that would become solid rock around them.

Some of them had survived, true. These were the ones who would not forget, who would tell their children, and their children's children, the story of Vesuvius and its mighty power. Of the gifts it bestowed, but also the danger.

The landscape was changed entirely, for the mountain had remade it. In time, grass would grow again on the spiny rock ridges. Trees would sprout and become tall, birds would make their nests, and the wildlife would return.

Even the people would wander back to the foothills, to take advantage of its fertility, to reap its treasures.

And deep within the mountain, the plates were ever shifting. Waiting.

54

The mountain surged twice more before it burned itself out and lay silent.

The population of Pompeii who had escaped to the south moved as a great herd toward the nearest coastal town. With no belongings, no shelter, they did what any refugee people would do. They relied on the charity of others.

Stabiae welcomed them. From its position on the bay, it had stood witness to the destruction that befell Pompeii and had news of other towns as well.

To the north of Pompeii, Vesuvius had obliterated Herculaneum. Through the previous day the wind had blown ash and rock away from the town. Though many fled, many others believed they were safe. When the mountain had overflowed near midnight, there was no time to escape. The searing mud flowed over the city and reduced every living thing to ash.

Here in Stabiae, only a smattering of the porous rocks that had first buried Pompeii lay on the ground. They had smelled the gases and seen the cloud, but they had survived.

It was rumored that the famed naturalist and writer Gaius Plinius Secundus, sometimes called Pliny the Elder, had sailed from Misenum, farther up the coast, to Stabiae. He apparently had plans to sail to Pompeii to rescue friends, but the prevailing winds confined him to the coastal town, and his weak lungs succumbed to the odors while watching the flames shoot above Vesuvius from the beach. They had found his body at morning's light.

All this Cato learned in the short time they had spent in Stabiae. The little family group of eight he had led from Pompeii bedded down in a brothel, opened to the refugees by its prosperous owner. His mother and two sisters, along with Nigidia and Ariella, took one small room, and he shared another with Micah and Lucius. There they slept for what felt like days, then took food and wine brought by sympathetic women of the brothel. He smiled to watch Octavia whisper to them when their owner looked the other way.

Sitting on the floor beside Ariella, he worried about Nigidia, the only one of their group with no family. She had lost everything, though they would not abandon her. Ariella's brother, Micah, hovered over her, assuming the role of protector. Cato caught Ariella's eye and motioned his head toward the couple. She smiled. Despite their disparate background, these two had both known mistreatment, exploitation. Perhaps . . . they could find support in each other.

Later in the morning Cato led Ariella to the beach, to look out over the sea and breathe the air where the wind had scrubbed it clean. He held her hand, their fingers intertwined, a tranquil silence between them.

She had not asked him any questions, but he had answers. "We will go to Rome."

Ariella did not speak, and he could feel her tremble beside him. He turned her to face him and held both her hands. "We will go to

Rome and you will be my wife. We will tend my uncle's vineyards and make wine. We will raise a family and fight against evil, together."

"How can we—"

Cato shook his head. "Do not speak of obstacles. We have defeated a mountain, Ariella. There is nothing left we cannot face."

Her torn tunic revealed the healing scar on her upper arm. He traced the cross with his fingertip.

She followed the motion with her eyes and whispered, as though to herself, "He was wounded for our transgressions."

Cato brought her face to his own and kissed her lips with all the promise of the future.

Across the bay, the first wave of rescue ships from Rome crested the horizon, their white sails billowing.

Ariella buried her face in his chest, and he bent to hear her words.

"And by His stripes we are healed."

THE STORY BEHIND THE STORY . . . AND BEYOND

In some ways, we owe a debt of gratitude to the mountain called Vesuvius and to those who perished under its flow. So much of what we know of life at the height of the Roman Empire has come to us through the frozen-in-time city unearthed in the region of Campania, near modern Naples.

The eruption occurred on August 24, 79 AD, and buried Pompeii under more than twelve feet of ash and pumice over the course of about twenty-four hours. The gradual ash-fall sealed in the city without air or moisture, preserving it exactly as it was on that day, frozen in time. Archaeologists digging 1700 years later discovered entire loaves of bread still sitting on counters, fresh from the ovens!

The population of the city was probably about 20,000 at the time of the eruption, and historians speculate that all but about 2000 of the townspeople escaped the devastation by simply fleeing the city while the ash was falling.

But not everyone escaped, as the evidence sadly attests. The plaster casts familiar to most of us from history class were created when pockets were discovered in the hardened ash—vacuums created by the decayed bodies of the volcano's victims. The plaster was poured into these cavities then excavated, giving us a vivid depiction of real Romans in the death throes of the eruption. I used some of these figures as inspiration for characters in *City on Fire*. To see the photos of the plaster casts capturing the moment of death of some of the characters, visit my website TracyHigley.com.

Over the centuries, dirt and vegetation gradually overtook the site until it was lost to the world, its location and even its name forgotten. Imagine, an entire city, preserved underground, waiting to reveal its vast riches of knowledge! The first hint of the hidden treasure came in 1599, when the digging of an underground channel to divert river water revealed some frescoed walls and inscriptions.

But it wasn't until the mid-1700s that proper excavation began, revealing a city with a morality very different from that of the culture excavating it. Much of the artwork and statuary was considered shockingly inappropriate, and debates ensued as to how much of it should be displayed to the public. Even today, many of the more explicit artifacts are housed in the "Secret Room" of the Naples National Archaeological Museum, which over the years has been alternately closed and re-opened and even today requires minors to be accompanied by adults.

Many of the details given to us by Pompeii—its graffiti, its buildings, its artwork—formed the backdrop of this novel. I had great fun finding places to add some of the intriguing details I found, and much of my research inspired specific characters and events. The name and position of Gnaeus Nigidius Maius came to me from graffiti found in Pompeii. Covering the walls are notices filled with electoral propaganda and announcements of the games to be sponsored by the candidate, including this one:

Thirty pairs of gladiators
provided by Gnaeus Alleius Nigidius Maius *quinquennial duumvir,*
together with their substitutes, will fight at
Pompeii on November 24, 25, 26.
There will be a hunt.
Hurrah for Maius the Quinquennial! Bravo, Paris!

While most of the characters in *City on Fire* are from my imagination, the characters of Maius, his slave Primus, and the gladiators Celadus, Paris, and Floronius are all names from the city walls.

The characters of the early church in Pompeii are also of my making, and I have tried to describe the function and reputation of these house churches throughout Rome with accuracy. I am indebted to Gerald Sittser, whose book *Water from a Deep Well: Christian Spirituality from Early Martyrs to Modern Missionaries* aided my understanding of the first century church.

The arena in Pompeii is considered to be the oldest Roman amphitheater yet unearthed, built probably around 80 BC. It was already nearly two hundred years old at the time of this story. The Flavian Amphitheater in Rome, later known as the Colosseum, was in its final stages at the time Pompeii was destroyed.

In outlining the events of Pompeii's final day, I have attempted to stay as close to the archaeological evidence as possible. Historians and scientists have been able to ascertain the rate at which ash fell from the first eruption to the final pyroclastic surge that buried the city, and from this I built the ending of the book and the end of the city.

In the years since 79 AD, Vesuvius has erupted many times,

though not with the devastation of that earlier eruption. Perched now over the populous city of Naples, it is considered dormant but not extinct and is an ever-present threat to Naples and southern Italy. The most recent eruption of Vesuvius in 1944 was caught on film because of the presence of American troops in Italy during World War II. Visit my website to watch Vesuvius erupt in a seventy-year-old live WWII newscast.

Over two million tourists visit Pompeii each year, and I was privileged to be one of them—during the original writing of this book and then again while re-writing it! To walk among the still-vivid frescoes, to stand in the center of the amphitheater, to gaze across the Forum at Vesuvius in the distance, was unforgettable. I even got the chance to climb Mt. Vesuvius and stare down into the crater. I hope you'll join me on the website to read my travel journal, look at photos, watch videos, and discover more about what is fact and what is fiction in *City on Fire*. There is much to experience in this amazing place, and I'd love to take you there.

Also on my website, you'll have access to a free short story—a fun modern-day tale that also includes a gladiator!

Thank you for joining me in this adventure in Pompeii. Our next journey together will take us on a tour of Egypt, Rome, and Jerusalem as we follow the intrigue and court politics woven into the ancient world, through the eyes of *The Queen's Handmaid* (coming Spring 2014). I hope you join me there.

Until then, visit me at TracyHigley.com and share your heart with me!

READING GROUP GUIDE

1. In what ways did you feel that Cato's relationships with his mother and sisters was unusual? Did you enjoy the way these relationships were portrayed?

2. Cato is challenged to stand up to Maius, even though he feels inadequate, and has failed in the past. Have you ever faced a similar challenge? How did you handle it?

3. Ariella is angry at God for the suffering he's allowed in her life and in the lives of her people. In what ways have you struggled with this issue?

4. Ariella is convinced she's invincible and doesn't want to admit weakness or a need for help. Can you relate? Are you able to seek help from others and from God?

5. Pompeii is a city reveling in its decadence. How did you feel about the way the author portrayed the society? Did it make you uncomfortable? Did you feel it was realistic?

6. In what ways do you think our society parallels Ancient Rome in its obsession with death and sex? Would you say the world is getting worse or improving?

7. What character did you most identify with? Why?

8. This story takes place in 79 AD. How familiar are you with the church's history in this period? What new things did you learn about the history of Christianity through the story?

9. Pompeii is considered a "lost city" because its location was unknown for many centuries. Why do you think we have such a fascination with "lost cities"?

10. In what ways do you feel that the author's travels to Pompeii and other ancient lands have informed her writing? Would you like to travel to Pompeii, Italy? Why or why not?

11. Cato and Ariella faced numerous obstacles to their relationship including religious, ethnic, and social differences. Have you ever had to overcome obstacles to pursue a relationship or friendship? Did you find it difficult?

12. Cato and Ariella are exposed to the gospel through the witness of a house church that is largely in hiding. How do you feel about the ways the Church today is reaching out? Is it more or less effective than the first-century Church?

13. The end of the story involves some specific intervention by God showing His power. Do you believe God still works in this way? If so, where have you seen or experienced it?

14. The eruption of Vesuvius and the escape takes up much of the latter part of the book. How did you feel about the author's treatment of this tragic historical event?

15. Romans 9:18–24 talks about the sovereignty of God in the events of history. How does Ariella reconcile her past and her nation's defeat with the idea of a loving God?

16. In Acts 15, the council at Jerusalem gathered to discuss whether Gentiles could become believers in Jesus. How did their conclusion affect both the church in Pompeii and the church today?

ACKNOWLEDGMENTS

The re-release of a novel written a few years ago is an exciting thing. Thank you to Thomas Nelson for taking on the project and making it fresh. I love the work all of you do to polish and promote your authors! Ami McConnell, thank you for the editing suggestions to bring new life to this work.

Though the content of the book has been updated, my gratitude to those who helped the story the first time around is unchanged, so I again offer my thanks to the following . . .

Pompeii has long held fascination for me—a lost city, frozen in time and then thawed, exactly as it was on the day the mountain spewed its fire and swallowed it whole.

Unearthing any story is, at times, a bit like digging in hardened ash, with an uncertainty of what one will find. I am grateful for the help and encouragement of all who worked alongside me to bring this project to light.

Karen Ball, your editing the first time around was stellar. Thank you for your wisdom and attention to detail. Thank you to my agent,

Steve Laube. You've been a cheerleader for my writing since we began, and your support and guidance are so appreciated.

A special thanks to Mitch Triestman, (otherwise known as Uncle Mitch!) for your invaluable help in understanding the Jewish mindset of the first century—and the present. Your excellent book, *To the Jew First*, gave great insight into Ariella's character.

A huge thank you to my daughter Rachel, for being my travel partner on this book's research trip. We will have stories to tell of Venice, Rome, and Naples forever, won't we?! It was such fun spending that time with you. I would do it all again in a heartbeat!

As always, the rest of my precious family has sacrificed and supported, encouraged and endured through the writing of yet another book. Ron, Rachel, Sarah, Jake, and Noah—I could do none of this without each of you and all you do for me. I love you very much.

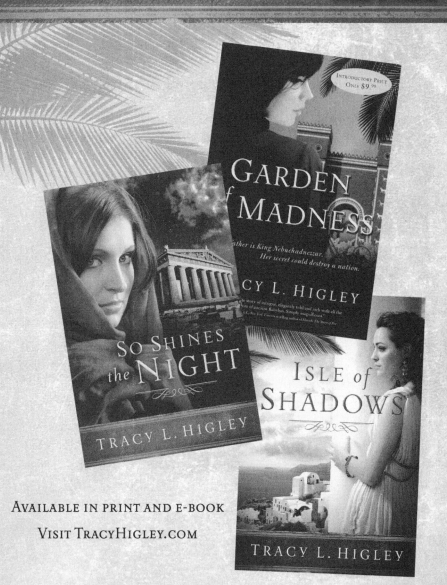

ABOUT THE AUTHOR

Author photo by Mary DeMuth

TRACY L. HIGLEY started her first novel at the age of eight and has been hooked on writing ever since. She has authored nine novels, including *So Shines the Night*, *Garden of Madness*, and *Isle of Shadows*. Tracy is currently pursuing a graduate degree in Ancient History and has traveled through Greece, Turkey, Egypt, Israel, Jordan, and Italy, researching her novels and falling into adventures. See her travel journals and more at TracyHigley.com.